SUPERTRAIN YOUR DOG— HE'LL LOVE YOU FOR IT!

Training will not break a dog's spirit; it will help make your dog a better pet and bring about an understanding between you. In fact, because training lets your dog know what he can and cannot do, it gives him a stronger sense of security. The final goal—a well-behaved, happy dog that can live amicably with you—is accomplished through love and understanding.

PAUL LOEB and JOSEPHINE BANKS, recognized as foremost authorities on animal behavior, have more than 25 years of experience in training thousands of dogs (and their owners) in every subject from feeding an orphaned puppy to exercising an aging canine. They co-authored *The Complete Book of Dog Training, You Can Train Your Cat*, and a column on pets for *Parents* magazine. Loeb and Banks train animals for private clients, as well as for movies and television commercials.

Books by Paul Loeb and Josephine Banks

Supertraining Your Dog
You *Can* Train Your Cat
The Complete Book of Dog Training

Published by POCKET BOOKS

SUPERTRAINING YOUR DOG

Paul Loeb & Josephine Banks

POCKET BOOKS

New York   London   Toronto   Sydney   Tokyo

POCKET BOOKS, a division of Simon & Schuster Inc.
1230 Avenue of the Americas, New York, NY 10020

Published by arrangement with the authors
Library of Congress Catalog Card Number: 80-10623

ISBN: 0-671-66666-5

First Pocket Books printing May 1989

10 9 8 7 6 5 4 3 2 1

POCKET and colophon are trademarks of
Simon & Schuster Inc.

Printed in the U.S.A.

To the gang: Inches, Sleepy, and Snap;
and in special memory of Plum

CONTENTS

Contents

Contents

SUPERTRAINING
YOUR DOG

INTRODUCTION

Entering one client's apartment, we found it to be completely bare except for a single couch that looked as if it had been attacked by a bunch of sharks in a feeding frenzy. The dark mahogany-stained parquet floors displayed large, prominent bleached-out urine spots. "Baby," the culprit, was not present. We could hear her, however, behind the bathroom door, where she was being confined so she could not rush the front door to knock us over, as she normally did when visitors arrived.

When Baby's owners had first brought her home, they had apparently allowed the dog to do anything she wanted. For their pet, they had adapted all the psychological methods of child rearing. But after six months their cute little five-pound bundle of joy had turned into a fifty-pound doomsday machine.

Overbreeding is blamed for the many stray dogs, but many of these vagabonds are actually untrained (or poorly trained) animals whose owners finally got so fed up they abandoned their pets. Many of the failures in training, in turn, come from misinformation about the correct way to handle dogs.

Though a dog is considered a member of your family, he is not an automatic member of human society. Thousands of years of selective breeding have facilitated a dog's adaptation into our families and our hearts. But a dog still needs special handling, with attention paid to his innate characteristics.

Don't interpret your dog's behavior in terms of human behavior, and don't project: People often see their dogs as human beings and discover their own motives reflected in the animals' actions. This is not necessarily misleading, but you should remember that your dog may be responding in ways that are entirely his own. Don't make the mistake so many people do of interpreting a dog's actions in terms of human behavior, and assuming he has your own motives and needs—dogs are still a species apart.

Introduction

When working with your pet, therefore, think of him as a member of his own species, removed from the wild and brought into what is now his new natural environment—your home. He can only act in accordance with the way nature created him, and can learn only if treatment and training are geared to that which he understands.

Your life with your dog will be far more pleasant if you pay attention to training your dog to fit your life-style. When very young, a dog learns through interaction with his mother and littermates. Once he is in your home, it's up to you to do the teaching. Your first step is to establish yourself as the boss. This doesn't mean setting up a fascist regime in your home and expecting rigidly correct demeanor from your pet at all times. However, lack of decisive leadership on your part can lead to anarchy and destruction. As social pack animals, dogs expect to either lead or be led. Therefore, if you don't lead your pet, your dog may well take over your home and you.

A dog learns through repetition and association. Your pet will do those things that bring consistently pleasing results, and discontinue those that bring displeasing ones. You should therefore use two types of training: *positive* to teach a dog to obey basic commands and to do tricks; *negative* to stop bad, destructive habits and disobedience.

All dogs need training up to a point. The exact amount can depend on your purpose for owning a dog, or on how far you want to take the training. Training will not break a dog's spirit; it will help make your dog a better pet and bring about an understanding between you. In fact, because training lets your dog know what he can and cannot do, it gives him a stronger sense of security. The final goal—a well-behaved, happy dog that can live amicably with you—is accomplished through love and understanding.

How these two types of training are put into practice can literally make or break your dog. "Supertraining" combines and utilizes the most practical and effective procedures of both types of training to make sure your dog stays well behaved.

—*Paul Loeb and Josephine Banks*
New York City

One

SELECTING AND CARING FOR A NEW DOG

The Physical Canine

Certain physical aspects of dogs are constant, and the dissimilarities amongst the various breeds are not as exaggerated as you might think from first appearances. Differences in size, shape, color, and length of hair and tails can be discounted. It is not the surface details but the basic characteristics that are important. The skeleton, which supports the muscles and protects the vital organs, is nearly identical for all dogs except for variations in size; as are the position of dewclaws and tails, and the shape of the head bones. Since dogs in the wild run in packs and hunt by running down their prey, usually on open ground, they are characteristically built for speed, agility, and endurance. Dogs have nonretractable claws (rather than the retractable claws of their ancestors), and can therefore run on the pads of their feet without interference. These claws are also better adapted for digging holes and for marking the ground for territorial purposes.

Pet dogs as they exist today are probably almost totally the result of selective breeding. No one is positive of the form or forms from which our dogs originated prior to human intervention, but it is known that they are relatively recent creatures. The dog is zoologically classified as a member of the family Canidae, which includes wolves, coyotes, jackals, and foxes. Other members of this family include dingoes and pariah dogs, which are domestics that have gone wild and interbred to develop standard characteristics. The present-day hunting dogs of India and Africa, though still part of the Canidae family, are not close relatives, but are from a different evolutionary branch.

Some theorists such as Darwin felt that domestic dogs were the result of interbreeding a number of different tamed wild canines. He believed it was impossible for the enormous differences among various breeds of dogs to be the product of domestication of a single species. Others claim a dog's direct ancestor is the wolf because of their similar skeletal structure and social behavior. But no matter what their origins in the murky past of pre-history, man took in certain Canidae that could fit into human society and were adaptable to perform certain tasks. Excavations of ruins from ten to twelve thousand years ago contain the remains of man and dog, indicating an already well-established symbiosis.

The Various Breeds

At one time, the type of dog you had would have depended on what region or tribe you came from; even today there are regional favorites. Today, however, the variety of breeds available is enormous. Myths have evolved over the years about the sources and backgrounds of varying breeds, but the dog originally reflected the human culture that developed. Thus agrarian cultures developed guarding and herding dogs, while hunting communities bred dogs especially fitted to the terrain and chasing food animals. Later civilizations indulged themselves in breeding dogs for companionship, show, or more specialized tasks. Most breeds originated on the continents of Europe, Asia, and North America, while only rudimentary use was made of dogs in Africa and South America.

Talking to professional trainers, handlers, owners, breeders, boarding-kennel owners, and veterinarians will help you learn something about the characteristics of various breeds. Attending dog shows might also help you choose the right dog for you. Each breed has certain selected characteristics, but if you allow for differences in physical size, agility, stamina, sensory performance, and emotional reactions, all are remarkably similar.

Most of the different breeds are classified according to function in several main classes. *Sporting dogs* generally have short to medium-length hair and range from medium to large in size. *Hounds,* either sight or scent, are medium to large dogs used for hunting. The *working* group is composed of dogs involved in herding, protection, and sentry duty—reliable animals for general basic obedience. *Terriers* are house dogs originally employed to ferret out and kill rodents; they are feisty and aggressive by nature. The *toy* group includes many miniature replicas of larger-sized breeds, and also some small breeds with no obvious basis in larger types. *Nonsporting dogs* include a miscellaneous mixture of medium to large breeds that don't fit into any of the other specific categories. *Mongrels* or *mixed breeds* are the most common dogs of all—generally of unknown ancestry.

The pads of a puppy's feet are a fair guide to how big he'll grow, but it's almost impossible to determine in advance which features will be retained.

In theory, at least, purebred dogs should have certain fixed or predetermined features. However, not all dogs that have fixed breed names or are bred to type are accepted as registration material for the official kennel club of any particular country. There is much overlapping, and the rules of the different kennel clubs are almost identical, but each has the option to accept different breeds. The three leading authorities in the world are the American Kennel Club, The Kennel Club in England, and the Fédération Cynologique Internationale in Belgium, which represents several European countries. Other kennel clubs include the Canadian Kennel Club, The Bermuda Kennel Club, Real Sociedad Canina De España (Spain), and Svenska Kennel Klubben (Norway).

Breeds Recognized in the U.S.

Sporting Dogs
Pointer
Pointer, German Shorthaired
Pointer, German Wirehaired
Retriever, Chesapeake Bay
Retriever, Curly-Coated
Retriever, Flat-Coated
Retriever, Golden
Retriever, Labrador
Setter, English
Setter, Gordon
Setter, Irish
Spaniel, American Water
Spaniel, Brittany
Spaniel, Clumber
Spaniel, Cocker
Spaniel, English Cocker
Spaniel, English Springer
Spaniel, Field
Spaniel, Irish Water

Spaniel, Sussex
Spaniel, Welsh Springer
Vizsla
Weimaraner
Wirehaired Pointing
 Griffon

Hounds

Afghan Hound
Basenji
Basset Hound
Beagle
Black and Tan Coonhound
Bloodhound
Borzoi
Dachshund
Foxhound, American
Foxhound, English
Greyhound
Harrier
Irish Wolfhound
Norwegian Elkhound
Otter Hound
Rhodesian Ridgeback
Saluki
Scottish Deerhound
Whippet

Working Dogs

Alaskan Malamute
Belgian Malinois
Belgian Sheepdog
Belgian Tervuren
Bernese Mountain Dog
Bouvier des Flandres
Boxer
Briard
Bull Mastiff
Collie
Doberman Pinscher

German Shepherd
Giant Schnauzer
Great Dane
Great Pyrenees
Komondor
Kuvasz
Mastiff
Newfoundland
Old English Sheepdog
Puli
Rottweiler
St. Bernard
Samoyed
Shetland Sheepdog
Siberian Husky
Standard Schnauzer
Welsh Corgi, Cardigan
Welsh Corgi, Pembroke

Terriers

Airedale Terrier
Australian Terrier
Bedlington Terrier
Border Terrier
Bull Terrier
Cairn Terrier
Dandie Dinmont Terrier
Fox Terrier
Irish Terrier
Kerry Blue Terrier
Lakeland Terrer
Manchester Terrier
Miniature Schnauzer
Norwich Terrier
Scottish Terrier
Sealyham Terrier
Skye Terrier
Staffordshire Terrier
Welsh Terrier
West Highland White
 Terrier

Toys
Affenpinscher
Brussels Griffon
Chihuahua
English Toy Spaniel
Italian Greyhound
Japanese Spaniel
Maltese
Manchester Terrier
  (Toy)
Miniature Pinscher
Papillon
Pekingese
Pomeranian
Poodle (Toy)

Pug
Shih Tzu
Silky Terrier
Yorkshire Terrier

Nonsporting Dogs
Boston Terrier
Bulldog
Chow Chow
Dalmatian
French Bulldog
Keeshond
Lhasa Apso
Poodle
Schipperke

There is no definite answer as to what kind of dog you should have, but some breeds do require more care than others. Long-haired dogs need to be brushed and combed frequently, not just for looks but for health. Short-haired dogs may require little grooming, but tend to shed more hair. (Allergic reactions to pets—and they are common—can cause havoc in the family. If anyone in your family has had allergies in the past—wheezing, sneezing, watery eyes, and itchy skin, for example—it would be wise to have them tested before taking on a new pet.) Poodles and Airedales do not shed, but they have special grooming requirements, as do many other dogs. If you don't want to be bothered, select a dog that has few grooming needs.

In addition to *your* preference, think of the dog's. Thick-coated dogs may be happier in cold winter climates, while short-haired dogs do better in the South. Each breed has its advantages and disadvantages, and in all breeds there are good, bad, smart, dumb, healthy, and unhealthy dogs. Go with the breed with the fewest number of drawbacks for you. If you want absolute perfection of looks, you'll have to wait for a full-grown dog, because that's the only way you can get a real guarantee.

Unless there is a special reason for getting a full-grown

dog, though, it is generally more desirable to bring in a young animal. Pups squirm their way right into your heart, and it is easier to mold their habits to fit your family's rhythm.

Canine Development

A dog's brain and body are remarkably coordinated in their development; and its senses also stay in relative synchrony with its motor abilities. The brain of a newborn puppy is still developing at birth. The brain's actual physical growth parallels the emotional, social, and behavioral growth of the dog. It is the development of the brain in conjunction with the newly developed abilities that indicate what external behavior a pup can achieve at various ages. In dogs, four major developmental phases occur, overlapping slightly, with some dogs maturing more rapidly or slowly than others.

1. The *neonatal* stage lasts for the first one or two weeks. At birth a newborn dog is blind and deaf. The pup never leaves the nest and is completely dependent on its mother for food and care. During most of this time the puppy merely sleeps, nurses, and tries to keep warm, seemingly responsive only to scent, sensitivity to touch, and changes in temperature. The eyes open at ten to thirteen days, but vision is not clear. A puppy has no control over the regulation of his body temperature. EEG's show a weak electrical-activity reading during the first two weeks of life; they also show that most early sleep is of the deepest sort. Reflexive nerves for suckling and crawling are already developed, but the mother must stimulate the pup's elimination by licking the genitals and anus.

2. The *transitional* stage runs from approximately two to three and one-half weeks. This is a period of rapid development. The ears open, and the pup first responds to sound. The eyes blink and focus (but do not achieve an adult level of vision until the next stage, at four weeks). The animal urinates without stimulation, and starts to defecate at some distance from the den. By thirty days, all twenty-eight puppy teeth are in. The pup stands and walks, following its mother,

and develops real control over the temperature regulation in the body. Toward the end of this second developmental period there is a sudden enhancement in recorded brain activity. The pup can stay awake for reasonable lengths of time, and develops adult sleep patterns. The pup is suddenly able to learn and able to tell one individual from another, thus indicating that socialization is possible.

3. The *socialization* stage extends from about four to twelve or thirteen weeks. In this time the pup learns with whom (or with what species) he will associate. Patterns of social behavior develop. The pup is now able to develop conditioned reflexes and show other evidences of learning.

This phase is devoted to the rapid honing of sensory, motor, and psychological capacities. Vision achieves adult level, and the pup's brain matures enough that the EEG's measuring brain activity record adult patterns of alertness. Most species-characteristic behavior patterns develop. Facial expressiveness appears, due to development of muscles that allow ear movements and control of the elevation of the lips. A repertoire of vocal patterns is established, and barking replaces the puppyish whine. Independence from the mother is initiated—and achieved. It is the time for the formation of emotional attachments. The pup learns to interact with his peers and his environment, which includes humans. This period is the optimum time for you to develop a good pet-owner relationship.

4. The *final* or *juvenile* period lasts from three to four months, until the dog reaches full sexual maturity. In this period the dog learns place orientation and adult interaction, and perfects motor skills and communication. Environmental fears emerge at four to five months. The dog may react fearfully in an unfamiliar situation or when a familiar environment is in some way altered, and he has to learn how to handle strangers and strange places. From twelve to twenty-four weeks, secondary socialization and environmental placement outside of the family or pack nucleus occurs. By fifty-two to seventy-six weeks, the dog reaches full physical and temperamental maturity. The mind follows the same timetable, but does not completely mature until one to one and one-half years, perhaps even later.

In comparing the development and life span of dogs and

humans, the first twelve to fifteen human years would be equivalent to the first year of a dog's life. Ten human years go into the next canine year, and five to seven human years equal each canine year thereafter. Life span varies according to a dog's condition and size. Generally the larger the dog, the shorter its life span. Thus a very large Great Dane may live eight or nine years, while a toy poodle may live twelve to thirteen or more. The record age for a dog was around twenty-six years, though the average is approximately twelve.

A Second or Third Dog?

Some suggest getting pairs of dogs, on the grounds that otherwise the single animal will lead a lonely existence. But not all dogs want pals—and those who do can become so attached to the other dog they no longer want to be bothered with humans. Some breeds such as beagles and hounds are pack-oriented, and get along well. But other aggressive animals such as terriers set up social hierarchies that lead to fighting. Two dogs of the same sex may not get along; and among three dogs, the matched pair may gang up on the loner. Therefore, if you must have two dogs, get one of each sex and have the female spayed.

Some people think a second dog will be company for the first, keeping each other out of trouble. Usually, however, the owner's problems are doubled, because two pets may become less trainable than one. If a dog is to be constantly alone, maybe you should get a cat as a playmate. If you must get a second dog, remember that experiences in early life are said to affect the attachments we make later on. Therefore, if you like the dog you have, it may be best to select a second dog from the same background. If the second dog is younger, it'll be easier for them to adjust to each other. The older animal may even accept the role of surrogate parent.

Where to Get Your New Pet

Most people get their dogs either from private homes, breeders, pet shops, animal shelters, or off the street. But where your pet comes from can be very important in determining what you are getting.

Professional breeders and pet-shop owners are business people. Animals are their merchandise, and they are usually interested in maintaining good health conditions. If you get your dog from a breeder or a reputable pet shop, you can feel reasonably sure it is healthy. You will be able to learn the animal's history, age, and pedigree.

Puppies from unreliable sources may be infected with various illnesses, and may have been improperly fed and treated. The problem is that even if pet shops try to carry disease-free, untraumatized pets, simply removing a newly weaned pup from home, transporting it, and putting it in with a bunch of other strange dogs almost guarantees problems. As commodities, dogs are big business. Some breeding farms that produce puppies for the pet-shop market ship them out crammed in crates: These pups are often weaned and taken away from their mothers too early and never get over the initial setback; some are suffering from stress or from being isolated or caged too long; while others have low resistances and are easily prone to diseases. Ask how long a dog has been caged in a store and when and how he was transported there. Also, check to be sure the store is clean and the animals look well cared for.

Societies that work for the welfare of animals are to be found throughout the world. Animal shelters make every effort to provide you with a healthy pet, and you will usually find a variety of dogs of all ages and mixtures, even purebreds. Many of the pets in pounds are ill, however, because of the stress to which they have been subjected. In order to find a home for the animals, the staff at a shelter will tell you everything you want to hear, and won't necessarily level about any training or emotional problems a dog may have. Many times you will indeed find a fantastic dog whose only misdeed is to have been in the way of callous owners who wanted to take a vacation. But full-grown animals have already been trained to adapt to another family, and they may have deep-seated bad habits that you will have to overcome.

If adopting an older animal, test him so that you'll be aware of any inadequacies from the very beginning. Problems can be overcome, but only if you know what they are. Play the detective and check for telltale spots on the rug or chewed furniture; play a little rough to see how the dog reacts. Take one of his toys to see if the dog is aggressive and tries to stop you. Some dogs are trained perfectly, of course, and for prospective owners who lack the time, interest, or energy to train a pet, an older dog may be the ideal choice. An older animal used to being around youngsters may be the better choice for a houseful of children. Older pets are generally calmer, more adept at watching out for themselves, and have the advantage of staying the way they look.

Usually your best source is a reliable, local breeder who loves dogs but is also practical, understands their needs, and takes pride in his animals. Here you are able to check out a dog's mother and father (dam and sire). And the right breeder will have spent time with the pups, getting them used to being handled and introducing them to different situations.

Keep in mind that getting a purebred does not mean you have a prize dog. Unfortunately, misrepresentation is not uncommon. If you are interested in showing or breeding the dog, select your pet carefully from a reputable source and ask for a frank opinion on the animal's possibilities. Be sure to get the official registration for the individual or litter. But be careful: Pedigree is not a registration. All dogs have a pedigree in that they have a family line or tree. To register a dog, both its dam and sire must have been registered. A purebred registry should have a pedigree and registration papers. Ask the man who sells you the dog to explain the registration procedure.

Selecting a New Puppy

Before getting a puppy, think carefully. He may not look or act like your dream image when he is full grown—or even after you get him home. Be aware in accepting that bundle of love that your pet is a member of the family and needs you to be home often enough to walk, feed, and be with him. If you go to parties, you'll often have to leave early. You'll have to get up earlier in the mornings, and have to plan ahead if you want to take a trip. Puppies and dogs need time, energy, and patience. Sometimes people get pets for their children, but if you do, know that *you*—not the children—will be caring for the animal.

Also take into account the basic considerations of your environment. The image of a dog running beside you along the beach or through the fields might not have any basis in fact. Working-type dogs such as Dobermans and terriers are highly active and need outdoor exercise. If you live in the country and have plenty of outdoor space, a larger dog can enjoy himself, but some suburban quarters can be even more cramped than those in crowded cities. Also consider the ages and number of your children; toddlers often manhandle small dogs, especially those that can be picked up easily. Smaller dogs have the advantage of living longer than larger breeds, need less exercise, and eat less. Larger dogs are impressive looking and appeal to the security-minded. But if you live in a small apartment, you'll probably be better off with a smaller one. Medium-sized dogs do well everywhere.

Health and Genetic Considerations

Few people will return an ailing dog because they get attached immediately to the new arrival, healthy or not. That's why it is really important to be very cautious about selecting a pup. A healthy puppy has bright, clear eyes and a clean, cold nose. He is alert, responsive, and lively. His skin should be firm; and there should be no sign of rash or eczema under the fur—which should be glossy. Ears should be clean inside, and the breath sweet. Diarrhea, a running nose, eyes that discharge pus, and dull, drab fur can all be telltale signs of ill health. If the pup seems to have an extremely high temperature, something could be wrong, so don't discount it as just excitement. Don't choose that quiet pensive pup in the corner. A tired, listless pup might be sick. Watch to make sure that the dog is moving properly and is not wobbly on his feet. Certain features can make a dog more prone to certain problems. Outsize ears, for example, can easily be infected with mites, drag on the ground, or get abnormal growths of hair. Other dogs have droopy eyelids, protruding eyes, extra folds under the eyes, or lots of hair around the eyes—factors that can affect vision and cause many problems of varying severity.

Mouths and jaws can also pose problems. Overshot and undershot jaws are prevalent in some strains of dogs. The affected animal doesn't have a proper bite, and can have tooth trouble and loss in early middle age. When the upper jaw protrudes beyond the lower, the lower jaw's incisors come up inside the upper jaw and can ulcerate the gums. There is no cure for an overshot jaw.

Unusually short-headed breeds (bulldogs, for example) tend to drool, dribble, slobber, and have breathing difficulties. Their tongues tend to protrude beyond the abnormally short upper jaw; or they may be unable to grasp food with the upper jaw, and so must eat by shoveling the food in with the lower. Some of these problems can be caused by the back neck glands being squeezed and having nowhere to go, or a soft palate that partially blocks the breathing passages. (There is an operation to correct this, but it is better to avoid it if possible.) Still other dogs have deep external folds on the lower lip that droop a great deal, giving the mouth a foul odor and often causing infection.

There are hereditary problems that, though not necessarily color-connected, tend to appear only in white-haired dogs. Hemophilia, the bleeding disease, is especially prevalent in male West Highland whites. (Fortunately, this disease is as rare as its human counterpart.) Some larger breeds of white dogs that show a certain amount of albinism may have defective hearing and vision; in some strains the defect is congenital. Test for these possibilities. But even a deaf or blind dog can be trained.

Skeletal abnormalities can cause a dog pain, discomfort, arthritic changes, even lameness. They have a definite hereditary genetic basis and are usually degenerative—they progressively worsen and become more painful with time. Surgery may offer conservative help. But in some cases treatment is aimed at pain reduction, and minimizing the time that the animal is actually lame. Such a dog needs short, frequent periods of mild exercise, with no excess running or jumping. The dog must avoid slippery surfaces, and must keep his weight down. Anti-inflammatory drugs, moist heat, and massage can help.

In miniature or toy breeds, a common defect is luxation of the patella, or dislocation of the kneecap. The kneecap slides out of the groove at the end of the femur, causing the leg to be held up and usually turned inward. Larger dogs, especially German shepherds, can suffer elbow dysplasia, an abnormality where the elbow joint fails to develop properly. This condition manifests itself any time from three months on, and causes intermittent lameness, arthritic changes, and some pain when the animal walks.

Hip dysplasia is another degenerative, hereditary joint disease that affects almost all the large breeds of dogs, with the exception of greyhounds. The condition is due to lack of muscle mass in the hip area, and is characterized by partial dislocation of the hip joint. The hip socket is malformed—such as the head of the femur being flattened or square rather than round—so that it does not fit properly in the socket. The joint may crack, resulting in varying degrees of pain and lameness depending on the severity and swelling. The seriousness of the disease varies. The basic symptoms are that the dog limps, has difficulty climbing stairs, and shows discomfort in his hindquarters. There is often an abnormal slope of the back toward the hips, but many apparently normal animals also have hip dysplasia. Often it shows up only on X-rays, but many of these undiagnosed dogs may be suffering pain nonetheless.

Increasing numbers of dogs suffer these problems, and hip dysplasia has reached almost epidemic proportions. Though present at birth, this problem is impossible to detect at that time. Authorities won't certify an animal as free of hip dysplasia until at least six months, though it may be twelve to eighteen months before diagnosis can be accurate. Therefore, if you are getting a dog of any of the larger breeds, be sure to see X-rays of the hips and veterinarian's certificates of soundness for the dam and sire. Some breeders don't think they should stop breeding dogs with only a small degree of hip dysplasia, because they say it would drastically restrict the numbers of certain breeds.

Scotty cramp, a disease of Scottish terriers, makes the dog hop first on one hind leg, then the other; or on both simultaneously, like a rabbit. The cause is unknown. Present from birth, the condition does not show itself until six months or older, and then only under stress or after excessive exercise. It is periodic in nature and incurable, but not really painful, apparently.

Certain congenital sight problems such as retinal disorders are also present at birth and are found in specific breeds. Retinal detachment is seen in Bedlington terriers. Two optic nerve defects (commonly known as collie eye) cause blindness, but progressive retinal atrophy is the most common cause of blindness in dogs: Starting out as night blindness, it becomes progressively worse. Irish setter pups used to be the most frequently affected, but it exists mostly in older dogs. Diagnosis usually requires examination by a veterinary ophthalmologist, or a visit to a large veterinary hospital.

Epilepsy is also believed to be genetic in origin, so avoid getting any dog whose relatives have a history of convulsions.

Cryptorchidism—failure of one or both testicles to drop into the scrotum—can be a problem and is another hereditary condition. The dog can be sterile, and in later life tumors (usually noncancerous) that have to be removed often develop around these undescended testes. This problem cannot usually be detected until three months of age; therefore, you should inspect the parents, though if the defect runs through the female you still may not be able to tell.

Evaluating a Dog's Personality Traits

It is most important to select a dog for stable temperament and trainability.

Either a male or a female—*dog* or *bitch* as they are called—will make a good pet, given proper training. Thus the question of sex is really up to you. The owners of females claim they are gentler, quieter, and better pets in general. Owners of males, on the other hand, claim their pets are livelier and have more outgoing, vigorous personalities. But for a first dog, a spayed female is easiest to train and handle.

It's best to match the pup's temperament to your needs and life-style. A retired couple would be wisest not to have an active, aggressive Weimaraner, and a big noisy family doesn't want a toy or mini breed.

Don't pick a dog whose temperament clashes with yours. A quiet, kindly person does not need an aggressive dog, and hearty extroverts are seldom content with a nervous runt of the litter. But actually the personality of a dog often reflects the owner, either because the animal adapts over time or because owners select dogs like themselves to begin with.

No personality trait is inherited as such, but genetic factors can dictate susceptibility to certain behavior. For example, shy, defensive behavior may be inherited, as is fear of noise and touch. Viciousness—or rather the aggressive nervousness

21

that leads to it—can be hereditary. Even a difference in sensitivity to pain has genetic origins.

It is risky to put a bunch of puppies together and try to decide which is best, although such comparison is usually the only basis for judgment. If you watch the animals playing together, you will see actions that can be related to temperament. A puppy who is constantly mounting others isn't oversexed, he's showing signs of overaggressiveness that could be a problem; while overly submissive actions can be indicative of lifelong infantile behavior. A litter of puppies all raised under the same environmental conditions will end up differently, because each is unique at its very conception and preconditioned to be affected by different stimuli. But a newborn pup will develop properly only if reared correctly in the proper environment. With erratic, disturbing training, a timid puppy may become shyer instead of achieving the confidence he could acquire with a different upbringing.

Thus the rearing a dog has received before you get him can keep on affecting him after you bring him home.

Be sure the animal has had lots of time to socialize with humans. Once past thirteen weeks a dog with no human contact may not be able to relate well to people. Puppies need experience with all kinds of people, other animals, and new situations. A dog that has had plenty of experiences and is exposed to a varied environment will be easier to train and be more temperamentally reliable. On the other hand an innately shy dog deprived of experiences as a pup will tend to avoid new things and will withdraw from new experiences and associations. Most dogs, fortunately, are highly sociable, and can be taught to overcome many of these early deprivations if the owner understands them. However, dogs that have been caged or kenneled too long may later show signs of emotional problems such as phobias, excessive timidity, or overaggressiveness. At the other extreme, puppies raised entirely by humans may not choose to play with other animals. They may see other dogs as different from themselves, and may consider themselves one of us. Species preferences and self-identification are acquired at a very young age; thus dogs raised with kittens may prefer cats to both dogs and humans.

Look at a nursing litter to see which pups fight for their mother's teats and which stay outside the group. Puppies that cry when isolated, or squirm and protest when picked up will need work. See how the dog reacts to new stimuli while alone and in a group. Make noises and snap your fingers not only to test for deafness, but also to see how quickly he reacts, and if he is sound-shy. To test for sight-shyness, place a forbidding-looking object near him to see his reaction. Isolate the dog from familiar faces in a strange environment to see how distressed he gets; does he shiver and cry, or happily explore the place? Look for fearful biting, overaggression, hysterical overactive struggling, and escape reactions. Test for sociability by watching how he follows a familiar person around.

Individuals within any breed may also have high activity drives, so when looking for a pup avoid pacing, nervous-looking dogs. Much like a hyperactive child in the household, a dog who's forever on the go may develop destructive tendencies and his constant, intense activity will soon become annoying.

Evaluating a Dog's Abilities

Training will not change the dog's natural temperament, so a shy, retiring puppy will not make a good attack dog. Nor is it easy to make a vicious dog truly trustworthy. So when getting a dog, keep training in mind, and select one who's not too quiet and nervous, nor one who acts too wild and woolly. An ideal dog should be responsive and anxious to please. Thus test for abilities and trainability, not intelligence. If you want a pet for a specific job, specialized training calls for certain abilities. If you want a hunting dog, for example, attach bait to a string and pull it to see if the dog will chase it. If he follows, allow him to take it, and check to see if his mouth is hard or soft, and whether he guards it or rips it apart. To test for retrieving ability, throw a ball out and see how he reacts. To see if a dog is water-shy, try putting him in a shallow puddle of water. Test his nose by seeing if he gets excited by an unusual odor. Does he readily follow a simple trail or ignore it completely? If you are looking for a dog to be guard trained, do a competitive aggression test. Tease the dog gently with a piece of heavy cloth or a toy to see if he grabs it and readily roughs it up. *No* reaction means he will probably be difficult to train. On the other hand, if he gets carried away, refusing to relinquish hold, he may be too aggressive to control.

Bringing a New Puppy Home

The new arrival in your home needs special attention, because it's a particularly vulnerable time for him. Unfamiliar surroundings and people can disconcert any animal, especially a young pup. Newly separated from his mother and littermates, alone—perhaps for the first time—a pup is bound to feel frightened. Make sure his first introduction to his new home is not too stressful, or it could cause emotional upsets that might be long-lasting.

Pups newly separated from littermates and mothers and put into strange surroundings with strange people, no matter how nice, are bound to feel frightened. Don't let your family, children, and friends "greet" the dog to excess, or you might end up with a different pet than you bargained for. Don't maul him; too much fondling and petting can hurt maybe more than it can help by making him more nervous and confused.

To *carry* a puppy, always lift him so his back is supported properly at all times, or you could run the risk of injuring him. Besides, he'll feel insecure without proper support. Don't pick him up around the stomach (unfortunately the method preferred by most children), grab him under the front legs, or lift him by the scruff of the neck. These methods are completely wrong. Pick your dog up and hold him by supporting him under the chest with one hand, while placing your other forearm under his hindquarters, cupping your hand under his stomach or around his rear legs. For added support, keep him close to your body. This closely-held cradling type position is the most secure for you and your pet. Make sure he is held tightly enough that he can't wiggle out of your arms, fall, or jump—but don't squeeze him so hard he can't breathe. Don't attempt to lift a larger dog at all. (If necessary, perhaps two people doing the job would be a good idea: one supporting the front and the other the rear.)

Since you're still strange to him, take every precaution against frightening him; move and speak quietly. Restrain yourself; give him the opportunity to make the adjustment. At the same time, don't ignore your new dog. The idea is to reassure him that his new living quarters will be a happy home without overwhelming him. Give him just enough attention to make him feel secure.

Dogs (and especially puppies) put through the trauma of moving to a new place tire easily. They need plenty of time for rest and sleep.

The location of your pet's bed is perhaps more important than the bed itself. A draft-free corner in a well-ventilated room is a good spot. The bed itself does not need to be elaborate, but it should be large enough to accommodate the animal comfortably. It should be raised slightly off the floor. A washable material should be used as a blanket, and since fleas and other bugs can hide in bedding, the whole affair should be washed at least once a month.

Outdoors is not always the best place for a dog, especially in cold climates. If your pet has a good coat—like a husky—he will like it outside, but a dog outside should be given warm shelter in which to sleep. The kennel should be weatherproof and situated so the prevailing wind does not blow straight into it. The permanent opening in the door should be just big enough for the dog to enter, and could be a hinged door if in cold climes. If there is no door, there should be an overhang over the doorway. Make sure—especially in warm climates—that there is ventilation and enough height for circulation. (You can add ventilation to the kennel by adding a mini-house with a roof atop and holes in the sides so as to ventilate without drafts.) It should be raised off the ground, such as on raised posts. There should be plenty of straw or other bedding, which should be changed frequently. A hinged roof makes cleaning easy, but it should be latched down so as not to be blown off by the first strong wind. If your dog is to be tied near the house, make sure there's shade at all times.

Never put a pup outside. Outdoor sleeping quarters and kennels are not suitable for a young dog, especially a puppy whose internal temperature-controlling mechanism is not yet perfected. Never put a young dog in even a warm outdoor kennel by himself. He will be miserable and lonely, which can be detrimental to his socialization. Therefore, unless he is to be an outdoor dog, your pet should stay indoors.

Wherever he is to be kept, be sure to provide water and some toys. Then allow your dog the opportunity to be alone to evaluate his new quarters. Rather than give him full run of your home immediately, introduce him to it gradually. Besides making your pet feel more relaxed, this will prevent him from getting into all sorts of mischief. Set up the constructive confinement from the outset by following the procedures outlined later, under Preventive Confinement. Even if you don't have the necessary equipment on hand to prepare the confinement chain, be sure your pet doesn't wander around. He should be confined somehow, even if just locked temporarily in the bathroom or put in a playpen.

A pup tires easily and needs plenty of time for rest and sleep, during the day as well as at night. Respect that need. Do not obedience train your pup for the first few days, but let him acclimatize himself.

Night is the most difficult time for a new pup. A ticking clock and a well-insulated hot water bottle wrapped in a blanket or towel might help relieve the loneliness of being away from his family, by simulating the warmth and sound of the littermates from which he has recently been separated. Even so, your new dog will probably cry out and whine from loneliness for the first few nights. Confining him near your bed at night is a good idea, since you can reach out to touch and reassure him.

If you don't want your dog to get into the habit of being in the bedroom at night, you are going to have to ignore any crying. If you run every time he cries, he'll learn to whine to get attention. Catering to those midnight cries may lead to a permanent whining habit. In fact, if this whining persists for several nights, scold him to stop the noise.

Feeding and Nutrition

Though dogs are essentially carnivores, an all-meat diet is not adequate to supply all their nutritional essentials. In the wild a dog feeds on grasses and eats the contents of the intestines and stomach of his prey to get the necessary vegetables, minerals, and vitamins. Meat cannot possibly give your pet all the vitamins and minerals he needs to develop properly and stay that way. A pup on an all-meat diet may get rickets and have teeth that don't come in properly. Older dogs can develop a condition called paper bones where their bones are weak and break easily because a very high phosphorous content throws off the balance with needed calcium.

Concoctions of your own may not be adequate to balance your dog's diet. Milk added to the food can cause soft stools or diarrhea, because dogs lose the ability to digest lactose (sugar in milk) early in life. Adding raw eggs is another mistake, since raw egg whites can interfere with absorption of other nutrients. Rancid fats can produce destruction of vitamin E, and food containing small splinterable bones can be extremely harmful.

Your best bet is to get your dog on a good commercial food and stick with it. Commercially prepared foods are probably better than most you could prepare. There is a variety of types available, including high-protein and the new natural products; whichever you select, be sure that it says "complete and balanced" on the label, and also indicates for what stage of canine life the food is intended. This ensures that the food contains all the ingredients required for the nutritional needs of your pet. The type you use depends on your animal's size, activity patterns, environment, tolerance, and preferences. Sometimes a dog has a condition that requires a special diet, and this can be recommended by your veterinarian. In general, however, a good completely balanced pet food will do.

There are three basic types of dog food: canned-moist, semidry, and dry. Each type has its pros and cons.

27

The *canned* foods are ideal since they contain all the required nutrients, plus have enough moisture and bulk to fulfill your pet's needs. But be careful to make sure canned all-meat foods are sufficiently nutritious. A canned meat product that also contains cereal and vegetable matter is your best choice. Canned foods will smell and go bad quickly after being opened, however, thereby requiring refrigeration—and becoming cold and unappetizing.

Semidry foods are an extremely convenient combination of meat, meat by-products, and cereal; they are highly palatable. However, they are expensive, tend to make the dog drink a lot of extra water, and are so compact that people overfeed their pets.

All *dry* foods are cereal-based, with some being especially formulated for puppies. Dry food is economical and convenient since it can be left out; however, it also makes the dog drink a lot and thus urinate more. You have to decide—perhaps through experimentation—which is best suited for you and your pet.

A pup needs more frequent feeding than an older dog because his stomach isn't large enough to hold all the food required for proper growth. A puppy up to six months is better off with three meals a day, then two meals until one year, and then one or two meals thereafter. However, if you cannot be home for these three feedings, give your pet two meals a day—one in the morning and one in the evening. Then when the dog is six to nine months old, cut him down to a couple of biscuits in the morning to help settle his stomach and a large meal at the end of the day.

Feed your dog in an easily cleaned dish that is exclusively his. Be sure you use one wider at the base than at the rim to prevent your pet from tipping it over in his hurry to get his dinner. If your dog is sloppy in his eating habits, use a few layers of paper under the bowl to protect the floor and save you from having to clean up after every meal. If you have several dogs, give each his own bowl.

It is best to give your pet his meal and leave it down for fifteen to twenty minutes. This should give him plenty of time to eat. Then remove the bowl and throw the contents away. Some dogs will hang around waiting for some tidbit before eating, and will eat only if they find there's nothing else.

Don't let him get away with this; your pet must learn to live by your schedule, not his own. By making sure your dog eats within a certain time span you can tell whether he is feeling up to par or not. Interestingly, when fed in groups rather than alone, a dog will tend to eat more—especially a younger dog. Fighting most frequently occurs around feeding time: The lowest dog on the totem pole doesn't get anything, while the top dog gorges himself. You have to control the situation and watch that each gets enough. Keep your pet's bowl clean and germ-free by washing it out daily.

In regulating food for their pets, owners often overestimate the amount of food needed, since most dogs will keep on eating as long as you feed them. The amount to be fed to your pet depends on the breed, age, weight, activity level, and condition of your animal. There is not much point to following tables on dog-food labels too closely, because each dog's metabolism is different. The amount you feed your pet depends upon his size and activity requirements. You should know your pet's activity by observation. To get his exact weight you can place a smaller dog in a basket and weigh, then subtract the weight of the basket. Larger ones can be weighed by carrying them in your arms while you step on the scales, then subtracting your weight. If you want, you can even go to a freight depot and weigh your pet on a large, flat baggage scale.

However, weight is not the only way to determine the amount of food he should get. Different types of dog foods vary considerably in their density. Thus for semidry and canned foods, an adult dog weighing five pounds and under needs one-third of a pack or can per day, while a thirty-pound dog needs one pack or can per day. For dry food, one-half ounce per pound of dog per day is a good guide, so a twenty-pound dog gets ten ounces of dry dog food daily. Watch to see how the amount suits your pet and adjust accordingly.

Your dog's bones should be covered with flesh and not too sharply outlined, but you should be able to feel them. If the pet is too thin, fill him out, but have his stool checked by a vet to be sure there are no worms. On the other hand, be sure your pet isn't overweight.

Before putting your pet on a diet, check with your veterinarian to be sure there is nothing wrong such as a hormonal imbalance or other problem. He may well advise a prescription diet. For weight problems caused by overeating, just cut down on your pet's regular food and give no treats. Do not put your pet on a fad crash diet, just cut down on the amount of food in each meal and let him lose gradually.

Variety is not necessarily the spice of life when it comes to feeding your dog. In fact, sudden or frequent changes in diet can cause diarrhea or vomiting. Some dogs get so attached to one type of food they won't eat anything else.

If it is necessary to change your pet's diet, you may have to be insistent. Keep in mind that a sudden change in diet can cause digestive upsets; a dog may even reject a drastic change in food. So when changing from one food to another, do it gradually. Add a little more of the new food at each meal and decrease the former food proportionally until the complete change is made. If your pet refuses to eat for a day or two, don't panic and give him a special treat. That's what he wants. Hold out until he gives in and eats. As with all carnivores whose food supply is not constantly available, a dog is well adapted to going without food for long periods.

Table scraps are not adequate nutritionally. Don't allow begging, and don't feed your animal from your own table. If you feed the dog from your plate when he comes nosing around, he may get accustomed to begging and won't develop good eating habits. Save scraps on one side for your dog, and feed them to him after cleaning up the dishes. Saving a little bit of a special treat seems only fair, but you're better off not feeding your pet too many table scraps.

Except in special cases, a complete and balanced diet usually needs no supplements. You can give added vitamins if you wish. However, if your dog is on antibiotics, give him a little yogurt to replace needed bacteria in the intestines. Growing pups, convalescing and aging dogs, and pregnant and lactating bitches may find vitamins useful.

Calcium, along with phosphorus and vitamin D, are necessary for proper bone formation; pups and nursing or pregnant females need lots of it. Bone meal and milk are the best sources. Since many dogs won't drink milk, put a teaspoon or so of powdered milk on the food. Where there is not a lot of sunshine, young pups need a teaspoon of cod liver oil sprinkled over their food each day to ensure that their bones develop properly.

Keeping the skin and coat in good condition is of the utmost importance. If your dog's coat is consistently dull and flaky, certain oily acids are missing. They are expensive, and so are kept out of many foods. Plain fat such as butter will help, and check to be sure any vitamin supplement you use contains fatty acids.

Flatulence or gas can sometimes be attributed to the food a dog eats. It is common in an aging dog because of diminished intestinal mobility; the system slows down through the aging process. Food is retained longer in the intestines, causing bacterial action on highly fermentable, poorly digested food. Gulping food is another cause; in fact, seventy percent of the gas in the digestive tract is said to be swallowed. Diseases of the liver, pancreas, and intestines are other factors. Less meat and more exercise will help control this problem. Crumble charcoal pills, available at your pharmacy, into your pet's dinner once a week. They absorb gas in the stomach, help relieve indigestion, and correct diarrhea. They are not digested, just naturally eliminated.

Water, unlike food, should be available at all times, unless there is a condition for which your veterinarian asks you to cut out or limit water for two or three days. With water available, dogs drink frequently a little at a time. If it is kept away and given at intervals, they may gulp it down, overdrink, and become ill. When there is a real problem with housebreaking, you may have to regulate the dog's water at night. Any dog who drinks an excessive amount of water should be checked by your vet. Unusual thirst is a warning signal; food can sometimes be the culprit. In general, however, a dog will drink only what he can hold. Only when there is a real problem with housebreaking should you regulate your pet's water as outlined.

What goes in one end must produce waste products in proportionate amounts at the other. Feeding and housebreaking are, therefore, directly related.

Two

THE
IMPERATIVES OF
HOUSEBREAKING

Why It Is a Must

When a dog comes into your home, perhaps the number-one priority is to teach him not to relieve himself wherever he feels like it. To an untrained dog nothing is sacred: not the new rug, not your bed, not the leg of a couch. Not only will you have to clean up the mess and tolerate the stench, you will have to cope with the residuals of urine's powerful acid, which eats into things, leaving a stain and smell that endure. There are no products available that definitely eliminate the residue, other than cold water dabbed on the spot to dilute it and draw out the stain. For the odor, tomato juice can help (since it works even on skunk odor), but it stains too.

Your dog is well capable of controlling his bodily functions. It's up to you to show him what's expected of him and then enforce it by making sure you and he keep to the rules laid down. Your dog must know you don't want him to relieve himself in your home, and that you mean what you say. Curbing your dog's bodily functions will not only keep your house clean, but is also a major step in his entire training. It teaches him self-control and puts him into the rhythm of your lifestyle.

Idiosyncrasies to Keep in Mind

For the first two to three weeks of life pups don't even control when they are going to relieve themselves: The mother completely controls the animals' excretory behavior. She licks the anus and genitals, causing evacuation through a simple involuntary reflex response to her stimulation, then ingests both urine and feces to keep the nest clean and hygienic. Since the nerve tracts to the frontal lobes controlling the bodily functions and elimination are poorly developed until four to five months, before this time you cannot be completely positive of your pup.

The "childhood" of a dog is very short in comparison to humans, so that physiologically a dog has attained the equivalent of three human years old at less than three months. Some human babies are two to three years old when trained, but mostly they are trained earlier. Few children are still wearing diapers at that age. Therefore, when a puppy is eight weeks old, he is ready to start house-training, and by three months your dog is well able to control himself and is ready for precision training. Your job is to insist that he strengthen both his willpower and control over the muscles involved.

Differences Between Males and Females

The urinary patterns of both male and female dogs are instinctive and depend on inherited physiological and psychological characteristics. The physical stance taken during urination is most indicative of the differences. Both male and female defecate in the same manner, and as pups they also urinate the same way—squatting, with all four legs extended, abdomen lowered, and tail raised. This is the stance generally maintained by most females, except for very dominant ones that take on male patterns to one degree or another. But males at puberty (around six months of age) take on a hind-leg-raised position and urinate against some object, though a timid type or one subordinate to a very dominant male may do so later.

One unsuspecting owner felt her tiny Yorkie to be a perfect candidate for paper training. She came home one evening to find the paper completely dry, and wondered why. When she went into the living room, she found her little puppy had grown up and had selected the side of her antique velvet Victorian couch as his first leg-lifting spot.

The spraying action created by such a stance makes it easier for male dogs to utilize their urine for social marking. The pressure of the flow in male dogs is so great that were they to squat, the urine would splash up on them. This is caused by the fact that a male dog's penis constricts the urethra, so that in order for the dog to urinate, he must exert positive pressure. In fact, the moment the pressure is relaxed, the flow stops. This physiological anomaly also lets a male dog be completely aware of when and how much he is urinating, and is why he can urinate constantly even with a nearly empty bladder.

Females are generally easier to house-train because they simply relieve themselves out of need. Thus they urinate and defecate once, and that's it. Males, on the other hand, make a whole social ritual out of eliminating.

Adult dogs have complete control over their bodily functions, but it is not just a full bladder that prompts urination—it can also be caused by the smell of another dog's urine. Dogs use urine as a signal to tell other dogs that they have been there and how recently. Because of this, they urinate on spots previously used by other dogs. Dogs also utilize their elimination products as social markers of various sorts. They thus relieve themselves in prominent places they have used before to constantly refresh the warning to other dogs to steer clear. They lift their legs to urinate on every object they pass in the street, and will defecate several times to mark off their territories and let everyone know they are around. Some aggressive females adhere to the same reasons and usages as males, especially during heat cycles when they leave little puddles around to let all the males know where they are located. Even with this idiosyncrasy, however, they usually don't lift their legs. The damage done by an untrained female is nowhere near as great as that done by male dogs who use your furniture as leg-lifting spots.

When in actual contact with another dog, your pet may also feel obliged to show his presence. A neighbor's small dog feels he needs to leave something more imposing so when in close proximity to another dog, he leaves a large mound. This same need to show presence is the reason male dogs, and on occasion females, scrape or rip up the earth with their hind legs.

Training a Younger Dog

Many times a dog (even a puppy) will be represented as already trained. Perhaps he *was* in his old home, but the training will rarely carry over to yours; the change in environment and the stress of moving somehow nullifies it. Therefore, get working on the problem immediately.

With house-training, you are exerting a dominating influence over your animal that can lead to a battle of wills. It is generally easier to train a puppy than a full-grown dog whose behavior is well established. Pups do not have bad habit patterns that may need breaking before training can be complete. The *degree* of training is what changes, not the basic techniques. Older animals will probably take longer and require greater vigilance and effort, but they can be trained. On the other hand, pups do not have as much control as older dogs, and need to eat more frequently; therefore they need to be given the opportunity to relieve themselves more often. No matter what type of training you select, the basic procedures remain constant. You have to get your dog to control his bodily functions, and to relieve himself when and where it is appropriate.

It's not that a dog can't control himself; rather the dog has never had to, and so has never strengthened either his willpower or muscle control. The time it takes to house-train a dog is, therefore, dependent on getting the dog accustomed to self-control.

Since defecating and urinating are pleasurable activities for dogs, and constitute one of their main social tools, curbing this instinct is a major step in training an animal. It teaches self-control, and puts your dog into the rhythm of your lifestyle. During housebreaking a dog will learn a lot more than mere control of bodily functions.

Housebreaking
or Paper Training?

Before starting to work with your dog, you should first decide what form of training you want for him. You can select among housebreaking, paper training, or a combination of the two. Make your choice with your pet and circumstances in mind. What is the size of your dog, his age, his sex? Do you live in the city or country? Are you home at erratic hours, or do you have a stable schedule and life-style? Just be sure that you want your dog to continue with whatever method you select, because once established, your pet's toilet habits become more difficult to adjust.

One friend with an Irish wolfhound puppy decided upon paper training. It wasn't long, however, before there wasn't enough paper in the house to absorb the mess—to say nothing of the odor greeting visitors.

Teaching your dog to relieve himself outside is probably the most practical choice, even in communities that have laws requiring that you clean up after your dog. A dog likes to go outside for walks rather than being restricted inside on paper. It is a big part of his life to sniff around and see what's happening in the neighborhood: new people, new dogs, changes in the environment. This investigatory behavior gives your dog something to do. Housebreaking and paper training develop almost the same habit patterns. The only real difference is that in paper training, paper is put down in the house; while in housebreaking, paper is never put down except outside the house.

The idea of training is never to let the dog relieve himself in the house unless he is to be permanently paper trained. At least at the start, you are to schedule his diet, water, and walk times to be sure you leave as little to chance as possible.

Feeding as a Training Aid

Food and feeding are major factors in your dog's overall training. Overfeeding your dog, varying his meal times, and constantly changing his diet can ruin your pet's success with house-training.

Feed your pet at regular times, and not later than 6 P.M. This gives the dog a certain regularity in his bodily functions. And do not overfeed your dog. Some people feed a fifteen-pound dog three cans of dog food a day and wonder why it has seven or eight bowel movements daily.

In selecting your pet's food, you may have to make certain adjustments. All dogs do not react well to the same foods. Foods with a high protein or salt content cause your dog to drink excessive water and thus urinate more. Some dogs are actually allergic to certain types of foods and may need a special diet. Get your dog on a diet that agrees with him, and stick to it. Keeping your dog on a constant diet of the same or similar food will help his house training, while sudden changes in diet or meal times are disastrous. Introduce new foods gradually by mixing small amounts with his accustomed diet. If changing the feeding times, do so by a few minutes a day. With changes, your dog's elimination patterns will adjust also, so be alert for mistakes until his body acclimatizes itself.

Leave water down for your pet at all times unless your vet recommends otherwise. If he is an excessive drinker you may have to supervise him, but never deprive him. Where there is a real problem with housebreaking, you may have to regulate your pet's water at night. Allow him to drink only a little when you first put the dish down and then some more a few minutes later. Otherwise he may try to get too much at one time.

Standard Procedures

The most basic method in house-training a dog is constructive confinement. Until your dog is completely trustworthy, he should not be allowed the run of your home. If he is, you will be running around mopping up puddles and picking up his messes all day. Dogs do not like to soil their immediate surroundings, so when confined they learn to control themselves. At first give him only limited freedom when he is good and you can watch him. As training progresses and your dog is relieving himself when and where you want, gradually allow him more freedom and less supervision. Your dog then learns that he earns his freedom with good behavior. But each of you should understand that confinement is not a punishment, only a preventive procedure to ensure that your dog gets loose only *after* he relieves himself where you want him to.

Whenever your dog is loose during training, keep an eye on him. If you see him sniffing about the floor, it is generally a signal that he is going to relieve himself. Call him to get his attention, throw something close to distract him, or pick him up quickly. This should stop him from doing anything. Then take him to where you want him to relieve himself. When he goes in the right spot, praise him profusely. Unfortunately, pups don't give warnings. They just squat quickly when the urge hits them, so you have to be especially watchful.

If possible, confine your dog near your bed at night for sleeping. Heavy plastic runners (such as the ones sold to protect carpeting) laid out over your dog's confinement spot will make it easier to clean overnight mistakes, and keep the mess off your floor covering. Most important, getting through the night is usually the first step in the battle, because a sleeping dog is not active and therefore has no urge to go. With your dog by your bed, you can quickly take him where you want him to go first thing in the morning. This ensures a minimum amount of early-morning mistakes. (Don't wait to shower and shave, just take him.)

Don't expect your dog to hold his bladder overnight, if overnight means ten hours. Eight hours is enough to ask. Properly scheduled walks or allowing your dog access to his toilet area is an important factor in training. At first, schedule frequent outdoor times during the day when your dog can relieve himself. Later you can cut down to three or four evenly spaced times—early morning, late at night, and another time or two during the day.

Housebreaking for City, Suburbia, or Country

Training a dog to go outside is the best procedure for most dogs, but none will do the right thing naturally. Since dogs are born, weaned, and raised indoors, they are thus imprinted from the time of birth to relieve themselves inside. Your job is to show your pet that this is unwanted and to train him to go outside, and possibly even to adhere to certain standards when there. He may have to learn to relieve himself while confined on a leash. Since you don't want to have to wait for him to decide to relieve himself, you will have to teach him to relieve himself as soon as he is taken outside. He may even have to know that he has to go at specific times and in designated places—or, conversely, not to be so regimented that he will only go at a certain time and place.

When housebreaking a dog, never put newspaper down in the house. It used to be that a puppy was first paper trained in the house, then taught to go outside while still having access to the paper. But a dog never really learns to hold with this technique, and at some point he has to *un*learn habits he has so proudly learned. He has to be weaned from the paper and taught to use the gutter or grass. If you prevent your dog from ever going inside, you'll thus avoid a lot of confusion.

Teach your dog to relieve himself outside from the beginning, starting with just outside your door. Even if he hasn't had all his inoculations, immediately take your dog outside to be trained unless he's ill. In this way your pet never connects the idea of toilet with your home, but gets into the habit of going outside from the start.

If your pup hasn't had all his inoculations, simply lay down a pile of newspaper just outside the doorway of your apartment building, on the front porch of your house, near the garbage or incinerator, or in the street outside your building. Carry your puppy to the paper and put him on it. Don't put him on the ground where he can pick up germs, and be sure no other animals come near him. Keep him on the paper until he relieves himself, using a leash to hold him in place. Be sure there is adequate paper for him to circle on. If he refuses to go within ten minutes, you can help him defecate quickly by using the cardboard match-suppository aid, as explained on the following page.

If he does what is expected, praise him—whether it was with your aid or not. This will make him connect the action with the paper outside. Then discard the soiled paper and take him back in. Play with him and give him a taste of freedom to show him what's to come when he is completely housebroken. When you can no longer be with him, confine him again.

If he does nothing outside, take him back in and be sure he is confined immediately. Don't let him loose—that's for dogs that do as they're supposed to. Take him out again later. No results this time should once more be met with confinement. Eventually, after he has held it in just as long as he can without doing something inside, he will do it outside if given the chance. When he does, you are well on the way to winning the battle.

Even if your pet has had all his inoculations, paper is always a good step in starting off your dog's training. It gives him a specific reminder, especially if you save some previously soiled paper and lay it atop the other paper as a signal. As his training progresses, you can simply eliminate it. This same method can be used to train a dog in areas where you must clean up after him when he defecates outside. Have your dog continue to always relieve himself on paper, then simply roll it up and throw it away. But if your pet has had all his inoculations and there is no cleanup ordinance in your area, you can simply take him outside to relieve himself. Be sure to get him *all the way* outdoors—not on your porch or in the hallway of your building.

When outside, most dogs learn to relieve themselves within certain specific areas. A country dog is usually able to choose the place he wants and so has a certain amount of freedom. If you would rather he confine himself to a restricted area, however, start him off that way from the outset. No one wants a garden that is fouled, so invest time in this training. Constantly take your dog to the same area you want him to use each and every time he is to relieve himself. Keep him there for ten minutes or so.

If your dog absolutely refuses to defecate when and where you want, use the match-suppository technique. Take a few cardboard matches with you as an aid. Moisten the plain cardboard ends with your saliva, then push them halfway into your dog's anus with the sulfur end out. Your dog will defecate to push the matches out, usually within a few minutes—and often almost immediately. Therefore, insert them when your dog is in the spot where you want him to go. (Glycerine suppositories are useless because they take too long to work.) Just be sure to use the right number of matches for your dog's size. A Maltese may need two or three while a German shepherd would need a half dozen. This match-suppository method takes a lesson from your dog's mother when she licked at the genital and anus area to cause your dog to relieve himself in his very early days of life.

Whenever your dog does what he is supposed to do, where he is supposed to do it, overwhelm him with praise. Then take him for a walk, play with him, let him free to roam your home for a while with you watching him. But don't let him loose to play too long: The excitement may strongly tempt your pet to go again. In housebreaking, preventing mistakes is more than half the battle.

If your dog is a city dog, he will probably need to go in the gutter rather than on the sidewalk. But he has to learn that this means going between the parked cars and not beyond that parking line. If he does, he could be hit by a passing car—whether or not he is on a leash.

To teach your dog to stay within certain confines, put him on a leash and take him to the same spot each time. Walk him slowly back and forth with a slack leash and stay quietly in one place to outwait him. If he refuses to go you can use matches, get him to defecate, and thus start him off on the right foot. Be sure not to jerk him hard when he is sniffing along the ground looking for a spot to relieve himself. Getting a dog to defecate while on the leash is not always the easiest thing in the world, since dogs normally like to go off by themselves where they can sniff around and take their time. The leash interferes with this freedom, forcing the dog to concentrate only on the job at hand. But every dog needs to learn to relieve himself while on a leash, because one day you may be traveling or visiting and be unable to let him free.

For this same reason, it can be really annoying if a dog becomes so imprinted with one spot that he refuses to go anywhere else. As soon as he knows where he is to go outdoors, you should occasionally take your dog to a different place. This way he will learn to relieve himself quickly, even in strange surroundings. If not, you may have to run to the park early Sunday morning in the rain because he won't go anywhere but on the grass. As a normal course, however, it's best if your dog has one spot right next to your home where he will relieve himself as soon as he's taken out.

In fact, your pet should be taught to go immediately when he is outside. This way you won't have to run around for half an hour to get him to go. So when house-training, walk your dog only *after* he relieves himself. Don't walk him for an hour and then insist he go; make him relieve himself first. Otherwise he may well learn to take a walk first—an idiosyncrasy that could be very annoying. In inclement weather you just want your dog to run out and do his business. Therefore, when you take your pet out, go to his spot and stay out only for a short while. Then if he does nothing, take him back in. Don't stay out all day with him, or he'll expect it in the future. The walk should be used as a treat. When he learns to go immediately, however, be sure to take him for a walk occasionally, or he may rebel and refuse to go until you do.

In the very early stages of housebreaking, you are probably going to have to run out six, seven, or eight times a day just to get your pet used to the idea. But later you should set aside normal, specifically scheduled walk times every day when your dog can relieve himself. These times should remain as constant as possible: definitely first thing in the morning, last thing at night, and at least one (and preferably two) other times in between. Others can be added if you want, but these are core times. During early training your dog should also be taken out after a lot of play or a large meal, because excitement can cause a weak bladder and stimulate the digestive system.

When a dog is in complete control, you can vary his walk times occasionally so that he learns not to mess up the house because you are fifteen minutes late. Once your pet is trained, use a random schedule at least occasionally so that your dog can learn to adjust if you have to stay out. To leave your dog for inordinately long periods of time would be unfair, however. Females, because of their less extensive social use of urination, are generally more reliable and need fewer walks, but all dogs need regular walking.

Corrections for Mistakes

The only time training with negative association is used in house-training is for your pet's misdeeds or mistakes. Since your dog can't be confined permanently but has to learn to live in your home, you must fix constructive confinement with a certain amount of freedom. And therefore the chances for mistakes in housebreaking do exist.

Whether or not you catch him in the act, handle the matter severely. Make your dog realize that you don't want such behavior. Vinegar and Tabasco sauce may sound like ingredients more appropriate to the kitchen than the dog kennel, but they are some of the most effective aids you can use.

Vinegar contains an acid that, when used appropriately, your dog will come to recognize as "your" odor as opposed to his own. Use it to indicate your authority over your dog. For example, vinegar is most generally used to cover the urine "marker" smell left by an unhousebroken dog. Rub vinegar into the spot where your pet relieved himself and, with a reprimand, make him smell it. This will show him that it is your house, not his.

Use the basic vinegar and Tabasco method whenever correcting a mistake, as an added reminder to your pet not to do it again. Get the paper towels, vinegar, and Tabasco sauce. Set them up near the soiled area. Bring your dog over to the mess, and hold him firmly in place between your legs. Clean up the mess right in front of him, and after you are done, wipe some vinegar over the area. Then put a dot of vinegar on your dog's nose and a few drops of Tabasco on his gums. Give him a good hard slap, place his nose to the vinegar spot, and let him go.

After this ignore him for ten minutes or so, then give him an easy command to let him do something good for you so you can praise him again. This way he knows that despite all, you still love him. But your dog must be shown in no uncertain terms that you don't want him messing up in the house, and the vinegar smell should remind him of your displeasure.

Catching your dog in the act and reprimanding him immediately is one of your best deterrents. This way you can associate an instantaneous, unpleasant experience with the action for optimum impact. Use a direct physical reprimand or the Rubber Arm technique described later in "Preventing and Eliminating Bad Habits." But even if you haven't caught your pet in the act, correct him anyway. Just be careful that your dog understands why he is being punished. He has to connect the reprimand with his deed and thus remember the misdeed. When administering the reprimand, take him over to the scene of the crime so it is clear in his mind.

Paper Training

Paper training is not a temporary procedure to be used as a stopgap until your dog gets all his inoculations and can go outside. It is for dogs that are *always* intended to relieve themselves on paper in the house. Before embarking on this method, be sure you are going to want your dog to consistently urinate and defecate on paper, in your home.

Since squatting is the normal urinating stance for females and males castrated early in life, you can paper train them without worry. However, it is really still a method best suited to smaller dogs. Large dogs urinate and defecate in large quantities and thus paper training can become a nuisance after a short while. Nor is it necessarily the best method for training an older dog, because old patterns have to be broken and new ones established. This can take a long time—especially if he is really well trained to the outside—because it will deprive your dog of a highly prized activity, and the sudden reversal of rules will cause confusion.

Male dogs of any size can be a problem in paper training because of their pattern of leg lifting. Castration may inhibit this behavior, but only if performed before leg lifting begins, at about six months. A timid dog, or one subordinate to a very dominant male, may develop leg lifting later, but it will always happen except in rare cases. Therefore, be sure your pet is a good candidate for the paper-training method. And realize that even with your dog going on paper, you are going to have a mess in the house. Additionally, all dogs need to go outside for exercise. You cannot completely cut your dog off from the pleasures of the outdoors, with its exposure to interesting sights, sounds, smells, experiences, and companions. However, paper training for the right candidate does leave you free not to have to walk your dog, and allows your schedule to remain flexible.

If you are sure it is the procedure you want, select a well-ventilated corner that you want him to use. Your dog's permanent toilet area should be well away from his confinement spot and where he is fed, since no animal likes to relieve himself close to where he eats and sleeps. Place several layers of newspaper on the floor to cover only a very small area; if it is a very small dog, a box filled with appropriate absorbent material like kitty litter will do. (Forget the old-fashioned method of leaving paper down all over the bathroom with the dog locked in and given unlimited availability. A dog will never really learn this way.)

As your dog becomes accustomed to relieving himself on the paper, gradually reduce the area the paper covers until there is only the equivalent of a single sheet. Do be sure it is still at least several layers thick for absorbency.

To eliminate confusion in early training it is especially important for the location of the paper to remain constant. Change the paper regularly. But when first training, leave a small amount of the soiled paper as a reminder to draw your pet to it. Later the paper and its placement alone will act as a trigger without the aid of a urine smell. Don't leave newspaper down anywhere except in your dog's permanent toilet area. If you do, it might be a temptation for him to go elsewhere. In fact, you'll have to keep your dog's toilet area clean if you want him to use it. Though animals return to an area where there is a smell, your dog will not wade onto filthy, soggy paper; nor will he go into a filthy box. Instead he will probably go onto a substitute such as your carpeting, or at least opt for right next to the paper. Then he will go farther and farther away until his toilet area extends throughout your entire home.

To train your dog to go on the paper, take him over to it frequently: right after eating, playing, training, or whenever you see him acting restless. These are the times when he is most likely to want to go, so be especially diligent about getting him to the paper then. Put him on the paper at several other set times each day to assure him that he has plenty of opportunities to relieve himself. On these occasions you can use the match suppositories to get him to defecate, and this will make him connect the paper with the action of relieving himself. One or two hours may be all that some very young pups can hold out. Therefore, when you see your pet getting restless while confined—or sniffing, circling, or squatting when free under your observation—pick him up quickly and set him on the paper. When he does what you want, praise him and reward him with some freedom. Make a fuss over things done right to let your dog know he is being good. Dogs want to please, so let them know they have at every opportunity you can get.

As your dog progresses in the training, give him more freedom and more of an opportunity to do the right thing. Instead of placing your dog right on the paper, place him a short distance away so he has to walk a little way to get to it. When he is going to the paper by himself, gradually put him farther and farther away so he has to walk to reach it. This will get him used to controlling himself and holding in, and it will teach him to give himself time to get there. Only when you are confident he knows what the paper is for should you allow him to be free by himself for a while. But watch him. Overnight is usually the best first time for total freedom, with the bedroom door kept closed.

Try never to allow your dog to make a mistake where there are no papers, and this will get him into the habit of always going on paper when he has to relieve himself. If he starts going off the paper for some reason, however, you may have to begin from scratch. If you actually catch your dog in the act of going where he shouldn't, follow the standard correction procedures: Walk over and slap him or throw something along the floor at him. This startles him and gets him to stop, while at the same time linking a negative connotation with the act. When he makes a mistake, clean up the feces and/or urine at once. Take your paper towels, Tabasco sauce, and vinegar over to the spot. Get your dog and punish him, using the Tabasco and vinegar method.

Reasons and Cures for Housebreaking Lapses

There are innumerable reasons why a dog has housebreaking lapses. No matter what they are, however, all breaks in training must be corrected, promptly and firmly. You have to handle mistakes with the understanding that one or two can turn into a full-fledged habit unless dealt with properly.

If a habit is already established, you sometimes may have to resort to retraining from the beginning. But if there is a sudden lapse in a previously perfectly trained dog, look for the obvious reasons first. Any extenuating circumstances should be corrected if possible. But you still have to deal severely with the lapse. You can't simply rationalize that it wasn't your dog's fault and do nothing, or you are asking for trouble.

The cause could be any of various medical problems, such as urinary or intestinal disorders. Sudden changes in diet or improper nutrition are other physically based culprits. Emotional factors can also influence elimination behavior, so dogs may urinate and defecate out of either aggression or fear—one to show dominance and the other out of nervousness or fright. Spite or anger at his owner may cause a dog to urinate or defecate, and even a new visitor in the house can trigger territorial marking or fearful piddling. Sexual drives are other causes; a female in heat will often break training and urinate frequently to attract males. Deviation from his regular walking schedule can cause problems too. Traveling is another reason; even changes in the weather can be an excuse. Usually, however, it is just a bad habit that causes a dog to break; this is the real problem animal—the dog who would just as soon go inside as out.

If the problem is medically based, have it treated if possible. If it cannot be controlled (as in the case of an older dog that has weak kidneys), work around your pet's needs. In these cases, give frequent walks and train your pet to use paper when necessary.

If your animal is eliminating in the house rather than outside because you fail to walk him on time, check to see whether his schedule should be reworked to fit both your needs. Even forgetting one walk can lead to problems. One friend did just this and had to suffer the embarrassment and indignity of her dog squatting at a New Year's Eve dinner party right on the stroke of midnight, just as everyone was toasting in the new year.

A dog who refuses to relieve himself outside because of inclement weather, despite the fact that you are walking him consistently, needs insistence. Confine him on wet days, and when you walk him, stand in one spot to outwait him. Punish him harshly for any misdeeds in your home. Dogs' refusal to go out in the rain has been the ruination of many owners. In fact, rain is one of the worst enemies in house-training, and much breaking of training occurs during rainy spells. That's why it's so important to train your dog to go as soon as he

51

gets outside. If you do, bad weather won't be so bad for either of you because you'll get back in promptly.

A timid dog who passes a little urine when greeting a person or larger animal needs to be handled with care. This nervous type of dog will often roll over on his side and urinate a little in submission. Try putting your hand on the dog and saying "good dog!" so as to prevent him from rolling over and thus lifting his leg to urinate. You can often tell when your dog is going to roll over by his submissive signal of raising his front paw as if to shake hands.

Stop this habit before it starts. Sometimes a puppy will wet the floor after someone calls him to come, and you should be treating him in the same manner as the nervous urinater.

In direct opposition to the nervous dog is the one who urinates aggressively—and who needs harsh treatment. This dog will urinate to claim his belongings and flaunt his dominance. A dominant dog may well urinate on the belongings of a visitor in your home—human or animal—and on the bed or couch that the newcomer used. He may even lift his leg on the stranger himself! The dog is unhappy about the intruder being there, perhaps out of insecurity, and wants to show he outranks the newcomer by claiming that everything is his in an outward demonstration. No matter what the reasons behind your dog's actions (or how amusing you may think he is when he does it), stop him or he will do it again and again. Soon he may even be lifting his leg to claim you, and may extend his aggression into barking and biting as well.

Spite is another reason for your dog to begin messing up in your home. Perhaps your pet resents it when you go out and leave him alone. One person's dog would always urinate if she came home and then went out again a short while later, whether she walked him or not. Stop any show of spite abruptly, and be severe in your corrections. If you catch him in the act, slap him or use the Rubber Arm technique. Additionally, use the vinegar and Tabasco method; take your dog to the spot and reprimand him. Because this type of dog invariably messes up when you're not in, a booby trap is a great deterrent. Hiding and catching him in the act when he thinks he is alone is also a good idea. Then reprimand him immediately, using the standard correction techniques. Your dog must learn that he isn't boss in your house, you are.

Visiting a friend's home or being in a strange place can cause your pet to break training. In new territories, dogs set down markers to establish possession and give themselves a sense of security. They also use urine to mark their path as they travel so as to enable them to find their way home. This is why people are constantly apologizing for their pets breaking training when visiting, especially if there is a resident animal. Then to compound the problem, when you leave the resident animal is likely to start lifting his leg over *your* dog's smell, and another friend is lost.

Teach your dog to behave himself and stay close to you when visiting a new place. Keep him on a leash so you know that your dog is under control at all times. Teaching him to stay near you in new places will mean that when you do let him loose, he'll know not to wander. This way you can watch him to be sure he's behaving. If he does mess up, use all the methods and the amount of severity necessary to stop the problem. If you don't, you will have to leave your pet home and constantly go home to walk him; or when on an extended stay, leave him in a kennel.

You can be understanding, but you must also be equally firm in stopping elimination transgressions during or just after traveling. The change in diet, new people, or a kennel atmosphere can upset your dog's routine so much he forgets his early training upon his return to your home. This is especially true of a kenneled dog confined in a cage and forced to evacuate therein. A dog in any new environment, even one returning to a familiar place after a stay away, should be confined for a while before being given his freedom. You should then watch him so he can be controlled until you are positive he remembers his lessons well enough to control his elimination patterns. Any breaks should be handled severely, with the standard methods.

Even though a female in heat (who leaves little puddles all over to let males know where she is) is basically hormone-controlled, you should still reprimand her for going where she shouldn't. To prevent problems, she should be confined during her heat cycle; spaying will stop the problem entirely. A male should never be taken near a female in heat except to mate, and then it should be in her home. If you bring the female to his home, the male will urinate over her spots when she leaves. And if you just visit a female in heat, your male is likely to mess up to show what a big shot he is—even if confined on a leash.

An otherwise completely trained dog will often have a special spot that draws him back irresistibly; he will go back to it over and over. This may be in an obvious place such as your rug. But if your dog seems never to go anywhere, look for a well-hidden spot in the cellar or behind a table. In such a case, besides dragging your dog over to the area and reprimanding him in the standard manner, you have to deter him from going back to the spot.

First try to get rid of as much of the odor as possible by scrubbing the area thoroughly with an antiseptic cleanser, deodorizer, or baking soda. After you have deodorized the spot to the best of your ability, douse the area with vinegar or, if you can safely do so, rub a foul or sharp smell such as camphor on the spot to repel him. Then cover the spot with a piece of screening, raised off the floor an inch or so to make it uncomfortable for your dog to squat there. Any habitual spot will draw an animal instinctively back to repeat himself, so you really have to work hard to get your dog to stay away. Therefore, every time you leave, remind your dog not to go there by taking him over to the spot and letting him smell the vinegar. And if you ever catch him sniffing around the area, tell him to stay away with a sharp "no!"

The recalcitrant animal who messes up for no reason except absolute orneriness needs special attention. This type of dog knows that he's doing wrong, but just doesn't want to stop or seem to care for whatever reason. First try the standard procedures for correcting him, then be much more severe in your actions; you really have to come down hard. This type of dog may take punishment for years, and never be completely trustworthy. Still-untrained male dogs two years and older are almost impossible to housebreak.

But no matter what the reason for their not being trained, simple or complex, come down hard. No one wants a dirty, untrained dog; if not housebroken, your dog will probably end up in the pound or worse. As a last resort, you may have to keep your dog constantly confined while you are not home, but try firm, even harsh, enforcement of the other procedures first. Few dogs are impossible if handled really consistently. But if not, confinement when you are not home is not such a horrible fate.

Paper and House Training Combined

Don't expect your pet to control himself if your schedule is really erratic. Additionally, a dog with a bladder infection or an older dog with kidney problems shouldn't be kept away from a toilet area. Under these conditions, give in a little and train your dog to go both inside on paper or outside when walked. The only problem with this type of training is that if paper is left down in the house, a dog will generally use it if he feels even the slightest urge. Therefore, leave paper down only when you are going to be out for a while, when you don't want to go out because the weather is bad, or as an overnight precaution.

Many people leave paper down all the time as a concession because their dog is not really trained at all, and they are afraid he might mess up. A dog will never learn to be clean in the house if he knows paper is always going to be down and available to him. If your dog is to be trained to use paper inside in conjunction with going outside, leave paper down *only* when you want him to go in the house. Simply follow the same procedure as for paper training and for housebreaking. Control which he is to do by either taking him out or leaving paper down.

If you have an erratic schedule or live in a community with laws requiring you to scoop the poop, a combination of house training and paper training may be a solution. Perhaps your dog urinates outside, but defecates on paper (either inside or out) to help you cope with the cleanup laws. If you sometimes can't walk him, you could just teach him to go inside on paper instead.

If you are paper training an older dog who has previously been accustomed to going outside, you may have to be really insistent. You will have to restrain him from going outside until he's forced to relieve himself inside on paper.

To teach your dog to defecate on the paper, place him on it and use the match-suppository technique explained earlier. Be sure to keep him on the paper until he does what he is supposed to do. Do this at the appropriate times—early in the morning and late in the evening or whenever you have observed he tends to relieve himself—until he gets the idea of what is expected. This could mean days of restricting your pet from participating in his favorite activities. But once he understands and adheres to relieving himself on paper, you can again take him out for walks.

A male who starts lifting his leg to urinate needs either an object to urinate upon or lots of room and extra paper so that he can lift his leg in the air and urinate outward. You can permit this with a small dog, but larger ones need too much space. If you have a very large dog it might be advisable to give your pet only specific times in which to relieve himself on paper, or the stench created could be a real problem.

Because he has to split his bodily functions, it may take a while for this process to click. However, if you are insistent and praise him profusely when he does the right thing and reprimand him for going outside, it shouldn't take long. But be sure to keep him confined until he is trained. If he has not been trained at all and you are starting this training from scratch, take your dog for walks to urinate, then bring him back and "match" him. If he is already broken to do everything outdoors, you will have to punish him for defecating outside and "match" him on the paper at the appropriate times. For a dog who is paper trained to do everything on paper in the house, "match" him on the paper while taking him outside until he urinates.

If you have a terrace or porch, you can have a special two-way-swing door installed for your dog so he can go in and out at will. You can then put paper or a litterbox in a specific toilet area outside. To teach your dog to go out there when he wants, push him through the door a few times to give him the idea of going in and out. Then push him through and take him to the toilet area. Proceed as you would for paper training. The only problem is that unless the outside area is fairly well enclosed, your dog may tend to wander. Additionally, a swing door big enough to allow exit and entry for a medium to large dog also admits other animals and children. If your terrace is secured, however, it can work beautifully for you and your pet.

Three

POSITIVE
OBEDIENCE
TRAINING

Reasons for Positive Training

You should not teach your dog to obey just for the sake of forcing your will upon him. Teaching him discipline keeps him living amicably with the people around him. You are responsible not only for your dog's safety, welfare, and happiness, but also for his training. And your life with him will be more pleasant if you train your dog to fit into your lifestyle.

Don't think you are going to break your dog's spirit. Instead, you're simply going to harness it. Some owners think they cannot love and train a dog at the same time, but training gives a dog something to do. Besides the fact that dogs want to please, keep in mind that their brains function better with training. Lessons make a dog more comfortable because they let him know what he can and can't do, thus affording a feeling of security. In fact, dogs who *don't* know what their owners want act nervous and insecure.

The rules of our society can be somewhat restrictive, so dogs have to be trained how to act. Some parks do not allow dogs whether on a leash or not. So that your pet can adjust his natural urges, you have to give him a new set of rules, not the ones he would learn from littermates or would need if running in the wild.

Pets vary in their ability to learn, with some being more adept at certain tasks. But it doesn't just happen; they all need some help from you. A dog comes to you with an unfinished education; you have to finish it. Every dog needs to be trained up to a point, after which he can be left on his own.

Your dog's training can be very basic, or it can be as advanced as you want. You are the one to decide how much education your pet needs; you can stop anywhere you want. All dogs must learn a certain amount, however, even if it is just not to urinate in the house and not to chew on your prized furniture. The real intention of training a dog is to make him a better pet and companion.

You are better off deciding how much you want from your dog from the beginning. The first thing to do is to make a list of the problems you have with your pet, as well as the things you want your dog to do. This will be a tailor-made guide for his training. Later you can adjust your expectations and revise your list when some new command needs to be taught or reinforced. Housebreaking comes first. Next you may want to teach your pet how to conduct himself in certain everyday situations, break him of annoying habits, and train him in responding to simple obedience. Fancy tricks come last.

Equipment You'll Need

- A twelve- to fourteen-inch chain or even a chain choke collar or leash, the length required depending on the size of your dog.
- Two S hooks, about one inch long.
- Two swivel leash fasteners of the button or slide variety. (A Chupeno Training Chain can be used in place of these items. This is a commercially available pre-assembled version of the device you will later be instructed how to put together from these items.)
- Several half-inch eye hooks.
- A regular buckle-fastening leather collar or, for short-necked dogs, a harness. Make sure the collar is loose enough so you can slip three or four fingers under it, yet tight enough so it won't slip off over the dog's head.
- A choke collar of adequate size for your pet. Size is determined by measuring the head of your dog at the widest point and adding an inch. When it is the right size, the collar should slip easily over the dog's head; and when pulled tight, it should be long enough to allow two to three inches of overlap. A nylon choke collar is best for short-haired dogs, but rolled leather that won't wear down the hair is better for long-haired dogs. Don't use chain chokes, which cut into your dog's neck.

• A six-foot training leash made of half-inch-wide cotton stripping, usually green in color. Don't use a chain leash. It cuts into your hands and is too heavy for you to manipulate with ease. Nylon leashes, though light, have a tendency to cut the hands and rub the skin raw.

There are two types of collars your dog must get used to: the regular collar and the choke. Put on a regular collar immediately even if you are not planning to leave it on all the time. This will get him used to something being around his neck. Most dogs will scratch the collar for a few minutes, but if distracted or soothed they will soon accept it. Tie a couple of short pieces of rag or cord to the collar where you would attach the lead so your dog gets used to having something dangling on him. Don't let him play with these or he may play the same game later when the lead is attached to his collar and you are holding the other end of it.

Once he's wearing the regular collar with rags or cord attached for a while, slip your dog's choke collar on, too. There is a right and a wrong way to do this. If you plan on keeping your dog on your left side, the leash—when fastened to the end of the choke—should extend from *over* and not *under* his neck. This means that if you have the choke on correctly, when you pull the leash straight toward you, it will form a continuous line coming across the top of your dog's neck. If you have the collar on wrong, however, the line formed will bend and curve under his neck.

Another test is to hold the leash up straight; if it forms the small letter *b* when joined with the collar around your pet's neck, it is correct, but a small letter *d* shape indicates it is wrong. This allows the collar to loosen automatically when the leash is made slack. If the leash is fastened to the choke collar incorrectly, the choke will stick. Another test is to put the choke collar on around your left wrist and pull tight. If on correctly, the choke will have an overlap on the upper part and will loosen when given slack. If not, it will remain tight. If it does, slip it off, turn it over, and put it on again.

Preventive Confinement

Once your dog is used to a collar, you can start getting him used to the areas where he will sleep and stay during the day.

Restricting your dog until he is trained is an ideal preventive (and curative) procedure. Confinement can be used for everything from housebreaking to stopping your dog from chewing up the house. If your dog has many destructive or rambunctious habits, he should be restricted to some degree until he has learned all his lessons. Children are kept in playpens to keep them out of trouble; the same is true for dogs. Your dog has to earn his freedom; it should be given to him gradually as he proves himself. Only when he is perfectly behaved should your dog be given complete run of the house.

Some animals can be confined and remain unaffected by it. For example, cats need little time for house-training and tend to become upset when forced to stay in the open. But closing a dog off in isolation can cause problems. Locking him away denies him the enrichment of being exposed to new situations and visitors. Your dog thus misses the opportunity to become closely attached to you, your home, and your family. As a pack animal, your dog needs to be with the family as much as possible. Don't make the mistake of sticking him in a corner of the kitchen. Rather than locking up your dog, restrain him in the open in a comfortable spot or spots around your home. This way he can see everything that is going on and feel secure in the knowledge that he is part of the household.

In selecting the places in your home where your pet can be restrained, you must make sure they're spots where your pet will be very comfortable. This is where your pet will actually be living until he is well behaved. He will leave only when you take him off to play or work with him. And since these spots will eventually become so familiar to your dog that he will return to them as secure, comfortable rest areas, be sure they are conveniently positioned. Don't put your pet near anything that could hurt him, such as a hot radiator or an object in which his collar can become entangled and choke him. Be sure your pet is out of drafts and away from the mainstream of traffic in your home. If you have a large home, select several positions so you can move your pet around with you. And no matter what size home you have, you should select a spot next to your bed where you can keep a watch on your pet during the night.

Once you've selected the areas for restrictive confinement, screw an eye hook into the floor or wall. Then, depending on your dog's size, get a twelve- to fourteen-inch chain choke collar or the equivalent length of chain. Place one small S hook, about one inch long, at either end of the chain, and fasten them to the chain by closing one curve of each S hook. Then take the two button- or slide-fastening swivel clips, and attach these to the other side of the S hooks. Close off the other curve of the S hook to fasten permanently. (Or get the appropriate-sized Chupeno Training Chain.)

When this is done, you will have a short chain with a swivel-clip leash fastener on either end. Next, take the buckle-fastening collar of the correct size for your pet. Too tight a collar will make him choke, while one that is too large may allow him to catch his paw in the collar and perhaps break a toe or rip a dewclaw. (Do not ever use a choke under any circumstances, or you could hurt your dog.)

Attach this collar to one end of the chain. Once this is done, you have a portable contraption that enables you to confine your pet easily. Simply attach the other end of the chain to the eye hook you have placed in the floor or wall. Or you can attach your pet to any stationary, solid object by clipping one fastener onto the chain itself to form a small loop. If you do this, make sure the chosen object is extremely stable.

Keep in mind that confinement is *not* punishment and should not be associated with it in any way. Therefore, be sure never to tease your dog while he is on the chain. In fact, play with him there so he understands it's a good place to be, and also to prevent him from developing a territorial, perhaps aggressive, reaction to the area. These confinement spots are simply places to stay until your pet earns his freedom as a reward for good behavior. Equip your dog's main spots with a bed to make him comfortable, water, and a couple of raw-hide bones or toys. But never put newspaper down in your pet's confinement area, not even if you are paper training him.

When first confining your pet, be sure not to leave him alone until he calms down and learns to sit comfortably and safely. Check his collar to be sure it cannot get caught and choke your pet, is tight enough not to slip over his head, and is not loose enough to be hazardous. Be sure he cannot injure himself on anything. Your dog must be aware of the limitations of his confinement, so for the first day or so, leave the house only for short periods of time until he calms down and accepts his lot. After your dog is acclimatized to this confinement, he should live on the confinement training chain until he's really well behaved, getting loose only when you can watch him. First let your dog loose for about an hour at a time, then give more and more freedom as he proves he deserves it.

If you're reluctant to utilize this training and won't tie up your dog, think about your rugs, furniture, and in fact everything that makes your home a comfortable place to be. In the final analysis, you will love your dog more if you keep him confined until trained, because he won't do any of those destructive things that can make you grow to dislike him.

The First Learning Session

Most people don't know how or where to start training their dogs. To keep the mistakes on your part and your dog's to a minimum, set up a special learning session right at the outset.

Training can be done without this lesson, but it is really highly desirable. You want your dog to get the right idea of what it's all about and start him off learning quickly. A good beginning sets up patterns for you and your dog. It allows you both to get to know each other, and lets your pet understand that you are boss.

If you have had your dog for a while, put him through the

session immediately. If you leave a pup or dog to his own devices—even for a short time—he'll start relieving himself in the house, chewing on things, crying and whining, and won't want to listen to you. But if he is a brand-new dog, be sure that he has been acclimatized to your home first, or he will become confused.

When you start training your dog, make sure that the area you choose is not going to interfere with the work to be done. Use a familiar, uncluttered, but enclosed area such as a room in your home. Until your dog fully understands what's expected of him, make the training area free from distractions such as loud noises, children, and other animals. Later, to accustom your pet to working anywhere and under all conditions, you *must* move your dog to unfamiliar areas and gradually bring in distractions. However, be sure to gradually build up your pet's repertoire of places and situations under which obedience is expected. Even the best-behaved dog will be uncertain when worked under new conditions in a new place, and unpleasant experiences may permanently discourage your pet from training. Be understanding and patient. This lesson should last for several hours, during which time you should bombard your dog with all the absolute basics of training: accepting a collar and leash, coming when called, sitting, staying, and lying down. These are the basic, most important positive commands, with ''come'' topping the list in priority.

The training techniques and schedule of this lesson are intended exclusively for this initial learning experience. For instance, it is probably the only time when all commands are given while the dog is on a leash. You want to control your dog and quickly get him to understand what is expected of him, so the leash is used for sure, fast results.

First accustom your dog to the leash. This is generally a simple matter if he accepts the regular collar. Once he has worn the regular collar for a while, remove it and slip his choke collar on. Attach the leash to the choke collar and allow it to fall or drag on the floor for a while to get him accustomed to feeling something around his neck. Later, when you pull on it, it will be familiar, and he will not be afraid. Don't let him play with this leash now, or he may constantly bite at it later. When you pick up the leash and put pressure on it, some dogs will fight like a newly bridled colt, but hold on firmly. If you insist, your dog will soon realize that there is no point in struggling.

Start to walk your dog around on the leash. He will probably either remain behind or lunge ahead. Just continue walking until he realizes there is no point to struggling and he might as well walk. When he does, reassure and praise him. Avoid taking him to strange surroundings, and as you walk talk to him and pet him frequently until he becomes used to the leash. Do not attempt to train your dog to heel at this time, simply try to accustom him to being restricted on the end of a leash. Teaching you and him how to walk *properly* on a leash comes in the regular training sessions.

Patting the floor or your knee and coaxing the dog to come along, will teach your pet to have no real fear of the leash. Do not drag him roughly at first. The dog may apply all four brakes and refuse to budge. Pull the dog slowly along the floor until he makes up his mind he is going to walk.

Keep in mind that dogs associate things, so repetition is important: As taught here these commands are just to start the association process in your dog's brain, a prelude to all training. Do not link commands at this point, but make sure your dog understands one command at a time.

The meaning of certain words can be quickly grasped. He should learn immediately to associate "no" with something wrong so you can easily repress undesirable behavior without punishment. Be firm when stopping bad habits, but never go into any negative training when you're teaching positive commands, because the two must not be connected closely in time. A quick, short expression such as "okay" should be learned to indicate permission is granted.

Start off with *come when called*. At this time, the command is taught by pulling the dog toward you with the leash. Within a short while the dog should come without pressure. When he does, quit. Simply sit yourself down on the floor or in a chair. Call your dog by saying the word "come." When your pet comes to you, praise him—and that part of the lesson is over.

The dog needs to be taught to *sit* right away. This will keep your dog quiet and still when you want him to be. With the leash on your dog, go to a quiet place where there are no distracting influences. Make your dog stand in front of you or at your side, and give the command "sit" while at the same time leaning over with the left hand and pressing down steadily on your dog's rump until he is in a sitting position.

As soon as he is sitting, keep him in place by holding him with one hand and petting him with the other while praising him. Don't keep him in place for too long at first. After two or three repeats of this, try just saying "sit" without any pressure. If he sits, pet him; if he doesn't, repeat "sit" and press back down.

This is usually enough for the first lesson. Repeat a few times during the day interspersed among the other work until it connects.

While training, never take your eyes off your dog. You should be aware enough of your dog that you can anticipate what is going to happen. This way you can constantly monitor your dog's reactions and correct or encourage him readily, as needed. On the other hand, don't let success go to your head and overdo the training. Your dog's concentration span is short, so be alert for signs of tiring. To ensure that your pet doesn't get bored doing the same thing over and over, vary your training routine. Your dog should look forward to work.

Stay is really for emphasis on all stationary commands, but the earlier your dog learns to stay still where he is put, the better. While it acclimatizes the dog to the training to come, it is also a lesson in self-control, teaching the dog patience and increasing his concentration and attention span. Place your dog in a sitting position, and say "stay" while gradually backing away from him the length of the leash. He'll probably try to move, but just keep replacing him in the sit-stay position until he obeys. "Stay" should be reasonably easy after he knows "sit."

Lie down is an optional part of this first lesson, but it's a good thing to get over with quickly. It lays the basics for some good tricks and helps make the dog realize from the outset that you are the boss. After all, it is a submissive gesture. Again it is better to have your dog on a leash so he cannot dart off, and you can use it as an aid. Tell him "down" and pull his front feet forward from underneath him as you apply pressure on his back to force him down. When he lies down, don't stroke and praise with too much enthusiasm, or it may tempt him to get up. To get a larger dog to lie down, give the command "down" and gently press down on the shoulders, draw his feet out from under him, grasp the dog's leash close under his neck, and pull him down. Practice until he goes down on command. Once learned, try combining lie down with stay by using the same techniques used for sit and stay.

The lesson lasts as long as it does so that you can take frequent breaks and thus separate the various aspects of training. The concentration span of your dog is short, so watch for him to tire. After short, frequent breaks, stop and give your dog a rest; walk him or do whatever you have to do to break the routine. Keep on working the animal until he knows something, but also give him time to rest.

The later training sessions may have slightly different methods, but these employed here give your dog a quick idea of what training is all about. By the end of this session you'll know the things about your dog that need the most work. You will be able to judge your dog's temperament and what type of methods he will need. Every dog that has had some preliminary training, who is not afraid of the leash and understands "come," "sit," and "down," will learn the subsequent exercises more quickly.

Though you may not realize it, a certain understanding between the dog and you has already been established through this small amount of training. After this, continually rework these commands in short, randomly spaced training periods to reinforce the teaching. Do not overlap commands in any one lesson. Keep them separated from each other until the dog understands one command at a time. This will ensure that your pet learns. Then gradually add the other basics, and finally add tricks to your dog's repertoire.

Basic Training Rules

There are no regularly scheduled sessions for teaching a dog to do something. Just work your pet in short exercise periods that can be given at any time of the day or night. The lessons themselves should be only two to three minutes in length, with five the absolute tops. Longer sessions are to be used only for complicated tricks after your dog is well accustomed to being trained and worked, or if your pet knows the command thoroughly but refuses to work. You need to devote only enough time to make sure the lesson sinks in. It's tempting to continue with a lesson that is going well, but it's best not to push your pet. If you do, your dog might become bored, flub the next try, and end the lesson badly.

There are certain common-sense rules you should follow:

1. Never work your dog after a hearty meal. If you do, your pet might relieve himself in the middle of training, because activity stimulates the digestion and bodily functions. Also, give your dog an opportunity to relieve himself after the lesson. The excitement can make it necessary for your pet to go—especially if he is a pup. If it's near feeding time, hold off and feed your dog *after* school. This way, the meal becomes a form of reward.

2. Play with your dog before and after training periods, not during. The lesson is for work, not play. However, don't be tyrannical in your insistence; keep it light but firm.

3. A dog is responsive to your moods. Therefore, you must have confidence that you can teach your pet. You must know what you want, and let your dog know, too. But at the same time, you must be restrained and treat your dog with patience. If you get impatient and excited during training, your pet will too. Use your normal tone of voice and steady body movements. Be slow and deliberate, never quick and jerky. Don't rush at your dog to correct him, but move slowly. No matter how annoyed you are, maintain a calm and quiet front. If you get visibly upset and irrational, nothing will be accomplished; even worse, you may convince your dog that training is an unpleasant experience. These sessions should be calm, efficient, and hopefully, enjoyable. If you feel you're running out of patience and are about to lose your temper, it's better to walk your dog through the command, quit the lesson, and start again later.

4. It's best not to work when the weather is really hot, or when either you or your dog are not feeling well. Use your discretion about when and how long to work your pet. Just be careful you don't allow this to turn into procrastination.

71

5. Everyone in your household must cooperate in training, but don't confuse your pet by letting different people use different training methods. You must all agree upon and follow the same procedures. In fact, it's best if only one person is designated to do the initial training. Later, when the dog becomes somewhat familiar with the commands, other persons can work him. Just be sure your dog is worked by only one person at a time. If three people issue different commands at the same time, your dog won't know what to do. Therefore, make sure no one gets involved except the person giving the command. No pet is well trained until all reasonable household members receive obedience and respect. But if you want your dog to be discriminating in whom he obeys, allow only certain persons to work with him and discourage obedience to others.

6. Avoid teaching in front of an audience, which will probably upset both you and your dog. If you do get caught in front of a group of people, however, carry through regardless. If you don't finish what you start, your pet won't learn to be obedient once distractions appear. When a dog starts to resist, perhaps the most common mistake people make is to give up or yell with rage. Your dog has to know that when something is said, it is meant. A command, once given, must be completed, even if you have to walk your dog through the command. Interruptions in lessons such as telephone calls should not be allowed to interfere with the training process. If the doorbell rings in the middle of putting your dog through a command, start the exercise again when the interruption is over. Be sure to finish the exercise so your dog learns that these interruptions are no excuse to goof off. Like kids, dogs need consistency so they know exactly where they stand. If you allow your pet not to finish, he will constantly try to get away with not listening. It is essential that the lesson not end with your dog having his own way. Your pet must complete work when commanded, even if his performance is not perfect.

How to Use Your Dog's Senses in Training

All sorts of training methods have been advocated over the years, but the problems with each have generally remained the same—whatever the outward manifestation of training, it never gave the dog a chance to be a dog. You can't expect respect and obedience from your dog unless you teach with an understanding and knowledge of what your dog really is. Dogs' incredible perceptiveness, plus their highly social nature and desire to please, makes them uniquely adapted to training. Their heightened senses allow them to pick up even the minutest signals. But you have to know what to do with your dog to train him properly.

Each species of animal is selective in the stimuli to which it responds, and an animal's behavior is made up of responses to these signals, sights, sounds, tastes, and smells from the environment. Knowing how your pet receives and interprets sensory messages from the world around him will help you understand how to treat him and what methods to use in training. What we humans see, hear, and smell is very different from what a dog perceives.

A dog's hearing is excellent, and it is the animal's second most important sense, after smell. The ear flap and external ear canal pick up and conduct sound, dampen incoming noises, and provide protection for the dog's delicate middle and inner ears. All dogs can manipulate their ear flaps by reflexively contracting the muscles that elevate the external ear in order to focus in on sounds. Most of the analogous muscles are still residually present in humans, so that some people can consciously wiggle their ears. But in us, the reflex reaction to sound is missing.

Dogs can hear higher and fainter tones than a human can. They are not as accurate as humans in discriminating differences in pitch and in the distance sound has traveled. However, they are especially adept at localizing the source of sounds, even to the point of distinguishing which noise comes from higher terrain and which from lower. A dog's hearing is so reliable that dogs are now being used to signal deaf people when the doorbell rings or in case of an audible danger.

A dog makes at least moderate use of its eyesight. Visual ability often varies greatly from one breed of dog to another, and some—such as hounds—have excellent sight. A dog's hunting instincts are triggered primarily by the movement of the prey, making it easier for him to follow. The placement of the dog's eye in his head gives him a visual field of 250° when the eye is at rest, as opposed to man's 180°. This lets the dog receive impressions from the side and rear without turning or revolving his head. Thus your dog can easily respond to hand signals even if he's standing by your side.

To help keep the eye moist and to protect it from injury, dogs have an opaque third eyelid that rises up from the corner of the eye nearest the nose. But despite their more expanded peripheral vision, canines do not have such a large binocular field. In dogs, that portion of the visual field seen by both eyes simultaneously is about 100°; humans have a binocular field closer to 140°. It is this lack of stereoscopic or 3-D vision which limits dogs' depth perception so they do not always gauge distances accurately. Since a dog's vision is generally limited, he does not rely on it alone, but uses other senses to augment it. Your dog may not recognize a specific person at a distance; he may have to get close enough to see features *and* smell *and* hear before recognizing who it is. Dogs do discriminate among intensities of light, so they see hues—shadows of light and dark. However, since there are no color receptors on the canine retina, dogs are color-blind. Their discrimination of form and pattern is mediocre, so they can seldom learn to distinguish visual symbols or shapes.

It is not that a dog's eyes are inherently inferior; he just uses them differently than we do, being primarily alert to movement. Generally, a dog learns more quickly by physical indications of what is expected than by voice. Perhaps this is due to a dog's reliance on body language as a means of communication. Thus you should have *two* ways of indicating what you want your pet to do: a voice command and a hand signal, which must be standard words and movements.

People often fall into the habit of using exclusively one method when both are needed. The only time a dog should be trained to obey just one type is in the case of a blind dog taught to obey voice commands only, or a deaf dog taught to obey only hand signals.

Estimates claim that hand signals constitute about seventy-five percent of a dog's training, and voice commands about twenty-five percent. But as the training progresses, voice signals become of equal importance. Some dogs can learn to respond to as many as fifty different commands. The trouble is that the variety of clear, effective arm and hand signals is limited, so that additional vocal commands can better increase your pet's repertoire. But if you are not consistent and use a different word or signal every time you give the command, your pet will never learn.

Neither commands nor signals should have any ambiguity about them. Both should be short, to the point, and consistent. Deviations in the commands given in obedience training can confuse an animal, and can lead to his refusal to respond. If your dog doesn't know what is expected of him, he will act as though being disobedient.

When hand signals are used, be sure to keep in mind that it is the motion that catches your dog's eye first. A dog's eyesight is designed to be especially sensitive to motion. Through work, some dogs develop such a heightened perceptivity that they learn to pick up even the slightest cues. A well-trained dog can, by observing the owner's subtle signals, appear to count or do complex reasoning tasks seemingly well beyond the scope of any animal's ability. The simple raising of an eyebrow or a twitch of the finger may be the signal. However, you must start off slowly and deliberately, gradually building to these refinements. Therefore, when first teaching, give broad sweeping gestures to indicate what you want. To give your dog the opportunity to be right, you must make sure you differentiate among the names and signals for the various commands. Each should have a definite word and hand signal to indicate what you want your pet to do; do not overlap or vary them from time to time as many people do. Constantly being given the same command and signal will

75

give your pet the security of knowing exactly what each one means and what is expected.

Though any word can come to indicate any action, it is best to stick to the standards. One dog sat every time she was told "up." Apparently this connection had come about by the dog sitting down in anticipation of being picked up every time her owner said, "Want to come up?" It didn't take long for the dog to sit, waiting to be lifted up whenever she heard the most emphatic word in the sentence, "up."

Sometimes teaching a dog to respond in seeming contradiction to the word being spoken is deliberate. One dog was taught to growl and look mean to the words "Be a nice dog." A funny reaction, but dangerous for a dog allowed to wander among children. Using an incorrect word to command your pet can be confusing to people who don't know your special secret code—and this can cause problems when leaving your pet at the groomer's or in a kennel.

Whether you use standard commands or your own special code, be sure to use only a single word or two. Going into a whole sentence will only confuse your pet. Give the command once—don't repeat it several times or you will constantly have to do it. Rather than just "sit," the command for your dog will become "sit-sit-sit." Don't snap or yell; use your normal tone of voice. The hand signal should be given just once too, and once you have given it, don't keep your hand in position—return it to your side. Finally, to test your dog to be sure he is proficient in both voice commands and hand signals, isolate them. First give only voice commands to be sure your pet obeys, then give only the hand signals.

Come When Called

"Come" is the most important positive command your dog can learn. When your dog learns this, you gain complete control over him. It is the first step in off-the-leash training, and it is the command that can save your dog's life in times of danger. As such, it should be the first thing a young dog is taught in positive training—"sit" is not an ideal first choice if your dog is in the middle of the street. Hopefully, once your dog knows this command you can take him to the park and let him run free, secure in the knowledge that he will come back to you when asked to do so.

In teaching this command, start by taking your pet into a familiar room where he feels comfortable. Make sure it's quiet and free from outside interruptions. Once there, close the door to avoid escapes and disturbances. Put on your pet's six-foot cotton training leash and choke collar. This collar and leash are to be used as aids in training your dog to come when called only long enough for him to understand what the command means. By its very nature, the "come" command requires that the animal be able to approach you when off the leash; it's for use when you want him to come to you from the other side of a room or to return to you when running loose outside. In the early stages, however, mistakes made on the leash are easily corrected. On the leash your dog is forced to come, because he'll be pulled or jerked if he doesn't. And if the leash is used properly, your dog won't show any reluctance. Therefore, in training your dog never pull the leash downward but always use an upward motion.

With the leash on your dog, sit down on the floor or in a chair. This puts you at your dog's level and makes you appear a less forbidding authority figure for your pet to approach.

How to Issue the Command

Before you can give a command you have to get your pet's attention. You can do this in many ways, but by far the most common are to either call out your dog's name or to snap the leash lightly. If neither of these work, try tossing something near your pet, and then call out his name. Count five to yourself to separate his name from the actual command, then use a combined voice and hand command. Bring your hand and arm across your chest, and at the same time say "come." A moment later, pull your dog toward you.

Use your normal tone of voice and give a clear hand signal. Coaxing, cajoling, or begging your dog is unnecessary. Don't scream the command repeatedly; there is nothing less effective than someone shouting at a dog and getting no response. When actually giving the voice and hand command to your dog, never exert any pressure on the leash. You want your dog to learn, right from the outset, to come because you *ask,* and not because a pull on the leash demands that he listen. If you pull or jerk on the leash and say "come" at the same time, your dog will connect the command with being pulled.

When reeling your pet in, keep both hands in front of you and gather the leash up in a hand-over-hand motion. This will encourage your dog to come straight at you rather than weaving off to one side.

When commanding your pet, move your body around as little as possible. If you move, he will assume you are going to him and not bother to come to you. Stand your ground until he gets to you. Don't lean over to pat your knee or thigh, which will tend to make your dog crawl and keep his head down when coming toward you and thus look submissive and unhappy. When calling your dog, sit straight so that the dog will come to you with his head held high in the air. Never actually repeat "come" or signal your pet to you from anywhere other than the spot from which you originally called him. Once you leave that spot, it should be to reprimand your pet for disobeying.

How to Use Praise

The only way to encourage your pet to be obedient is to let him know the right thing is being done. To do this, a pleasant experience or reward of some sort must follow the desired action. When calling their pets, some people tempt them with a reward of food, feeling that this will make the dog come running. But you shouldn't resort to this unless your dog won't listen any other way. A reward works fine as long as your dog is hungry, likes what you offer, and isn't involved in something more interesting than the food. Your dog should come to you because you ask, not because you are tempting him. After all, with food as a reward, all you are teaching your dog is to come for food, not to come when called.

Since dogs love to please, praise is usually incentive enough. It is probably the most effective means of showing your dog you are pleased.

In praising, however, just keep in mind that stroking soothes and reassures, while patting makes a dog nervous. Many owners pat their dogs on the heads as praise, but dogs don't want to be tapped. Stroke your pet and say "good dog." Let your pet understand in no uncertain terms that you are pleased; make a big fuss over him so he will enjoy being worked and trained. Only if you praise your dog profusely when correct will he understand what is right. Once a lesson is well learned, of course, you will not want or need to continue with an extreme overt show of enthusiastic praise. As the training becomes well established, you can gradually decrease your enthusiasm.

As a general rule, your dog should learn to work because you ask, not because of bribery. Food is sometimes used as an added incentive for complicated tricks or as an absolute last resort, but it's best not to make a habit of this form of reward. Extra food will put weight on your dog and make house-training more difficult. Besides, if your pet learns to work for treats, he will work for anyone with food—especially if the other treats are better than yours.

If it must be used, however, food should be given on a random basis. At first, reward your pet every time he obeys. Then when he understands, treat him every few times in an irregular pattern. After he is really well trained, give your pet a treat only once in a great while, just to show that there is always the possibility of reward. But be careful not to set up an inadvertent pattern to your rewarding. If you do, your dog will soon catch on and obey only when he anticipates a food reward. Slot machines are perfect examples of the effectiveness of random rewards.

When you praise your pet for doing right, do it in such a way as to use it to your advantage. Correct praise can help you make sure your pet consistently does well. At least in the early stages of training, praise your dog by chucking him under the chin to keep his head up and make him look happier. A dog with a lowered head looks as if he is cowering even if he really isn't. Therefore, when he does as he's told, place your hand under his muzzle and hold his head upward so that he is looking up at you *before* saying "good dog." At the same time, this will hold him in place. Until completely trained, chances are he'll stop being good as soon as you say "good dog."

When teaching this command, the way you praise your dog is very important. Don't say "good dog" as soon as he starts to come toward you. If you praise him too soon, your dog may think he's done what you want, and he's likely to stop coming toward you and return to whatever he was doing. You want your dog to know that when you call, he must come *all the way* to you.

Wait until your dog is right next to you before praising him. Then make sure your pet stays beside you by reaching out to hold him in place. Only after you are touching him should you say "good dog." And be sure to hold him underneath the chin so as to keep his head up in the air. Give him the look of being proud of what he's doing instead of that hangdog, droopy-headed look.

Once you are sure he has learned his lessons well, you may not have to hold him in place. But until you're positive your dog knows the command, be sure to follow this procedure for praising. If not, he will learn he doesn't have to come all the way over to you.

Repeat this a few times, then move to a different spot. Again sit down and call your dog, but don't pull him all the way over to you. Simply pull him along about a foot, let the leash go slack, and say "come" again. If he doesn't come, pull the leash another foot, then let go of the pressure and say "come" again. Continue this until your dog either comes to you of his own volition or is eventually pulled over to you.

Even if your dog only comes to you six inches on his own, it means he understands the basic concept of the command and responds to it. Repeat this procedure over and over until your dog comes to you of his own accord, with no external pressure.

Once you feel sure your dog is responding to the command enough so that he will come even a short way on his own, again move to a new position and again sit with him. Give the command for your dog to come. Wait a few moments to give him the opportunity to respond without any further encouragement. If he doesn't, this time—rather than pulling—gently jerk the leash. The idea is still to see if you can get your dog to come to you from the end of a six-foot leash of his own accord. Therefore, again work it a foot at a time, but this time with jerks rather than pulls. Once your dog comes immediately on the word "come," the jerk following it is unnecessary. That is why you must wait a few seconds till you see if he will come *before* exerting the jerk. The jerk is only to nudge the dog to come toward you and to show him what's expected.

After he has an idea about what the command means and comes at least reasonably consistently when you are sitting down, stand up and try it. Place your feet apart to block your dog from going to either side. Then proceed as you did when you were seated, first using the pulling method then the jerking one. Just be sure you don't lean over. Stand straight and gather the leash up as he comes toward you so as to control your dog and make sure that he stays squarely in front of you. Keep a tight hold on the leash and keep it somewhat taut, thus forcing your dog to keep looking up at you.

"Come" Without a Leash

The second level of training—teaching your dog to come without a leash—is designed to instill in his mind that you can reach him no matter where he goes.

Take your dog to a different but still familiar room. But this time make sure the room is sparsely furnished. There should be a minimum of sofas, beds, or anything that your dog can run under or behind. To have success in this part of the training, you need to keep the barriers down between you and your dog.

Again close all the doors so he cannot escape. Again make sure that there are no distractions in the room such as other people, pets, or noises. In all new training you want to try to keep it as simple as possible so your dog can concentrate on the task at hand. First review the basics learned while using the leash, just to be sure your dog understands and comes readily to you from the full length without any encouragement. You only want to refresh your pet's memory to be sure he's ready to learn without the leash. You just have to know that your dog has it firmly in his mind that the command "come" means to come to you, to be touched by you. Once he does, you can teach him that it also applies when there is nothing attaching the two of you.

To start off-the-leash training, plant yourself in one spot, sitting or standing, whichever position your pet responds to most readily. Once your dog appears relaxed, say his name, count five silently to yourself, and then call him to you, giving both voice and hand commands: Move your hand and arm toward yourself in a large beckoning gesture, at the same time saying "come." If he doesn't come, take something soft that won't hurt, such as a magazine or slipper, and toss it at or near him. After it lands, immediately call him again, using both hand and voice commands but not saying his name.

Just be sure you don't keep repeating your pet's name over and over. It's the command that's important, not the name, which you can be sure your pet knows. If after you say his name and give the command your dog looks toward you but refuses to obey, don't call out the name again. Simply repeat the command, and if he refuses to obey, either treat your dog as disobedient and correct him with negative training; or if it is a new command, walk him through it. (Prefacing every repeated command with your dog's name is annoying. But when you do use your pet's name, be sure to give a command to follow it up. For whatever reason, many people call out their pet's name but forget to follow it up, as if their pets are clairvoyant and know what is wanted. Once you call out your dog's name, your pet will be uncertain and on edge unless you tell him why you are calling him.)

The "come" command means coming right up to you when you call. It does not mean coming three feet near you, or coming when your dog feels like it. Wherever and whenever you call your dog, he should come to you immediately. You shouldn't have to take one step off the spot where you're standing; he should come to you. If you start making concessions, allowing him to come to just a few feet away or letting him not respond once in a while, soon he won't listen at all.

Even if you run into some distraction such as the doorbell or phone ringing, don't forget the lesson. Once you give the command, make sure your dog comes to you. This doesn't mean working your dog for hours on end; if he comes to you the first time you tell him, call it quits. But if after about three minutes your dog has still not obeyed, remember the spot from where you called him, and get him and walk him back over to that spot.

Don't run after your dog when he does not respond to your call or he'll only run farther away, either thinking it is a game or becoming nervous. Running after him repeatedly saying "come, come, come" only makes matters worse. The dog then knows that he doesn't have to come to you, you are going to him.

If he absolutely will not come, walk over to him methodically. This may mean rousting him out from under chairs or behind any other hiding spots. Take him by the collar or scruff of the neck and give him a good shake or a slap. Then let him go and walk back to your original call spot.

When you get there, again call your dog to you, using both voice and hand commands. Even if he is slinking along right by your side, call him again when you get back on the original call spot—following is not coming on command. When he gets to you, touch him under the chin and praise him profusely while holding him in place. If he does not come right up to you but only close by, reach out and bring him into place. But don't grab at him, which will frighten him off.

The premise behind the teaching of this basic command is to show your dog that when you call him, it's bad for him to be anywhere except at your side; and when he is there, only good will happen to him. Therefore, one of the cardinal rules in training is to never, under any circumstances, call your pet to come to you and then reprimand him or inflict any kind of discomfort (including grooming, bathing, or medication) when he gets there. Never ask your pet to do something, and then seem to punish him when he does it.

However, in almost direct opposition to this principle, you must keep in mind that when you tell your dog to do something and he doesn't listen, your pet is being disobedient. If you have to call your pet two or three times before he comes to you, and he fully understands what he is supposed to do, your pet is misbehaving. When this happens, you have to correct him through a negative training procedure. Your dog will continually test you to see if you mean what you say and if obedience is really necessary. If you don't insist, your pet will quickly learn that he really doesn't need to pay attention.

When you re-call your dog after reprimanding him, he may start to walk toward you, then waver and look as if to go the other way. If so, call him again quickly to remind him. If he ignores you and refuses to come, throw something hard at him. This may make him run to you for security and protection. If he absolutely refuses to come but continues to run off, go and get him. Pull him all the way back to the spot you originally called him from. You must get him there, and once you do, praise him profusely—even though you brought him.

Repeat this training until your dog learns to come to you on command. If for some reason he will not listen to you, no matter how often you drag him back to the spot or how many Rubber Arm objects you throw at him, go back half a step— *reach him anywhere*. Attach a length of cord measuring fifteen feet or so to your dog's leash. Then rework the command as you would if your pet were on a shorter leash. This may help you teach your pet that distance does not affect the need for him to obey the command. However, do not resort to this method unless it's absolutely essential. Once you have established the idea with the lengthened leash, again proceed with the second stage of training—and take off the leash. When he gets to you, praise him in the appropriate manner by holding him in place and chucking him under the chin in an upward gesture.

No matter what form of encouragement you give your pet to teach him to obey, be careful that your dog has no fearful experience when learning—such as having a noisy fire engine go by while you are giving a command. Your pet may well connect the experience with the command, and he will thus anticipate the same thing happening every time he hears the command itself, and may never learn to obey.

Distractions and Unfamiliar Places

In working any particular exercise, allow your pet to become proficient before bringing in distractions. You want to be sure your dog will obey at all times when given a command—even when the command is least expected. Eventually you should expect obedience from your dog even when he is playing with other dogs or being petted by a visitor. He is not always going to be working under ideal controlled conditions, which in reality are rare; therefore he has to learn to cope with changing circumstances. Working in an ideal setup at first is important so that your dog thoroughly understands the concept of the command. But once he does, you should make the atmosphere more realistic and closer to normal everyday living conditions.

Therefore, once your pet is coming to you without a leash consistently in a quiet, familiar room, first try varying the environment. Simply take your pet into different rooms in your home or to a friend's home and work him in the "come" command there. For distractions, bring a few different people to watch you work. However, be sure that you don't gather together what would constitute an audience. When one person gives a command, no one else should interfere. What you really want is to have people around who might normally be there, plus the usual household noises such as the television or radio. Then test your pet's proficiency in this command by calling him when he's involved with a toy, or even at play with another dog. He has to come under all circumstances.

Don't bombard your dog with everything all at one time, of course. Introduce distractions gradually and make sure he is ready for each new stage. Too much at one time can cause a traumatic experience that might ruin your dog's training.

He may think the same bad thing will happen each time the command "come" is given, and so refuse to listen. When you call him to you, he should associate only good things with you.

Outdoor Training in an Enclosed Area

Dogs respond to the outdoors as a symbol of freedom and often make a dash for liberty, forgetting all their lessons. Only after your dog learns to come to you consistently in the house, and has been taken methodically through every training step along the way, is he ready to be taken outside.

Even then, your pet's first outside training experience should be in a semi-enclosed area such as a fenced-in garden or a dog run. There have to be enough restrictions to ensure that you can control him while teaching him to come back to you outdoors. Before you can finally allow him off a leash in the park or on a beach, you must be absolutely sure of your dog. Teach him thoroughly in an enclosed area first to avoid problems later.

The best way to proceed is exactly as you did when teaching the dog inside. Take a quick review by having him come from the end of a six-foot training leash. Then use a leash that has been extended with an attached cord. Once your dog responds immediately, move on to the off-the-leash training procedures.

The most effective off-the-leash outdoor technique is the Rubber Arm method, which makes your dog think you can reach out to get him anywhere. It is perfect for reinforcement when he refuses to listen. If you use it to correct any regressive behavior your dog will learn that once outdoors, when you call his security lies solely with you. You can't use a magazine or a slipper as your Rubber Arm tool because you need something with more heft to reach your dog at a greater distance. You can use small chains, a choke chain, or even your house keys (with a bright ribbon attached to help you recover them from the grass). Just keep the size of your dog in mind. A Yorkie and a shepherd logically require different throwing objects. The idea isn't to hurt or frighten your dog, but to let him know you can reach him wherever he is.

When you are outside and your dog is running around, call him to come once. If he comes, praise him. If not, he is being disobedient because he knows the command. So take your Rubber Arm training aid and try to hit him with it. The object shouldn't hurt him, but it must actually physically touch him.

The moment *after* it does touch him, say "come" and give the beckoning signal. Be sure not to make the hit and command simultaneously. You must hit first, and then immediately call him to you. When he comes running to you, take hold of him as you did indoors and praise him abundantly, holding him under the chin to keep his head up. He should get a good reaction for obeying. If he's really stubborn and absolutely refuses to budge, exert more velocity as you throw so that your aid hits hard enough for him to understand that he must listen to you.

Consistent refusal to obey requires that you go over to him, *calmly* give him a good hard slap, and walk back to your call spot as you would indoors—but this degree of disobedience generally means you have to go back a few steps and review the training.

Once this part of the outdoor training is complete and your dog comes to you consistently, take him somewhere where there aren't any really well-defined restrictions. Before you can do this, you have to be absolutely positive your dog will return to you when called. Even if your dog responds so well to the command that he comes back every time, you should still subject him to the Rubber Arm technique at least once while in an enclosed area. This will remind him that you can reach him anywhere, that he must come even when completely free, or there'll be trouble.

Outside, with No Restrictions

Freedom to be outside without restrictions is reserved only for those dogs who really obey when called. It can come only after working with your dog through all the preliminary stages. Once out in the freedom of your local park, nearby countryside, or beach, you must vigorously reinforce your pet's training by using the off-the-leash Rubber Arm technique. Even the best-trained dogs wander around, getting so involved in new sights and sounds that they lose track of their owners. Never allow your dog to run off in a new area, but keep him in sight at all times so you can readily call or signal him to come back. If he appears to be wandering off, call him back close by your side and keep him there. Don't hesitate to throw your training aid at him if he doesn't respond right away. And if you use something like a chain or keys that rattle, just a shake of them should be enough of a reminder so you can call him and get him to come to you.

You will find far more complete information in the section on Off-the-Leash Training. However, these directions apply only if you want to work hard with your pet. Coming back while off the leash is really essential: Even if your dog isn't allowed to wander as a general rule, you want to be able to get him back if he accidentally gets free.

Correcting the Most Common Mistakes

Many dogs are perfect about coming when called except when there are other dogs around; then they just don't seem to hear the command. Because your dog is in the midst of a mass of other animals, you can't use your Rubber Arm technique. You have to leave your call spot, walk over to your dog, and give him a whack to show him that you really mean that you want him. Don't let him get away with not coming because he's involved in play and you don't want to interrupt his social life.

If your dog assumes an oversubmissive posture when approaching you after being called, treat it as an emotional problem. If it is just a matter of habit, you have to make your dog at least look happier about coming. Pick him up the minute he comes to you or simply grasp him immediately when he gets near you, and hold him in place to give him security while you praise him. Bring his head upward toward you by always chucking him under the chin. A treat or a favorite toy held high in the air will also force his attention up.

Some dogs run to everyone but the person who called them, as if looking for protection. This of course makes everyone think that the owner giving the command—namely you—is a complete tyrant. To overcome this trait, you must enlist the aid of the same people to whom your pet runs. To teach your dog to come only to the person who calls him, make him associate something unpleasant with everyone else. Once you're sure your dog knows the command, take him into a familiar room where a couple of family members or friends—three people at most—sit around casually. Call your dog to you. When he starts running from one person to another they should give him no sympathy, but ignore him. If he persists, they should reprimand and chase him. If several people throw things at your dog when he disregards a call to come, he will run for protection to the person calling him. Equally if not more efficient is to have each person he goes to ignore him completely. You either throw something at him or go over and drag him away from the person to whom he ran. Then call the dog again from the original call spot.

If there are two or more owners, there is often a problem of one interfering with the other. In this case, each one of you should work the dog separately at first; the second owner must ignore or chase off the dog once the other gives the command. Your dog must learn to go only to the person who calls.

Some dogs come so slowly that they appear to be in slow motion. Lack of praise while the dog is learning is often the reason. People get so carried away by the dog's obedience that they forget to let the dog know they are pleased. During the all-important early lessons, be sure to overpraise your dog profusely to get him coming excitedly and happily.

But usually there is no excuse for this slowness. Getting speed out of the slower-moving breeds such as bassets is not always possible, but most dogs can be hurried up. To speed up an average dog, have another person stand close behind him. Call your dog and then have the person tap your dog's hindquarters, throw something close behind him, or make a noise. This should get him off to a flying start.

If your dog comes to you, but just keeps going when he gets there, throw your Rubber Arm aid at him as he goes by. After it lands, repeat the command "come." If he darts off to either side instead of coming directly to you, put him on a leash. Walk backward very slowly while making him follow along quietly just in front of you. Once he is walking along nicely, let him out to the full length of the leash. Tell him to come. If he goes off to either side, snap him back into line and again repeat "come." Do this until he comes right straight up to you—and when he does, praise him profusely.

If your dog tears madly toward you, all but knocking you to the ground, you need to be slow and methodical to calm him down. If you lean over as soon as your dog starts tearing toward you, he may tend to slow down—so stand up straight. Then when he gets to within a few feet of you, reach out to stop his advance and hold him in place. Praise him profusely—at that distance. You have to teach your dog that you want him in front of you or by your side, not all over you.

Wherever he's praised is the spot he'll learn to come to. After all, it's your attention he wants; if he gets it in a certain spot, he'll stay there. If it is a question of jumping on you, break the habit as detailed under Socializing Your Dog.

Handling Breaks in Training

If you have gone through every recommended procedure and your dog persists in running off, you may have to trick him to get him back. First try simply calling out his name. When you get his attention, say "good-bye" and walk off in the other direction. If he pays not the blindest bit of attention to his name, throw your Rubber Arm aid. When he looks at you, say "good-bye" and walk off.

Most dogs learn "good-bye" at an early age. You say it constantly when you leave the house. The knowledge that this word means departure, along with your turning your back on him, indicates that you are leaving. Since you mean food, housing, comfort, and security to your dog, the chances are very good that he will follow and not allow all those good things to walk away from him. When he follows and comes to you, don't say anything, simply leash him and take him home. This type of dog is obviously not well trained and needs to be reworked in the "come" command before being allowed free again.

If you are out in the country and have a car, drive slowly away and call out "good-bye" to your dog. When he starts to chase, don't stop. Let him run for his life to catch up. This should teach him that if he doesn't come quickly, you're likely to leave. Then in the future, if your dog wanders out of sight, the sound of the car engine and your call of "good-bye" might be enough to get him to come.

To set up an incorrigible dog, take him to an enclosed area and let him run off and play. Then call him. If he doesn't come, hide and wait until he looks for you. Wait while he frantically searches to make him feel insecure. When he does eventually find you, he'll be so happy that he may be reluctant to go off again.

When set free, if your dog is tempted to run off in the opposite direction the moment you call and nothing seems to bring him back, tie a ten- to twelve-foot cord to his collar.

Let it drag along the ground. Allow him to run around and play so that he thinks he is completely free. Then unexpectedly give the command ''come''; preferably when he is involved in something. If he refuses to come, quickly step on the end of the cord.

This will give your dog quite a jolt when he takes off in any direction other than straight toward you. You could even tie the end of the cord to a stationary tree or post without your dog's realizing he is tied. Then if your dog should dart off, he will be jerked back. Your dog will soon realize the cord is there, but if you get in one or two good jolts, he should learn his lesson. If he refuses to come even after this, take the end of the cord with both hands and give a series of jerks to get him to you. When the dog finds there is nothing to be gained by running away, which he associates with unpleasant experiences, he should come without the use of the line.

If you have to go after your dog, he may see you coming and suddenly start walking toward you. Keep going toward him. He's coming only because he saw you start after him, not because you called. Therefore when you meet, don't praise him, but turn away from him and walk back to the call spot.

When you correct your dog for not coming, never do so while your dog is on the spot from where you called him. All corrections must be inflicted at a distance away from that. When your dog finally does what he is supposed to do and comes to that spot, only good should happen. He must be stroked and praised for obeying. This is the only way that your dog can understand when he has done the right thing.

Refinements on the Basic "Come" Command

In training a dog to come when called, you could theoretically train him to come to you on any signal—a whistle is a perfect example. To do this, however, he first has to be trained to respond to the *word* command "come." After that, you can set up all sorts of secondary signals, simply by giving the sound or signal, following it immediately by saying "come." Then eventually eliminate the word "come" and just give the secondary signal.

Thus to teach your dog to respond to a whistle once the dog knows the command "come," give a blast on your whistle, call your dog, and make the hand signal. Soon he should respond when you give a blast on the whistle alone. You can train him to respond to a particular whistle, or to the generalized sound of any whistle.

You can even teach him to respond to a silent whistle, since a dog's hearing is so excellent that he can hear higher and fainter sounds than we can. If your dog is rewarded only when he responds to a certain whistle, he'll soon discriminate and react only to the one that is exclusively "his." The problem with training to a specific whistle is that if you lose that one whistle, you might get stuck with a dog who won't know how or when to return to you. You will then have to start over and recondition him to a new sound. This idea of teaching your dog to respond to generalized stimuli can be extended to any sound or signal, but it is usually best to stick to the standard ones. Choosing an exotic or ambiguous one can lead to confusion.

When their dogs come after being called, some people want them to sit, lie down, or stand in front of them or at their sides in a heel position. These refinements can easily be added—*after* your dog learns these other commands. For now, when your dog comes to you, simply reach out to hold, place, and praise him exactly where and in what position you want him to stay. He'll soon learn that's where he is to be.

Test your pet's proficiency in the command by gradually increasing the distance from which you can call your dog. Additionally, try him out when he's involved in other activities and least expects it—but demand obedience. Deliberately put him in difficult situations where he is distracted by noise or other dogs. Then after he learns the other basic obedience commands, use them in conjunction with each other. Just be sure he knows all the commands separately first. You can then call your dog to you to obey another command. The "come" command is the basis of absolute control, so make sure your dog understands it thoroughly and obeys under all circumstances.

Four

THE STATIONARY COMMANDS

What They Are

These commands are intended to hold your pet dog in one position or another rather than have him actually *do* something. Once a stationary command is given, your dog should stay in the commanded position until released. After all, you wouldn't expect the animal to bounce up from a sitting position. Since your dog is supposed to stay still in one spot, be slow and methodical when commanding him. If you move around, your dog will tend to fidget around too.

"Sit," on a Leash

The "sit" command is probably the easiest of all the commands to teach, since it's a natural, comfortable position for your dog to assume. To start, place your dog in a corner while you stand directly in front of him. Here he is well controlled: Two walls block his rear, and you prevent his escape from the front. For added control in early training, put your dog on a leash and slip it under your foot rather than holding on to it.

Once he is in position, tell him "sit" just once, in your normal tone of voice. At the same time, point your finger downward to the floor in front of your dog's nose so he can see it. But don't *keep* your finger pointed down, which will tend to teach your dog to look down—just what you want to avoid. And make sure there's no pressure on the leash when you actually issue the command.

Since he has never heard or seen any of this before, it won't make any sense to him; so when you first command him to sit, he'll probably ignore it. But if he's been initiated into the concept of training by learning to come and participating in the first session, your pet should understand that the word and action mean something. However, he doesn't understand exactly what, so you have to show your dog what the command means. To show him exactly what you want, jerk backward slightly on the leash and/or push hard on your dog's rump to force him into a sitting position. After a few seconds, praise him and let him go.

Repeat this procedure. When issuing the command, don't twist your body into a position that you think symbolizes the command "sit." Take a relaxed stance. And when asking him to sit down, be especially sure not to lean over. If you start to do this, your dog will think the signal includes your body being stooped over.

When actually issuing the command, don't touch your pet or put pressure on the leash—issue the command first. Then if your pet does not obey, push or place him in position. Do not reissue the command, however, while still touching your dog. Before repeating the command, always release your hands from your dog or ease up pressure on the leash, or your dog may well associate the push or pull as part of the command. He will then wait for a physical touch before he obeys.

But *do* touch him after he obeys, to hold him in place. If you don't he may take the praise to mean he can leave. Remove your hands just before you tell him to stay or give him another command. He should leave only on his release word and signal.

When you feel your dog vaguely understands what you want, don't push him into position immediately but wait about five seconds. If he obeys right away, praise him, but hold him in position for a few moments before releasing him. If your dog just stands and looks at you, however, give the command again. If he doesn't listen this time, push him down forcefully to show you mean what you say. Don't give up or assume your dog is stupid; he *will* catch on. But you must work your pet methodically. If a dog fails to perform, go back and firmly start again.

Don't repeat the command several times. Don't snap or yell; simply use your normal tone of voice. Make sure you don't lean over, and be sure your finger is pointed in front of your dog so he can see it—but don't keep your finger pointed down toward the floor. Praise him under the chin to keep his head up. Continue this until he responds and sits readily on command.

Once your pet sits for you in the corner when you are right in front of him, start increasing your distance from him when giving the command—but have him remain in the corner. Once you are standing outside arm's length, chances are your dog will decide to take off before you even issue the command. To counteract this, attach a cord to your dog's leash to lengthen it, and then rest it under your foot, being sure it is very slack. This way, when your dog attempts to take off, he'll be brought up short and you won't have to keep leaning over and dashing to grab him.

At first, back away from your dog so that you are only three feet or so away, but still directly in front of him. Give the command and signal once. If he obeys, walk back to him immediately and take hold of him under the chin to praise him. If your dog just stands there, go over to him and push him down sharply or give him a whack across the rump to force him into a sitting position. When he starts to obey, gradually back off until you get to the full length of the extended leash.

As your dog obeys and is consistent at one distance, gradually back away a foot or so farther. Thus if he sits at three feet, increase the distance to five. Don't be in too much of a rush, however; sometimes you can push ahead too fast. So if he doesn't sit for you at five feet, go back to three and increase the distance to four the next time.

Once your dog is obeying reasonably consistently, let the extended leash lie on the floor rather than resting it under your foot. This will get him used to feeling unrestricted while you still retain control. If your dog tries to move out of the way, you can quickly step on the leash with your foot or reach down for it to put him back in place. Your dog has to know that when you say something, you mean it. Work methodically with the extended leash until your dog is obeying consistently.

Don't keep on working and working your pet once he does sit. If he sits for you, quit, wait a while, and go on to your next lesson—either in the same or a different command. When he is listening consistently, simply remove the leash.

Free from Restrictions, Without a Leash

Once he is proficient at sitting in the corner with the extended leash on the floor, he has to be taught to sit on command in front of you. He knows exactly what the command means; now he has to learn that it applies in all locations. To begin teaching your dog to sit in the open, teach him to sit by your side. Stand your dog on your left side. Say "sit," and at the same time bring your right hand over in front of your dog and point to the floor.

Wait about five seconds for it to sink in. If he obeys, praise him under the chin with your right hand and hold him in place with your left. If he doesn't pay attention, pull his head up by the loose skin on the neck, which can be used as a handle, and push down on his rump. As he starts to descend, release the pressure and repeat the command "sit." Be sure not to say "sit" until you have stopped placing pressure on your dog and he is sitting of his own accord. Once your dog is seated, praise him. Keep this up until your dog responds without any physical encouragement from you.

Next stand in front of your dog and go through the procedure. If your dog not only refuses to sit but actually runs off in the opposite direction, throw something at him to stop him in his tracks. Go over to him, give him a good slap, and bring him back. Repeat the sit command and make sure he complies.

Keep doing this over and over until he finally obeys. And when he does so with you right on top of him, proceed to gradually increase the distance from which you can command him, as you did when he was in the corner. After he will listen consistently from at least a few feet away, go on to teach him to stay as punctuation. Until he understands the stay command, you can never completely trust him to remain in position.

Avoiding Problems in Teaching This Command

If you find you can't work with your dog any longer because you are getting tired of him absolutely refusing to listen, or because a distraction such as the doorbell interrupts the lesson, push him into position and hold him there. Simply tell your dog to sit, push him down, say "good dog," and finish there by releasing him. This will ensure that he always finishes by doing what he is asked.

Be sure your pet assumes the correct position when told to sit. If he lies down instead of remaining seated and he is on a leash, jerk him up hard so he understands from the start that when told to sit he must do just that. (It is almost impossible to snap a heavy breed to a sitting position, so exert numerous quick jerks in succession to annoy the animal until he sits up. Remember, a heavy dog requires more severe handling to make an impression.) Once he's off the leash, place your foot under your dog's stomach area so that if he lies down, he is forced up. If he attempts to get up without being told, make him sit again by snapping the leash or slapping him down hard until he remains where he is told. Any dog who growls and shows his teeth, or even attempts to bite when made to sit, should be stopped immediately. Reprimand him thoroughly as you would any aggressive dog.

"Stay" and "Okay"

"Stay" serves the purpose of a punctuation mark. The "stay" is for emphasis or punctuation; for example, when you are going to leave for a while, when you turn your back on your dog, or even when you pay attention to something else such as being involved in a conversation. It is a reminder to your dog that the stationary command given is to be held until you release him with a special release word or signal. The command telling your dog to stay is simple and graphic: Say "stay," and hold your open hand out toward your dog with the palm facing him. To make sure he understands, at first push your hand right into his face in an emphatically visual signal. Later you can be more subtle.

To teach your dog to stay, take your pet to a corner and have him assume whatever posture you wish. Once he's in position, move your right hand quickly and firmly toward his face, as if you were a policeman stopping traffic, and say "stay" once. Turn your back on him and walk away a few feet, then turn to face him. If he has followed you—as he's sure to do in early training—give him a slap or a shake and take him back to the original stay position. If he runs off, throw something at him to stop him. Then go and bring him back into position. Repeat the entire procedure over and over until he stays where he's told. When he does, go back to him. Upon reaching him, touch him first to hold him in place, and praise him. Then quickly tell him to stay once again so that he doesn't think he's free to leave. Once told, he has to stay until freed by his special release word and signal.

Praise is not a release. When you say "good dog" and praise your dog, the chances are he will stop being good. Therefore, touch him just the way you did in teaching the "come" command. However, don't make the praise something to be associated with authority.

When first making your dog stay, don't try to walk off a long distance from your pet. Go off just a few feet. It is best to remain close and be certain than be doubtful at a distance. After he is staying easily from a few feet away, gradually walk away a little farther each time to get him used to staying alone and not leaving until released. But every time you turn your back and walk away, watch over your shoulder discreetly to see whether he has run off or is following. When your dog moves even slightly or indicates uncertainty by fidgeting, hold out your hand in the stay signal and again tell him "stay." If he does actually leave, don't run after him or turn around to grab him until you have reached the spot where you originally intended to turn around. When you do turn around and he isn't there, go over to him, give your dog a slap and tell him "no." Then pull him back to the stay position.

Once again, tell him to assume whatever position you want and add a "stay." Then walk away. Turn back when you're ready. If he is still there, hold out your hand as a reminder for him to stay. Then walk back to him, touch him, say "good dog" and quickly tell him to stay again. When you are ready to let him go, give your release word, and nudge him to indicate he is free to leave. If you are demanding and keep taking him back, eventually he will freeze to the spot when told and stay until you release him.

Do not repeat this exercise for more than two to three minutes at a time, or the dog will become bored. But don't allow your dog to be careless in the early lessons, or he won't be trustworthy later. As with all commands, give them only once. When your dog is staying, don't keep saying "stay, stay, stay" to keep him in place; the same is true for telling him it's okay to relax. If you feel he needs a reminder to stay put, repeat your hand signal to be sure he stays. If he continues to stay when told to leave, nudge him up again.

Don't use your dog's name when teaching him to stay or go off, because it's best to avoid saying his name when he is to be alone. In addition, be especially careful never to say "stay" and then add "good dog." If you do, your dog may leave. Say "stay" last to keep him in place until you're ready to release him, which you should do with your special release command.

When in training, a dog is on the alert. Therefore, it is very important to let your pet know it is okay to relax and go on to other things. Every dog needs a release word and signal to let it be known the time has come to stop listening at attention. (Even guide dogs for the blind are given this courtesy. As soon as their harness is removed, guide dogs know they are off duty and can relax.)

To tell your dog to go about his business after finishing a task, or to release him from the stay command, select a special word or phrase *and* a signal. This will let your dog know he can relax. "Okay" is the most commonly used word, and the signal is either a clap of the hands or a waving-off gesture.

This way, when you want him to relax, you simply say "okay, get out of here" and clap your hands or wave him away.

Teach your dog to obey the release command simply by using it consistently every time you want him to end a command. After you finish praising your pet, push him gently off the stay spot, tell him "okay," and clap or wave him off, then pet him again quickly and walk off casually. Your dog will readily understand this means he is free to go about his own business. Be insistent that this is the only time your dog is allowed to go off. Your dog should not leave until you permit him to do so.

If your dog consistently creeps forward when told to stay, stop him before it becomes a habit. Keep pushing him back into place. Don't allow your dog to jump up every time you return. If you do, soon he will start jumping up whenever he sees you coming. If he gets up too soon, push him down hard quickly and tell him to stay. If your pet whines when left after being told to stay, go over to him, hold his muzzle closed or slap him and tell him "no."

Testing and Polishing Your Dog's Ability

To make sure he knows exactly what "stay" means, test your dog by taking him out of the corner to the middle of the room. Place him by your side, give him a stationary command, and tell him to stay while giving the appropriate signal: swinging your open left-hand palm back into your dog's muzzle. Then take a step forward and walk in front of your dog. Turn and face him while holding out your hand in the stay signal. If he has moved, get him and take him back. If he stays, walk back to his side, hold him in place, and praise him. Then take him to different places and repeat the procedure. This will teach your dog to be obedient and stay wherever you tell him.

To ensure that he knows to stay until released, circle around behind him to see if he moves. At first you may have to hold your dog by the muzzle so he can't get up or turn his body to watch you. Then after circling, go back to your dog's side. Create a little activity to get your dog accustomed to a certain amount of confusion. Tempt him by running past him, throwing toys in front of him along the ground, making noises, even walking other dogs past him. This way, you prepare your pet for the unexpected. Just be sure not to use your dog's name or call him to you while trying out his proficiency. If he shows any sign of moving, warn him by issuing another stay command and signal. If he actually goes off, reprimand him and bring him back.

After your dog will stay for you wherever you tell him, extend the time he will remain. Most dogs hate to be ignored, so test your pet by sitting down in a chair and pretending to read. When he breaks, correct him by throwing something hard enough to make an impression. He knows the command by now. Then drag him back to the stay position.

Eventually you should be able to go out of sight and have your dog stay. But when first teaching your dog to remain where he's told, stay out of sight for only a few moments. With his owner away, a dog will get nervous and excited. If your dog should follow you or sneak off, reprimand him quietly and drag him back to where he was told to stay. Place him in position, command "stay" again, and leave. Repeat this procedure until your dog stays. Your dog must not be allowed to move until permission is given. When he does obey, increase the length of time for your dog to stay until you can remain out of sight for a few minutes.

Sit Up and Beg

This is an easy command—for the right candidates. It is *not* a good idea to teach a dachshund or St. Bernard to sit up. Unless your dog's back muscles are strong to begin with and are made stronger through practice, your dog won't be able to sit up straight.

Don't get impatient with a dog who's having difficulty with

this trick. Just like people, not all dogs have a good sense of balance. However, if you have a small- to medium-sized dog with a good strong back, he should be able to do it with reasonable ease.

As usual in early training, if you think your pet may run away, put on his leash. The voice command for this trick is "up" or "beg," and the signal is to raise your open hand, palm up, in an upward gesture. (To avoid confusion, be sure not to teach your dog to sit up and beg when also teaching the basic obedience command of "sit.")

You can use several methods to get your pet to sit up, but there's really only one best place to start—against a wall or preferably in a corner, for support until he builds up his confidence. Use a carpeted area at first in case he falls over. When you are teaching a trick, make sure your dog can't hurt himself—and never rush him, or he may never learn. Keep placing your dog in a corner and sitting him up in a begging position so that his front legs are up in the air and his rear on the ground. At the same time tell him "up," raise your open hand upward, and hold your dog in place. As you repeat this procedure, gradually release your hold on him until he's supported by the corner walls alone.

Once this is done, build up the time he's able to stay sitting up there. When it seems as if he has the idea well enough so that he is supporting himself, rather than being supported by the walls, try him away from the corner.

Place your dog in the sit position and give him the command and signal to sit up. If he will allow it, lift him to a sitting-up position by his front feet. If he doesn't like to have his paws touched and gets upset when you try to lift him that way, you may have to resort to the less desirable method of lifting him gently by the collar or leash.

Once you have your dog sitting up, hold him in place for a few seconds, then praise him and give him a tidbit as a reward. *After this*, release him. When he understands the act of sitting up when told, you could also try holding a morsel of food over your dog's head just out of reach. Tell him to sit up and give the signal. Tempt him with the food to get him to reach for it. As he does, gradually move the food higher above his head, thus forcing him to raise himself up to get at it. But don't hold it so high or move it up so quickly that your dog stands up on his back legs. You want him just to sit on his rump with his front paws up off the floor. If he does get up, therefore, lower the food until his rear is again sitting on the ground. Otherwise take the food away completely, make your dog sit down, and start from the beginning.

Once he really understands, try to get him to sit up with your hand and voice commands alone, without touching him or tempting him up with a treat. With work, he will eventually sit up on his own wherever and whenever you tell him. As with most other commands, it's just a matter of insisting until he does it.

"Lie Down"

Though seemingly simple, the "lie down" command can be difficult to teach because it is basically a submissive gesture. To your dog, lowering his body to a crouching position is reminiscent of submitting to allow a dominant animal to mount him. Your dog may not be eager to take such a demeaningly humble posture simply because you ask him to, and even though lying down is the most natural position for a dog to assume, you may have a difficult time getting your pet to do so on command. Older, dominant males are usually the most reluctant, but the stubborn streak against submission can show up in the tiniest female poodle. So for the best results, your dog should trust you totally before you attempt to teach this command, and he should already have had some obedience training.

The command for lie down consists of saying "down" or "lie down," and signaling by holding your open hand palm downward in front of your dog. Once trained, your dog should drop the instant he sees your hand signal or hears the command. Just be careful that when indicating you want your dog to lie down, you don't lean over to almost touch the floor, or you may end up having to do so continually.

To start teaching this command, sit down on the floor or in a chair beside your dog. Put your dog in a sitting position

107

without telling him to do so. Tell your dog "lie down," and lower your open hand palm downward to give the signal. As usual with a new command, your dog's response will probably be to simply look at you with an unknowing, blank expression. Pull his front legs out from under him with one hand, and with the other push firmly down on his back. When you get him to lie down, praise him, but continue to hold your hand on his back to keep him in place. Repeat this procedure several times to let him get used to the action and start to connect it with the command.

Next, put the leash on your pet. Sit in a chair next to him and slip the leash under your shoe between the sole and heel. This way the leash can slide freely back and forth under your instep. Again place your dog in a sitting position without commanding him, then give the hand and voice command for him to lie down. If he doesn't obey within five to ten seconds, repeat the command. If there is still no response, pull the leash slowly but firmly through the opening between the sole and heel of your shoe. Don't jerk, just gradually put pressure on the leash.

This will lower your dog's head. No matter how much he struggles, hold him in position. If you have an extremely large dog, you could use both hands to pull on the leash. Don't choke him, but give him just enough slack to permit him to breathe without giving in. When your dog stops struggling, ease the pressure on the leash slightly and push against his back, making him lower his entire body. Don't take your foot off your dog's leash. Keep it there so that if your dog leaps up, you can pull him down quickly.

Once your dog is lying down, hold him there and praise him calmly. Then after a few moments release the pressure and pull your dog up to a sitting position. Repeat this procedure several times more, being sure not to continue the lesson for more than a few minutes.

If your dog braces to tense himself and refuses to give in and lie down, hold him in position until he relaxes slightly. Once he does, immediately place the pressure on him again until he settles to the ground. Don't give in to your dog—if you do, he will test you forever. Remember, it's not force that gets him down, but rather firm, insistent pressure. It may take time, but if handled quietly and surely, all dogs will eventually give in. You have to be absolutely persistent, and give the necessary encouragement and a sufficient amount of praise when your dog obeys. Constant repetition will soon connect the words "lie down" and the signal of a hand, palm down, with the desired position.

When exerting pressure to make your dog lie, be sure to give him every opportunity to comply. As soon as your dog starts to go into the down position by himself, let up on the pressure immediately, and repeat the command using both the word and hand signal to reinforce your pet's understanding. Once your dog is lying down, don't be too enthusiastic with praise unless you are holding him in position; otherwise your dog may be tempted to jump up in excitement. Instead, hold him in place and stroke your dog calmly and gently.

After your pet has mastered the command when you're sitting next to him, he must learn to lie down while you're standing up. Put his six-foot training leash on him, and place your dog close by your left side or right in front of you. Holding the end of the leash in your left hand, hook it under the instep of your shoe so it can slide freely. Be sure to place your full weight on that foot so that you won't be thrown over backward if your dog struggles.

Stand erect—your dog is the one that is to lie down, not you. Give the voice command and hand signal. Wait five to ten seconds. If he obeys, praise him. Otherwise give the command once more, and give him ten seconds or so to comply. If there's no response, immediately exert pressure on the leash, compelling your dog downward by forcing his head to the ground. Then hold him in place until the rest of his body drops down as well. If it doesn't, lean over and push him down with your hand.

As your dog starts to go down, release all pressure immediately and quickly repeat the command to help him connect the word with the action. Always give your dog every opportunity to obey of his own accord. When he is lying down, hold him in place and praise him profusely but calmly.

Once you feel your dog has the command down pat, allow the leash to hang slack in your hand or loose on the floor. Give the command once, and wait five to ten seconds. If he doesn't obey, repeat the command, giving him another ten seconds to comply. If there is no reaction, hold the leash in both hands and place your foot squarely on it, stepping close to your dog's collar. Step slowly downward, and put your full weight on the leash. This should apply enough pressure to make him lie down.

Off the Leash, Without Restrictions

Once your pet listens instantly on the leash, remove it and work without one. If he knows the command, follow procedures that allow him to demonstrate his knowledge. Put your dog by your side and place him in a sit position. Give the voice and hand signals for him to lie down.

If he doesn't obey, try raising your foot up as if you are going to put pressure on an imaginary leash. Your dog may respond to that reminder. If he doesn't, simply lean over and push him down. Repeat this several times until he understands that the command applies with or without a leash. Be thoroughly insistent, because if your dog doesn't obey when you're right on top of him, he isn't going to listen from a distance. If you're sure your dog understands the command and yet refuses to obey, push him down with more force or even slap him down severely. Don't tolerate stubbornness.

Any attempt your dog makes to run off should be stopped immediately. Go get him, give him a slap, and bring him back to repeat the command. If he's really incorrigible, put on his leash but don't hold it. Let it drag on the ground so that you can easily grab or step on it if he makes any moves in the wrong direction. The moment he starts off, throwing something right at or in front of him may also get him to reassume his position.

After your dog is obeying the command without a leash, you have to teach him to obey at a distance. Don't try to do this by immediately crossing to the other side of the room and telling him to lie down. Chances are he probably won't listen. Start off by giving the command when you're only a few feet away, and gradually build up the distance.

First put the leash back on your dog and make him sit by your side. Then hold the leash and walk a couple of feet away from him. Drop it on the floor but make sure it's within easy reach if he attempts to run off. Command your dog to lie down. If he starts to run off, quickly pick up the leash or step on it lightly. This will keep him in place and may even be enough of an incentive to get him to obey. If not, pull the leash taut, step on it closer to your dog's collar, and gradually walk up it toward your dog, exerting more and more downward pressure on the collar. Then if he has not lain down, by the time you are almost on top of him you can slap or push him down harshly. Once your pet obeys from the end of a leash, take the leash off and gradually increase the distance from which he will obey. To learn this properly, however, your dog has to know how to stay when told.

Eliminating Problems and Adding Refinements

Once in the "lie down" position, some dogs try to creep forward on all fours. If this happens, move toward your dog or walk toward him up the leash. If this doesn't work, a good slap should show him that the forward thrust is unwanted; or throw something down hard in front of him. When commanding, don't hold your hand too close to the ground—that will tempt him to come toward you rather than lie down. Saying your dog's name when he is lying down will also tempt him to get up or creep forward. If your dog backs away from you, this could be a sign that he's afraid, so ease up and back away from him.

Instead of lying down on command, some dogs dart off frantically in one direction or another or roll over on their backs. Don't laugh at this antic. The minute your dog starts to roll, push him quickly back into the correct "down" position. Repeat this until he no longer rolls over. For a dog

111

who gets aggressive about being made to lie down and growls or even shows his teeth and lunges to bite, reprimand harshly.

Some dogs are really stubborn and won't learn to lie down with any of the standard methods. For them you have to think up little tricks. One owner took his dog to her favorite sleeping spot on a small rug. There he told her to lie down, and sure enough she did, because that's where she always slept. After repeating this a few times, the owner took the rug and placed it somewhere else, and again put the dog through the "down" command. She felt so secure on the rug that she again responded readily. Soon she was so used to obeying the order to lie down that the command became generalized, and she obeyed without the rug.

When your dog has learned lie down, simply add the "stay." To do this, follow the exact directions given for teaching "stay" and its release. Be ready to correct your dog at a moment's notice—the mistake made all too frequently is that the correction is too slow in coming. The instant he breaks from the "down" position, your dog should be reprimanded. Once told, he has to learn to stay until released by your special word and signal.

At first back slowly away just to the full length of the leash. Then take his leash off. When he is obeying and staying while you are close by, increase the distance until you can go out of sight. Later build up the time he will stay for longer and longer periods. Don't repeat the command unless your dog actually breaks or you think he is going to move out, and you could possibly keep him in place by so doing. If he breaks, go get him, slap him or use the Rubber Arm corrections and bring him back. To test that your dog knows the "stay" command, tempt him to get up (without calling his name).

"Roll Over"

It will be easier for him to learn to roll over if your pet already knows how to lie down on command. You must be careful your dog doesn't confuse this roll-over exercise with the lie down. Therefore, it's better not to actually tell him to lie down; rather, place him in the down position and start to work from there. This will eliminate any connection in the commands.

Sit on the floor or in a chair to get close to your pet, with his head next to you. Take a treat and reach over, bringing it just in front of his nose. Gently bring the treat over his head and around to the other side so that the dog must follow the treat. Your voice command is "roll over," and your hand signal is making a circle toward the right. Later, a slight circular motion of your hand or finger, or just the words "roll over," will be sufficient.

Hold the treat just out of reach of his nose and tempt him with it, and as his nose moves to follow the smell so must his body. If it doesn't, gently help him along. When the dog finishes a complete roll, give him the treat. Repeat it going the other way. Then go back and forth a couple of times until the dog starts to roll.

If, instead of rolling over, the dog jumps back up to get the treat, hold him down with your other hand to help him roll over. Just don't let him get up and go the other way. You want him to roll; eventually he will. When he does it, don't ruin everything by going through the exercise too often, or he may well become bored and refuse to do it.

When he is doing this continually while you are seated, it's time to try to see if he'll do it while you're standing. You may have to first put the leash on your pet until you're sure he won't take off. If you hold the treat above his head, away from his nose, he may tend to get up. A long dowel stick can be helpful to keep him down and nudge him over.

Give the treat only when the dog completes the command. This way he will understand he will get his treat only when it is done. When the dog shows no hesitancy and rolls over quickly when told to do so, take the leash off. Then gradually cut down on the treats so that they are given on a random basis, every once in a while with no definite pattern. When he's really good with you working up close, start moving away and issuing the command. At first stay in his sight so he can see your hand signal. When he learns it thoroughly, test with either a hand or a voice command.

"Play Dead"

Depending on how this trick is executed by both dog and owner, it can be an amusing performance—or simply look as though your dog is lying asleep on his side or back. To be effective, your dog must assume the correct position promptly and express the appropriate body attitude. A good basis for this—perhaps even a prerequisite—is for your dog to know to lie down and stay (when told to do so) until given his special release word. This trick is simply an extension of that command. Be careful your pet doesn't confuse the signal with the circular one used for rolling over. Be very definite and use a good strong voice signal. In fact, your voice command of "bang" or "play dead" is a major source of the amusement in this trick.

To teach your dog to lie on his side and play dead, stand over him and make him lie down *without* commanding it. Issue the voice and hand commands by saying "play dead" and giving a semicircular motion with your hand. Then physically turn your dog onto his side and hold his muzzle flat on the floor in a suitable "dead" fashion. When the dog relaxes and stays for a few moments without struggling, release him with his special release word, then praise and treat him. Repeat this several times until your dog has some concept of what it means. Gradually increase the length of time you hold him in his "dead" position.

For playing dead lying on his back, start out as if going to make your dog roll over. Use the commands for "play dead," and a procedure similar to the tempting one used to teach "roll over." Here, however, stop the dog once he is halfway over and resting on his back. Sit down on the floor or in a chair and make your dog assume a "lie down" position with his head near you. Hold your hand with its tidbit of food just in front of his nose and give the signal for him to play dead. Then move your hand in back of your pet's head so that he follows the tidbit with his nose. His body should naturally

114

follow as his head comes around, but if it doesn't, help him. When he is on his back, hold him in place for a few seconds by holding him physically and using the "stay" command. When he is doing it, give him a treat and then release him with his special word.

Once your dog understands what this command is all about, gradually eliminate your aid in turning him over. Additionally, make him remain in position without holding him. When he does it without any help and will stay until told to relax, command him from a standing position. If more control is still necessary, keep him on a leash and use a long stick to hold and nudge him into place.

As he learns, remove the leash and gradually increase your distance from him as you give the "play dead" command. Increase the length of time he will stay "dead" until told to leave the spot. Don't try to make him stay too long, however; keep your pet in position only long enough to make the trick effective. Once he is proficient, give tidbit rewards on a random basis, but always be lavish with your praise.

Up from Down

Once your dog completely understands the "sit," "lie down," and "stay" commands, you can teach him to sit back up from the down position. While standing right in front of him, tell your dog to lie down and stay. Wait about fifteen seconds. Then tell your dog "sit up" and give the reverse of the down command as a hand signal—that is, with your hand open, palm up, raise your hand in the air. After this, wait about five to ten seconds. He knows what "sit" means, but now that he is lying down, he probably won't make the connection. Therefore, give him the benefit of the doubt: Again give the command. This time, as added incentive, clap your hands quickly and push your hand straight up in the air while telling your dog to sit up. If your dog still doesn't sit up— either through stubbornness or because he doesn't understand—nudge him up by placing your foot under his chest or stepping lightly on his front feet. You don't want to hurt him, just gently nudge him so that he'll get up. When he does sit up, quickly tell him to stay, and praise him under the chin. If he refuses to sit up that way, put the leash on him and jerk him up. Your dog should learn to sit up immediately on either voice command or hand signal.

Repeat this training in one- or two-minute sessions until you are sure your dog understands the command. After he is obedient, start to gradually increase the distance from which you issue the command. First give it at three feet or so from the dog and tell your dog to sit up. When he does, punctuate it with a "stay." (If you forget to add the stay, your dog may well feel free to do as he pleases. He has to stay where you want him until you let him go with your special release word.)

Stand for Inspection

When given this command, your dog will remain standing rather than flopping into the more relaxed sitting or lying down positions. Often when walking your dog, you don't want him to sit down every time you pause. Additionally, at times your dog will have to submit to being checked over by a stranger—such as a veterinarian or groomer—and not run off, wriggle around, or object nervously or viciously.

To prevent a dog from sitting or lying down every time you stop walking, hold your dog on a short leash. When you stop, command your dog "stand," while bringing your arm across in front of you and thrusting your palm in front of his nose in a stay gesture. At the same time tighten the leash just enough to take up the slack and prevent your dog from sitting. (Don't jerk on the leash, which will make him sit.) If he doesn't have a leash on, drop your left hand to your dog's side and touch him to keep him standing. Do it quickly, however, or you'll have to lift him up from the sit position. In fact, until your dog knows what it's all about, you may have to place your hand underneath him and consistently lift him to a standing position.

If your pet is really incorrigible, loop the end of the leash around his entire body to keep him on all fours. You can also slip your foot, with the toe pointing up, under your dog just as he comes to a halt. When your dog feels the foot under him, he will quickly come to a stand. With an excitable dog, however, this method may make him leap up nervously.

After your dog knows how to stand on command by your side, teach him to stand and stay at a distance from you. First put him on a leash. When he is standing, walk out to its full length, but remain facing him. Remind your dog to stay with a hand signal. Once your dog is standing with the leash on at full length, take it off and follow the stay/release procedure as outlined.

If he moves forward, walk up to greet him and bounce the palm of your hand against his nose. Since you won't be right next to him to administer corrections, place something underneath your dog such as a toy or other obstruction. That will make him get up if he happens to lie or sit on it. Even try standing him so that he straddles a low bar or solid barrier. When he feels something underneath him, your dog will quickly learn to correct himself. With a little practice, he will learn to stay standing. When he does, gradually increase the distance you can stand away from him without him breaking. Then expand the time he will stay until he will remain for a few minutes.

Small dogs often learn to stand for inspection more quickly if first taught on a table. Simply place your dog on a table and tell him "stand," then "stay." If he doesn't, stand him up and hold him in place. Persistent refusal to stand can be met by looping the leash under your dog's stomach, and pulling him up every time he sits or lies down. Repeat over and over again until he learns. When proficient on the table, transfer your dog to the floor.

After your dog stands on command and will stay for a period of time, he should learn to accept being handled by other people and tolerate activity around him without moving. Have a friend nonchalantly move around your dog. Be firm and insist that your dog not get nervous around people. But don't overdo it: Your dog may become upset if you expose him to too many people. Ask a friend to handle him so he learns to accept examination from someone other than you. It should be casual petting at first. Later the "examination" can be more thorough, and the person should touch your pet's hindquarters and open his mouth. If your dog sidles off to move away, put him back in place; if necessary, hold him while the other person puts hands on him. Under no circumstances should a dog be allowed to growl. If he does, he should be smacked hard. However, dogs with questionable dispositions should be muzzled until they get used to being touched and until owners see how they react toward strangers. Even a shy dog will accept training and over time will learn to allow strangers to touch him. The difficulty here is that the dog's confidence must be won before much progress can be made. Some dogs are suspicious of everyone that comes around and should be approached slowly and carefully.

Linking the Stationary Commands

Keep each stationary command separate so that your dog doesn't mix them up, or when you say "sit," your dog may lie down—and vice versa. Until your pet is perfect in each command, be sure that there are rest periods between training sessions involving different commands. Don't allow your dog to anticipate a command, because it may be the wrong one. To make the command specifically clear, always use *both* voice and hand command so that he'll respond to either.

Work the stationary commands once or twice a day for about a minute or so each time. At first if he doesn't listen within a few minutes, walk him through—you cannot give your dog a command and then quit. He must complete what he has been told. If you permit your dog to have his way, he will try the same thing again. Conversely, if your dog does as told for you within a matter of thirty seconds, the lesson is over.

But once your dog understands all the stationary commands individually, it is time to link them. First test that he understands exactly what each hand and voice signal for the stationary commands means. After you're sure he has them down pat, you should be able to orchestrate your dog's actions and connect the stationary commands with others. (In fact, if you have taught your pet to stop on command, you have already begun this process.)

When you start linking your commands, however, just be sure to alternate the order in which they are given so that he doesn't learn to anticipate you. He should anticipate only when you are teaching a trick or command that requires a series of actions to perform, and that should be something deliberately taught by you and not left to his own discretion. Do a series of downs and sits, alternating the one with the other, being sure that your dog goes up and down in the same spot. Then try a series of commands such as telling your dog to sit and stay, then calling him to you with the motion saying "come," and perhaps stopping him in midwalk and ordering him to lie down. Or tell him to stand, back away and tell him to stay, then have him sit back up, and finally call him to you. Issue the commands in various differing orders. Once he has an idea of listening to a chain of commands, try using voice commands only, then only hand commands. This way you get your dog to use his brain, and can be sure he really knows and understands his lessons.

When you call your dog to you, there may be times when you want him to sit right in front of you. Were you training for obedience trials, a dog should first sit in front of you after being called, then go around by your side and sit close to you there in a heel position. To teach this, put your dog on a leash, play it out to the end, and say "come." As the dog starts to walk, back up a few paces so that he has to come forward. As he is doing so, gradually take up the slack in the leash with both hands. Stop when the slack of the leash is almost gone, and tell your dog to sit. If necessary, reach over the dog's back and push him down to the sitting position.

Keep the leash taut to prevent him from darting off, and stand with your feet apart to stop him from going past you. When he is in position, he should be squarely in front of you and as close to you as possible. If he sits too far away, pat your thigh and perhaps take a small step backward to coax him to come closer. If that doesn't work, pull the dog in slowly on a tight leash and hold him there until he sits properly.

Dogs who sit crooked can quickly be made to sit straight by nudging them lightly on whichever side is out of line. However, do not make this correction unless you hold the leash tightly so that your dog cannot jump away. To get your dog to go around your side after first sitting in front of you, pat the thigh by which you want him to stand (usually your left) and pull your dog around to your side on a tight leash. If you don't want to bother having him sit in front of you but only by your side, pull him to that position consistently instead of in front of you first.

Once you feel your pet understands what is expected, remove the leash and call him to you. If he doesn't sit in the correct position in front of you or by your side, lean over, place him in position, and push him down to sit. Then if he is in front of you and has to go to your side, pat your thigh to get him there.

It shouldn't take long to teach your pet this little linking refinement. However, if he is stubborn, slap him into position. Once he knows the command and will not do it, he is being disobedient and needs some strong nudging. Letting your dog get away with disobedience only teaches him not to listen to you.

Five

OUTDOOR OBEDIENCE

Walking on a Leash

Learning good leash manners is a must. Even if you don't plan on using one, you cannot teach your dog to walk without a leash unless you first teach him to walk correctly *on* one.

In the first part of training, your dog is taught simply to accept the leash and learn to walk by your side in a straight line. You should start the training inside to give him a feeling of what walking by your side is all about before taking him outside where sounds and sights can be extremely distracting. Throwing everything at your dog simultaneously can cause problems. Besides, working the lesson indoors first will allow *you* to acquire a certain agility handling the leash, and a feeling of oneness between you and your dog. This way, he'll know exactly what's expected of him when he does go out, even if he doesn't know what is out there.

You need your six-foot cotton training leash and a nylon or rolled leather choke collar. Just be sure to always take the choke off your dog when he is free, because it might catch onto things and choke him.

To hold the leash for training, place your dog by your left side. (If you prefer him on the right, read right for left, and vice versa.) Take the end of the leash with your right hand and hook the end loop over your thumb. With your left hand, grasp the leash a little more than halfway down and allow it to remain comfortably placed a short distance above your dog's collar.

Your left hand is then held casually at your side, while your right hand is held at waist level or a little below. You want your arms to fall as naturally as possible so you can relax when walking your dog.

This method of holding the leash gives you much more control over your dog. You need to be able to readily let him out to the end of the leash or pull him in very close, and holding the leash with both hands allows you to easily slide the leash in and out at will. Your right hand pulls or releases,

123

while the leash itself slides through your left. Your left hand can also grasp tightly for control, though you can keep a relaxed grip if your pet is well behaved.

Use both hands in training; you'll frequently need both to exert enough force to correct your pet. Use your left hand to control the leash and also to stroke your dog encouragingly when he's good, or to make corrections when necessary.

Your right hand is the guiding hand. Use it to pull in or let out the slack, as needed. If you don't hold the leash properly, the excess will dangle down and get in your way.

Do not hold the leash so taut that your dog is dragged around instead of being able to move by himself. The leash needs a reasonable amount of slack so that you can administer proper corrections for mistakes. On the other hand, if the leash is too long, your dog will readily get out of position. Position yourself so that the leash and your hands are constantly prepared to correct your pet.

Let your dog wear his collar and leash for a while around the house while you practice holding and working the leash. Simply play with it by alternately letting the slack out and taking it in again. Once you feel that both you and your dog have a sense of working together, go on to the first real lesson.

Staying by Your Side

Start the training in the house to make sure your dog has some idea of what it is all about before being transferred outside, where the sounds and sights are extremely distracting.

In this lesson, instead of moving forward as you would expect, you go backward. Take a step or two backward, then snap your dog's leash. Don't say a word, just jerk on the leash a few times by snapping your left hand back quickly and then letting go of the pressure again almost immediately. Repeat again and again until your dog comes back to your left side.

If your dog refuses to budge, pick him up and place him at your left side so his front feet are aligned with your legs.

Don't pull him back into place. The idea is to annoy your dog so that he comes back into position on his own, not because you dragged him. Besides, most dogs—especially the larger breeds—are too strong to be pulled back into place. At the same time, pulling teaches your dog that constant pressure around the neck is simply the price of a walk outside.

When done properly, a quick, sharp, unexpected jerk never loses its effectiveness. Tighten the leash momentarily by snapping your hand back, then release it quickly and keep it loose until your dog moves out of line. He must know the difference in the sensation of the leash when he is doing right or wrong. In this way, when teaching your dog to walk by your side, the leash should always be kept slack except when making a correction.

When he is in place by your side, check to be sure the leash is slack and then reach over to praise him. Just be sure you praise him *only* when he is at your side, in perfect alignment—on your left side with his front legs aligned with yours. He should be standing or sitting straight forward; sitting a foot away from you or sitting out on a crooked diagonal is wrong. If necessary, adjust him bodily to make him sit right. Even if your dog is only out of line a slight amount, he needs to be put in the right place before being praised; otherwise he will never understand exactly where he should be. He will learn to stay exactly where you consistently praise him. If he learns that this is the only place he is going to be praised, this is where he will go. Repeat this exercise again and again. After a few tries, see if he has learned anything by giving your dog a few seconds to come back to you after you step backward. The movement of your body should tell him he's not by your side and to go to you. If it doesn't, jerk him into place and finally pick him up and position him, if necessary.

Keep stepping backward until your dog learns to step back with you. When he learns to come back with no pressure on the leash, you are ready to begin the training in earnest.

Walking Straight Ahead

The absolute fundamentals of leash training your dog to walk with you are to get him to move out when you do, stay by your side when you walk straight ahead, and come to a halt when you stop. The logical start is to teach him to begin walking when you do.

Place your dog on your left side, making sure his front feet are right next to yours. Adjust the leash so you are holding it correctly with both hands. Tell your dog to start by giving a slight jerk forward on the leash. Do it just enough to get your dog to move out. Then, if you feel it is necessary, say "let's go" while stepping off and walking at your regular pace. Eventually, when he is off the leash, the slight movement of bringing your hand forward plus the simultaneous moving of your foot will wave your dog onward. Keep in mind that you do not give the verbal command unless you are actually in motion. Then while you are walking, keep the leash slack as long as he stays close by your side.

If he tries to cross in front of you, knee him out of the way. If he lags behind, goes ahead, or wanders off to one side, bring him back into place with a quick, sharp jerk on the leash.

If a dog refuses to respond to an ordinary jerk of the leash, use a series of quick, sharp snaps. Your dog may be so distracted that one jerk on the collar may not be enough to get him to look in your direction, let alone to walk in place by your side. Therefore, give a number of short jerks one right after the other, each a little harder than the previous one. If your dog is errantly stubborn, you may need to take the leash in both hands and jerk in a downward and backward stroke. Just be careful to always snap back and to your side, or you are likely to hit yourself.

A stick such as a three-foot-long dowel can be of use in helping keep your pet in place. This stick is held in the left hand with the lead and is tapped against the dog to nudge

126

him into place when necessary. It is an aid for use in guidance, not for reprimanding when he does things incorrectly. However, it might be helpful in chasing off other dogs.

If you use the verbal command "heel," always do so when there is no pressure on the leash. To get your dog into position, jerk on the leash and quickly let go of the pressure. *Then* say "heel." Give the verbal command only as you're actually moving. Don't say it just before you start to walk, but only after you've given the nonverbal signals and have started off yourself. If he is out of line, jerk; then let go of the pressure and tell him to heel. Soon he'll start to associate voice, hands, and body movements with walking close by your side. Give him plenty of praise when he is good—but only when in exact position.

As the signal to halt, a moment or so before you stop, prepare yourself by pulling back slightly on the leash and adjusting your body. Ensure that he stops along with you by jerking backward slightly on the leash just before you stop. Your dog will soon associate this movement with halting, and will stop on that cue alone. Eventually he'll pick up even more subtle clues in your posture, and will recognize your unconscious signals such as mere hesitation. When he does stop—whether he is sitting, standing, or lying—make sure his front legs are even with your legs. This may mean placing him every time you stop and correcting him repeatedly until he understands what you mean.

When first teaching, you must demand your dog's attention throughout the training session and keep an eye on him at the same time. This lets you make sure he is paying attention and staying close by your side no matter where you move. If you don't watch him, you may not catch mistakes and correct them in time.

It is unnecessary to keep telling your dog "heel" in order to get him by your side. You have to teach him that when being walked on a leash his proper place is close by your side unless he's told otherwise. When you leave and want him to stay while you walk away, always give the appropriate command, such as "sit," plus the emphasis of "stay" to keep him there while you move on. If you don't say anything, however, your dog should keep moving along with you. When you stop, he is not to keep on going, but is to stop also. In other words, walking by your side means stopping and starting when you do, and moving as you do in various directions. Through training, let your dog know that the most comfortable place to be is by your side. Once he understands this, there's no need to constantly remind him. Better to use a jerk on the leash as a reminder rather than the word "heel." Your pet should be stroked and praised only when he is exactly by your side, in perfect placement. Stick to the rules consistently whenever you walk your dog. If you exert great control one day and let him run around uncontrolled the next, the lessons will be completely negated by the times he is allowed to do as he pleases. Dogs are inclined to take advantage of all they can, so it is best to put in hard work and be insistent from the outset. Until it is second nature for him to stay with you, keep after your dog. Once he learns, you can both relax and enjoy your walks.

All dogs need exercise, but it is a mistake to take a young pup for long walks. Like a small child, a pup tires quickly; and romping about the house or in the garden provides all the exercise that is necessary at this age. At about four months you can begin going for short walks, and gradually make them longer. But never overstrain a growing dog. And if he gets accustomed to excessive exercise, he will always expect it.

Once your dog understands the basic concept of walking calmly along with you, refine his skills. Teach him to start and stop immediately by walking along in a manner similar to a wedding march: Take a step forward and then stop, take another step forward and then stop again. Give the appropriate signal at each step until your dog is proficient and stops and starts exactly as you do. After that, stop every few steps rather than on every step. Don't set up patterns such as stopping every three or four paces, but use a random pattern.

Stop and start suddenly. If he goes out ahead of you, snap the leash to bring him back into line. In fact, if your dog continuously keeps going when you stop, jerk the leash hard *before* you stop to let him know you expect compliance. To correct the incorrigible dog, let him go to almost the full length of the leash. Then take the end with both hands and snap back to your side with all your might. When he is at your side in the correct position, praise him.

To teach him to stay exactly in line by your side as you walk along, jerk the leash and knee him out of the way, or nudge him in the rump. Don't wait for him to go to the very end of the leash; start snapping the leash if he leaves his exact spot beside your leg—you want him there at all times. Whenever your dog is out of position, whether moving or standing still, you should correct him.

When you start out walking, do so on the foot closest to your pet to make it easier for him to follow you—but don't step on your dog's foot. As you progress in this part of the training, watch that your dog is inclined to use your leg as a leaning post. Discourage him by knocking against him with your leg. Don't get too close to him by stepping backward or sideways; rather insist that he come to you. Jerk at the leash until he is in place; if he refuses, pick him up and place him.

The Unmanageable Dog

If your dog halts at every spot to relieve himself, drifts ahead, lags behind, heels wide, lurches at passersby, bites at your arm, plays with the leash, attacks other dogs, pulls you through doors, or rushes ahead into elevators, he needs additional training work.

When your dog wants to relieve himself, you should allow him to sniff around a little: That is normal pre-elimination behavior. Do not, however, allow him to sniff constantly and stop to urinate a few drops on everything he passes. When you feel he needs to relieve himself, walk slowly and give him a chance. Otherwise keep walking at your normal pace and make your dog stay by your side. If your dog keeps sniffing along the ground or smells everything he passes, correct him. When he lunges off to whiff at the nearest fire hydrant or lamp post, jerk hard on the leash or give him a slap on the rear. For a dog who always has his nose to the ground, the cure is a hard kick at the ground between his nose and the spot he's smelling.

If he drifts ahead, don't try to catch up with him. Instead

slow down and let out the leash. Get a good grip on it and jerk sharply straight backward by your side—not up and not down, but straight back. Then stop moving completely and motion your dog into position. When he's in the proper position, again hold the leash as you would normally and continue walking.

A really unruly dog can be brought under control if you turn around quickly and go in the opposite direction every time he lunges ahead. A series of these fast, unexpected turnabouts should get quick results. If your dog lags behind, try to get him to move faster by snapping the leash in a series of short, fast jerks. If you have a short-legged or slow-moving breed, you might have to slow your pace slightly to match your dog's stride. But more usually this is just a bad habit on your dog's part, and you should walk at your normal pace and jerk him along.

A dog who refuses to walk at all, but sits and applies all four brakes, can usually be made to start by a quick jerk on the leash. If he absolutely refuses, give him a hard nudge in the behind. Or take the leash in both hands and walk ahead of him to the full length of the leash, and give a series of very hard jerks to get him to come to your side. Once you get your dog to move and he is walking properly, praise him encouragingly.

Jerk your dog back into place consistently each time he heels wide. If he's a stubborn dog who constantly gets way out of line, try walking him close to a wall so that he is forced to walk correctly. Walking him between two people can also help teach your dog to stay close by your side. But a dog who walks so close that he is under your feet needs a few nudges with your leg or foot to keep him out of the way. Persistent cuddling requires forceful thrusts. Never give in to your dog, or you may have to do so consistently. He has to obey you and come into position himself.

Lunging at passersby or other dogs in either friendship or aggression is annoying and dangerous. Whenever you see your dog showing interest in an approaching person, immediately jerk hard on the leash as a warning. This should stop him fast. You should not allow your dog to bark and pull uncontrollably. The moment he starts, turning in the opposite direction and snapping hard on the leash is another method of coping with the problem. In his excitement, he may not be listening to you, so you must use physical means to control him. Flipping the end of the leash sharply across his nose can help; having a second person throw something at him can also work. If your dog shows extreme aggressive tendencies, corrections must be severe.

While walking on a leash some dogs grab playfully at their owners' arms or at the leash itself. If your dog does this, don't pull away. That will only encourage him to grip harder and perhaps accidentally tear your clothing. Hold still and bring the end of the leash down across his nose immediately. If he doesn't listen, slap him on the side of the muzzle. He must back off. When he lets go, praise him. One or two such lessons should teach him not to play this way.

Simply being restrained by a leash and asked to walk by your side can cause some dogs to get hysterical. They growl and jump around, climbing all over the person holding the leash, even lunging and trying to bite. Handle the problem severely with a sharp slap on the nose, a boot in the behind, or an object thrown at him.

Your dog should allow you to pass through a doorway or other aperture without rushing through and knocking you down. To teach your dog not to rush ahead, make him sit and wait for a moment after the door is opened. Then quietly pass through, with him by your side. For a dog that loves to tear ahead through every opening he sees, an excellent cure is to crack the door ajar just enough to admit his head. When he starts through, close the door quickly but gently so as to catch him just behind the ears. Hold your dog for a moment while he struggles to free himself, then release him by opening the door wide, and jerk him back into position by your side. Thereafter, your dog should be only too happy to let you go first. Another method is to have a second person stand on the other side of the door and throw something in front of or at your dog if he goes through first. He will soon learn to avoid this by letting you go first or staying right by your side as you go through.

If your dog rushes up and down stairs while on the leash, he can cause you a nasty fall. Dogs often do this because they are not sure of themselves on steps and try to get the trip over with quickly. You have to show him it is safe with you.

Approach any steps slowly, with your dog on a slack leash. As he lunges ahead, jerk the leash back sharply. Then when he walks with you, praise him to reassure him that everything is secure. And to make sure it is, keep a tight hold on the leash to stop any slips.

Don't hold the leash too tight, or you won't allow yourself enough slack to give the proper jerk. Holding your dog so tightly on the leash that he can't get his breath will make him fight it, but taking either hand off the leash or changing its position can cause you to immediately lose control of your dog.

Stopping at Every Curb

If you live in the city, it is imperative to teach your dog to stop at every corner before stepping off into the street. If you don't, he could get hit and possibly killed by a car, whether he is on a leash or not. Walk your dog up to the curb and stop short. Every time he attempts to step off the curb without you, jerk him back as hard as you can. Then back away from the curb about five to ten feet, turn and again walk to the curb, and stop short. If your pet stops with you, praise him profusely.

Once he obeys, keep the pressure loose on the leash but keep taking him to the curb and working him until he really knows to stay with you. Once proficient, test him by stepping off the curb and stepping back on quickly with one foot and see if he steps off and back on exactly with you. If not, jerk him back quickly and reprimand him. As an ultimate test, run toward the curb and stop short. If it works and he stops, you're in business; but if he is a truly recalcitrant dog, frighten him back by throwing something in front of him every time he steps off without you. When he stays with you, praise him. He should know it's safe for him to walk off only when you do.

Teaching Your Dog to Sit
(or Stand, or Lie Down)
When You Stop

Depending on the situation when you stop, you may want to command your dog to sit, lie down, or stand and stay. You may even want him to generally assume a specific posture such as sitting every time you stop. But don't start this type of demanding training until you are positive your dog is well behaved when walking by your side in a heel position, and he has been schooled in whatever stationary position you expect him to assume.

To teach your dog to sit whenever you stop, give the voice and hand signals for your dog to sit each time you come to a halt. If he doesn't listen, pull up and back on the leash until he does. To instill standing, tell your pet to stand and stay by bringing your hand down in front of his face quickly every time you stop, and tell him to stay. To ensure that he does stay standing, put an extra leash around his midsection and pull him up every time you stop.

For getting your dog to lie down, give the command "lie down" and signal him by bringing your hand, palm down, in front of his face. Noncompliance should be met by bringing the leash under the instep of your foot and pulling so as to force his head down, and at the same time exerting pressure on his back to make him lie.

After he has learned this little refinement of assuming whatever stance you want him to when you stop, be sure to command him to take different postures occasionally. This will keep him pliable rather than automated, and will make sure he's on the alert, ready to obey any of the different commands you might give him when coming to a halt. However, once your dog is accustomed to always assuming a set position every time you stop, you might have to exert a reasonable amount of pressure to make him assume a different one when ordered to do so. He'll get so used to one way that he can't understand why the plan should be changed. Therefore, if you want him to do something other than the routine, be sure you signal in plenty of time—either as soon as or just before you stop—to let your dog know what you want. To be sure your dog understands, you have to be insistent. If he doesn't do as told, check that he is exactly in position by reaching your left hand over his back. If he's not where he should be, correct him by putting him exactly where you want him and in the stance you want; but when he is in place, praise him profusely.

No matter what posture you have your dog assume, when you want him to stay while you move off, tell him to stay— and always move away from him with your right foot stepping out first. (This is the leg farthest away from him, as opposed to the leg you'd start out on if you wanted him to move with you.)

Every time you stop, your dog should stay by your side, in whatever position you ask. To be sure he does, you have to be prepared to make corrections when he isn't perfect. A dog who stands wide or crooked should be forced to come in closer by a hard slap. Just be sure it isn't you who's at fault. If your dog sits too wide, perhaps it's because he's afraid of getting his toes stepped on every time he halts. If this is the case, correct your mistake, and make your dog come in by himself rather than you moving to him. This way he feels secure in the knowledge that he controls his own actions, and that you are going to stand still and not walk into him. A dog who sits too far to the rear may be doing it for a similar reason. Instead of making your dog come in close, you may be tending to move backward to get nearer your dog. If so, stop it. However, if it is just a bad habit on your dog's part, have a friend walk along quietly behind him and the moment he starts to sit, toss something at your dog's rear to get him to move up. If you have no assistant, lean over to nudge his rear end along. (When you make corrections like this, make sure your dog is on a leash, or he might run away. Only when he is perfect should he be let off the leash.)

Turns

After your dog walks with you in a straight line, teach him to stay by your side as you turn. Right- and left-hand turns are really quite simple; you just have to let your dog know what you want. For making a left-hand turn, grasp the leash short with your left hand to keep him under control. Jerk the leash gently to get his attention and let him know that you might be stopping or preparing to do something. At first, actually come to a stop before making your turn. Then as you turn, jerk him along—he should come right around with you.

Soon he will be ready to turn when you do, without the intervening stop. At that point, simply take a step forward on your right foot and pivot on it to make a ninety-degree turn to the left, then step out with your left to guide your pet properly.

Once he is reasonably proficient at this, make the turn when your dog isn't looking or is a little ahead of you and doesn't expect it. If he doesn't make it around and gets in your way, strike your knee against him, if he is a large dog. If he is small, use the inside of your foot. Make several turns in a row to be sure that something sinks into his head.

Making a right turn is just a little more difficult because of the position of the leash. To get your dog to make it around to the right, you have to continually jerk the leash with very short jerks. Keep jerking until your dog makes a complete turn. To make the ninety-degree turn to the right, pivot on your left foot and step out with your right. Warn your dog by giving a slight jerk on the leash. If he misses, jerk the leash sharply to the right. When your dog catches up and is in the correct position, pet him immediately. Repeat the lesson over and over for best effects.

Continue working these two turns until he does them with ease. Don't forget to signal your intention to your dog. When about to make a right turn, jerk the leash slightly to the right to warn your dog. For the left turn, a slight touch with your left leg signals him that you intend to turn in that direction. Test to be sure he knows these two turns by walking straight ahead and then suddenly turning in either direction. If he doesn't turn with you fast enough, hit him forcefully with your leg or use a series of annoying jerks to get him going in the proper direction.

After your dog knows the simple right and left turns, he is ready to learn the U-turn or about-face: Both you and your dog turn around completely and go in the opposite direction. To U-turn to the right, knee your dog on the outside while you pivot forward with your left foot. Just before making the turn, indicate the way you intend to go by giving the leash a jerk in that direction. Then after making the turn, give another jerk to get your dog going. In the left U-turn your dog is on the inside while you pivot on your left foot. Help him along by pushing him around to the left with your leg or foot. When executing the right U-turn, your dog is on the outside— you should jerk him along to get him around. Use the same corrections in making these turns that you used with the plain left and right turns.

In early training, all turns should be made smartly to keep your dog at attention and on guard for sudden changes in direction. During turns, if your dog walks slightly behind you or goes off to the side, a slap on the side of the rump will bring him back into line. If he goes out farther, a good hard jerk on the leash will usually work.

The first few times you make turns, your dog will probably keep going a few steps before realizing you aren't with him. To avoid such misunderstandings in the future, correct him so he learns to pay attention to your signals. Let him go out to the full length of the leash. Then just before he reaches the full length, take the end of the leash in both hands and give the leash a sharp jerk. If needed, add a boot in the rump.

Testing and Refinements

To make sure your dog completely understands walking by your side, run him through some variations. Vary your speed by alternating your pace from normal to slow to fast, and make sudden stops. Your dog has to learn to stay by your side no matter how slowly or quickly you go. Take him through several turns, or practice by continuously circling to the right, then reversing and circling continuously to the left. Zigzag and make sudden three-quarter turns. This will help keep your dog more alert for frequent changes.

The figure eight is a favorite practice device to hone a dog's ability to stick close by your side. Drumming this exercise in will make it clear to your dog what is expected of him. Place two objects about six to eight feet apart and walk your dog around them in a figure-eight pattern. (Posts and trees are fine for use too.) When circling is done to the right, keep your dog on the outside, and take small steps so you won't get too far ahead. When circling to the left, your dog is on the inside: Take long steps to make it unnecessary for him to change pace. If he attempts to pass on the wrong side at any time, jerk the leash tight with a snap, and hold your dog in position until he comes around to the correct side by himself. Then praise him. This will teach him to stay close to you when passing people, other dogs, and stationary objects.

Working your dog by your side until he's perfect will ensure you have no problems when walking him. Then once your dog is perfect in heeling on the leash and will come whenever you call, it is just a matter of going on to the next step— teaching him to behave with his leash off.

Off-the-Leash Training

Off-the-leash training—probably the ultimate dream of most dog owners—is basically a logical extension of all the other commands. Your dog is eligible for this work only when he is perfect in basic obedience. Don't be too anxious to get him working off the leash, because if he's not properly prepared you'll have nothing but problems.

Since your dog should behave off the leash as well as he would on one, be absolutely sure he is ready by giving a review of all the basic obedience work. Run him through coming when called, sit-stay, lie down-stay, and walking on a leash. Be sure he thoroughly understands both voice and hand commands. If he's really good at the basics, you can go on to give him a taste of freedom.

Staying Close by Your Side While Off the Leash

When free, your dog should walk close by your side and not wander. Only when you give him permission should he go farther away from you and relax to do as he wants. If, however, you send him out to perform certain obedience tasks, he should do so immediately and return when asked.

Before trusting your dog where there are no restrictions, practice first inside or in an enclosed area. When he sees grass and smells outdoor odors, he will be tempted not to do any work. Therefore, acclimate him to obeying where you have complete control. Proficiency at walking by your side on an extremely slack leash is the best way to be sure he is ready for this part of training. Simply drop the leash on the ground and let it drag along. This gives your dog the illusion of freedom, but still leaves you a means of control. The moment he gets out of line, grab or step on the dragging leash so that he is snapped backward.

Be very definite: Correct him promptly and bring him back when he is even slightly out of place. To let your dog free without a leash outside, you have to establish definite control. Be especially insistent at this point in the training to ensure that he'll always be in the correct position by your side. Later, when he is reliable, you don't have to be quite so emphatic.

To make sure he is perfect before removing the leash, go through the step-by-step sequence you used to teach him to walk on a leash by your side: First walk a few steps backward; stop and start suddenly. Turn to the left and right. Zigzag. Really put him through his paces, and if he's reluctant to obey at any point, work him harshly until perfect.

After the leash is off, your control comes through the thorough basic obedience training you've already accomplished. Your dog has to know that getting freedom doesn't mean he can forget all previous training. The privilege of being off the leash is paid for by trustworthiness. Therefore, when taking his leash off completely for the first time, again review the basic commands and the step-by-step heeling procedure.

When your dog is walking free by your side and lags behind, hook a finger into his collar and pull him along, or use the scruff of his neck to bring him close to you. If he tries to go forward, bounce the palm of your hand off his nose. If he darts out, throw something such as a rolled-up leash or your keys at him; then call him back close by your side. Every time he is out of line, bring him back, using whatever means are necessary.

Once your dog is off the leash outside there are no definite foolproof rules and techniques to follow; the main idea is to get results without causing any unfavorable reactions. Some people carry a stick to nudge a recalcitrant dog into place. Others have a second person make corrections by throwing something at him or even nudging him in the behind.

Make your dog see that his security rests with you; that you are all-powerful and can reach him anywhere to control his actions. Use your Rubber Arm technique; if necessary, attach a line to his leash so as to extend it, then allow it to fall free and review walking by your side. When first outside, be really strict and keep an eagle eye on him for any mistakes. Only after he is perfect can you give him the real freedom he wants.

Hanging Loose Near You

If you don't want your dog to stay glued by your side, indicate that he is free to wander off a little: Give him his release word and signal. Say "okay" and wave him off, giving him a nudge to let him know he's free. Don't militaristically point away from you—that's a definite signal to go to a specific area and obey a certain command. Here you just want to signal freedom, so indicate it in a loose manner.

At first he may be a little confused at being allowed free, but it won't take long before he understands. Outside, most dogs have no problem leaving your side to run around and have fun by themselves at the slightest invitation. However, your dog has to learn that he can go only when you indicate; even then, he must understand not to wander out of your sight. Keep him in sight and under control at all times so you can call him back if need be. Never allow him to drift out of sight—especially in a strange place—because once away from familiar surroundings, your dog may well keep on wandering and soon get lost.

Some dogs get so carried away by new experiences that they start wandering. Teach your dog to stay near you by putting his leash back on him and working him harshly; then review him off the leash and vigorously correct any mistakes. Some difficult dogs need to be given their freedom gradually and have corrections strictly enforced. They should be worked thoroughly close by your side and have their memory refreshed every now and then with a little discipline.

Dogs who chase or bark at joggers, other dogs, or any other distractions should be stopped emphatically. The minute your dog starts out to bark or chase, throw your Rubber Arm tool at him. Don't move or say a word, just throw it. This should stop him in his tracks. Once it lands and you want him to come back to you, call out his name (if he hasn't already turned his attention to you) and say "come."

With an off-the-leash dog, not coming when called is perhaps the biggest problem. No matter how good he is normally, once your dog knows there is no leash on to correct him, he may think he can do anything he wants. This usually happens because you were careless in earlier training, and means you have to go back a few steps. The natural reaction is to run after the errant animal. But this is the worst thing you can do—it will only make the animal run farther and faster.

First try the standard methods of throwing something at him or going over to him, calmly and methodically giving him a slap, and walking away. Then go over and drag or jerk him partially toward your spot, go back to the original spot, and again command "come." Rework him rigorously in the come exercise. Unpleasant corrections, such as having a second person throw something at him, should make him run back to you for protection and can help cement the command.

If there is no one around to help, use the Rubber Arm technique. Every time your dog refuses to listen, throw something at him from a distance, and after it lands, tell him to come. Otherwise simply walk over to him and drag him back to where you want him. (Further remedies for really recalcitrant animals are to be found in the section on Come When Called.)

Going Out or Away from You

In this command the release word and signal that you use to tell your dog to wander off from your side and enjoy some freedom is extended to indicate that he must go away from you to a specific area, and perhaps even obey a further command when he gets there. Affect a more intense attitude in your voice and hand commands. Point to exactly where you want your dog to go, and tell him to do so. Once this lesson is learned, you will be able to send him to bed or out of the room. If he tends to follow you or your car when you leave home, you will be able to send him back. With proper training you should also be able to direct your dog exactly where you want him, and after he learns the basic concepts of jumping over hurdles or retrieving, you'll be able to command him to do so from a distance.

However, teaching your dog to go in a specific direction isn't quite as simple as signaling him that he's free to go. It's hard sometimes for your dog to understand why he should go away from you for no apparent reason. (Moreover, it's hard to praise or reward him at a distance.) Clinging to you is not generally a bad trait and, in fact, should be cultivated in early training. But if you have a specific reason for asking your dog to go off when told, he should even be given special prodding to make him do so. Just be careful to do the training with care, or your dog may feel he is being punished.

Going to Bed or Leaving the Room

Start off teaching your dog to go to a specific area by working in your home. Since his bed—whether literally a bed, or just his favorite sleep spot—is a secure place for him, sending him there is probably your best first step. Take him a few feet away from the spot. Tell him "go to bed," and point toward it. If he rushes to it, go over and praise him profusely. If not, push him in the direction of the bed or even take him there. The actual voice command is the word "go"; the hand signal is your arm pointed toward the spot where you want him. Here, however, your pet will understand the word "bed" if you use it constantly.

After a while, the action of going to bed will become generalized to mean going to the particular spot you point to. Once he goes to bed readily when told, gradually increase the distance he must cross to get there. This will get him used to going away from you when told to do so.

After he learns to go to bed on command from a distance, teach him to leave the room when told—either to go to bed, or simply to get out. The doorway from one room to another makes a definite barrier for your dog to pass, which makes it easier for him to understand the action of going. Point toward the door—a graphic destination for him to reach—and tell him, "Go out of the room." If he hesitates, shove him through the doorway. Then go over the threshold and praise him, at the same time telling him to stay and holding him in place. It shouldn't take long to teach him to leave the room and stay out. If he tends to sneak back, be emphatic and insist. Keep him out by employing the methods you would use to teach him to stay or stop as enumerated in the following section. Once you get him to stop coming back toward you, send him back to the room he left. He should know—at least at the outset—that you will follow sooner or later.

"Whoa" or "Stop"

Learning this command could save your dog's life by allowing you to stop him before he starts out across the street in the face of an oncoming automobile. Along with "come," this command assures complete control over your dog. However, it may tend to slow down a dog in responding to the "come" command. A properly trained dog probably won't slow down too much, but some shyer dogs may not react well to this command. Therefore, don't make a practice of stopping your dog every time he is called, nor in the same place. If you do, your dog may anticipate the order and automatically slow up, waiting for you to tell him to stop.

In order for a dog to learn to stop moving when told, he must know the "stay" command thoroughly. Once you have halted him, you may also want your dog to sit or lie down and stay, so he should have learned the sit and lie down commands. Only when he does can you teach him "stop" or "whoa."

Be sure to work inside or in an enclosed area at first so as

143

to have control. Place your dog in a sit-stay position and walk away a short distance. Call him to you. When he comes half-way, step forward quickly and push both hands toward him as if you were a policeman stopping oncoming traffic, and say "stop" or "whoa." If he stops, quickly tell him to stay.

If your dog ignores the command and continues to come forward, run toward him and physically stop him. If he shows no response, the next time you call your dog, tell him "stop" or "whoa" and then throw a chain or his leash on the ground just in front of him. Then repeat the command and signal. A loud stamp with the foot or throwing a heavy book or magazine with a thud in front of him might also help. Startling your pet this way should make him stop short.

Once your dog stops when asked, you have to teach him to respond to the next command you issue from a distance. Immediately after you stop him in his tracks, tell him to sit or lie down. When he obeys this, tell him to stay in that position. Keep him there for a short while until you release him or call him to you as your next command. Or you could test him simply by walking to see if he stays. Just be sure you don't set up patterns such as always walking back to him or always calling him after telling him to stop. Praise for stopping on command at a distance has to be in verbal form, and you must make sure you say "stay" afterward to keep him in place. Your dog should go free only when you release him. By this point in training, your dog should know that "good dog" is praise, not his release word.

Outdoor Work

The early indoor lessons should serve as a good background to working outdoors. By performing them, your dog has already grasped the concept of going to a specific area when told. But, when first outdoors, you want him to go away from you only a short distance in a specific direction. The first few times you order him out, don't try to get him to go out too far or to perform too perfectly. Simply send him out a few feet to a definite—and preferably familiar point—then halt him with "stop" or "whoa." (If he doesn't know this basic command, you shouldn't let him off the leash.) If he goes out and stops when told, go out and praise him. After he continues to listen well for several tries, gradually increase the distance each time. Change the direction and distances you ask him to go, because using the same place constantly will teach him to anticipate. But take it easy, and don't rush. Better to have a well-executed, short "go" than a botched long one.

If he doesn't listen or walks out only a foot or so and then waits or goes off in the wrong direction, take a different tack. Your dog has to learn to go out in the direction ordered and stop when told. To make sure he does: Stand him by your side, point in the direction you want him to go and walk him there. Say "stop" when you've walked him out several feet. Then take him back to the start spot. Do this several times until you're sure he understands and responds.

If this doesn't work, get yourself a long line about thirty to forty feet long and a pulley or ring. Attach the pulley or ring to a fixed object, such as a tree, at about the height of your dog's neck. Then run the line through the pulley or ring, and fasten one end of it to his collar. Carry the other end of the line back about ten feet. Place your dog by your side, point in the direction you want him to proceed, and give the command "go." If he doesn't move, either pull him forward by reeling in the slack line or by simply walking slowly backward, holding onto the rope. If he's slow, give a jerk on the line.

Refinements and Problems

Avoid using your dog's name, because he will tend to come when he hears it. And be sure "come" and "go" commands are not taught too closely together, or he may become thoroughly confused. During training, always walk to him before sending him off in the opposite direction.

You may have to resort to reinforcing the training where

your dog needs it most. If you have difficulty getting him to go in a straight line when commanded, train in a long narrow passageway such as between two walls or fences. If he will only go in one direction, take him to an open field and send him in a number of different directions in rapid succession. To get him to go farther—or if he comes toward you when he should be going in the opposite direction—run toward him a couple of steps, give an overhand throwing signal, and repeat "go." To stop any untimely return, use your Rubber Arm aid thrown just in front of him—or behind him to get him moving out farther and faster.

Once he obeys the "go" command to the point where he will go wherever told, start sending him off to do obedience work. Here your dog has to learn to go off to do something specific such as jump a hurdle or retrieve an object. First you give the command you want obeyed, then point toward *where* you want your dog to go to do as told. For this you may need to use more definite methods, whether inside or outdoors.

Six

ADVANCED TRICKS

Jumping

It's really spectacular when you point to a barrier, tell your dog to jump, and have him take off and soar over it. But before you can teach your pet jumping he has to be already trained in basic obedience. Any form of jumping you want your dog to do requires a certain amount of control, especially since all jumping eventually needs *distance* control. Even the command signal is the same for all. Combine the word "jump" with the signal of pointing your hand toward the object or barrier to be hurdled. This holds true for jumping across a stream, over a fence, or through a car window. The signal remains constant unless you want to add an *across, up,* or *through* to the command. Teach the jump exercises in the given sequence: That way, they are most readily understandable and thus the easiest to teach.

Over a Solid Hurdle

This is the best type of jumping to start your pet off with; it is also the most common type of jumping and the one most people want their pets to do. Once your dog learns the basics, they can be generalized to other jumps.

For your dog's first jumping hurdle, place a six- to twelve-inch board between two rooms in your home. (To be sure the task fits the size of your dog, adjust the hurdle to suit him.) This will give your pet two definite goals: jumping over the hurdle and passing through the doorway. If you have trained him to go and leave the room, it will be a familiar action. Work in a carpeted area. Make sure the board is well secured, and even pad the top of it. These few precautions will ensure

149

that your pet won't hurt himself in his initial jumps, thereby refusing to jump in the future.

To start his training, put the leash on your dog. Stand in front of the hurdle, point your arm toward it, and say "jump." Then walk briskly toward the board with your dog, and step over it. Your dog will probably jump over it after you; when he does so, say "jump."

But if he doesn't, pull him over the board. Let go of the pressure as he is coming over. When the dog is actually on the way over, say "jump" again to make sure he connects the action with the word and understands what it means. When your dog is over the hurdle, praise him. Do the same thing going in the other direction. Continue for a couple of minutes, then give your dog a tidbit as a treat, lots of praise, and release him. Do this regularly until the concept of the word "jump" sinks in.

When you feel your dog understands the command, encourage him to go over the hurdle without you stepping over with him. Stand on the same side of the hurdle as your pet. Make sure there is enough slack in the leash so that he is not pulled or encumbered in any way. Tell him "jump" and point toward the hurdle. If he doesn't do it himself, nudge him over. When he gets to the other side, tell him to sit or lie down and stay to prevent him from returning before you command. When you're ready, call him back to you.

If he hesitates, jerk the leash to get him started back over. As always, say "jump" as he is going over. When he comes back over to you, praise him lavishly. Keep up this exercise until your dog works without a nudge and with no pressure on the leash.

Once proficient, gradually start raising the height of the jump in accordance with your dog's size. If he refuses to jump high enough put the leash on and jerk him forward and upward as he goes over to show him to jump higher.

Once your dog goes over a solid hurdle set up across a doorway in your home while on a leash, remove the leash. Sit right in front of and extremely close to the hurdle and order your dog over. If he jumps, praise him profusely. If not, nudge him over. Once he is on the other side, quickly tell him to sit or lie down, then praise him. Then call him back and praise him again when he comes.

When he obeys from up close, place him about four feet in front of the hurdle, while you stand right next to it. Call him to you, and when he approaches you, tell him to jump over the hurdle. If he does, praise him profusely and tell him "stay." Let him wait for a short while, and then call him to jump back.

When he does this with ease, place him a few feet back from the board. This time, stand next to him. Point toward the board and tell him to jump. If he doesn't comply, take him by the scruff of the neck, walk him toward the board, and gently nudge him up and over. The next time, after issuing the command to get him started, simply walk over to the board with your pet. As he improves, do not approach the hurdle as closely. Eventually you will need to take only a step or two, and then none. Just take it easy and go at a reasonable pace. If he will go two feet away from you to jump, but not six, try him at four feet away. Soon he will get the idea of approaching and jumping at a distance from you.

Don't call your dog's name when working or he's likely to start straight back to you. Just call to get his attention; if you can't, throw something near him to attract him. Some dogs get out of control and need to be made to sit and stay for a few moments before being given the command; then, the minute they land on the other side of the hurdle, they must again be made to sit and stay or even lie down. Allow your dog to jump only on command, and discourage him from doing it on his own. This will prevent him from jumping out of confinement or over things you don't want him to scale.

Once he's proficient at jumping from a distance, go on to the next step—directing your pet while you are not standing next to him. First sit him a short distance from the hurdle while you stand two feet or so away from him (but not right next to the hurdle). Call out his name to get his attention, then point toward the object you want him to go over and say "jump." If he doesn't listen, go over to him and drag him to the hurdle. Nudge him over, then praise him.

As he obeys, gradually increase the distance at which you can command him, while at the same time making him go farther to reach the hurdle. In teaching this trick, be sure not to use only one type of hurdle. Practice jumping with a variety of different sizes and colors. If you don't practice your dog's jumps in a number of places and conditions, your pet may refuse to jump a barrier unlike the one he's used to, or under unusual circumstances. However, don't push your pet too fast and try to get him immediately to jump anything you point to. Go easy, and be thorough. Also, tell him to jump at times when he least expects it, so you can be sure he understands it as a command, and doesn't need you to go through the preliminaries of making him sit in front of the hurdle. You should be able to call his name to get his attention, point toward the hurdle, tell him to jump, and have him do so.

Once he is good with one hurdle, go on to another so as to acclimatize your dog to jumping many different objects. Always use your hand command and point to the jump you want your pet to go over so that he gets to know that the object you point to is the hurdle he has to clear. This way you may be able to direct your dog's jumping to such a degree that eventually you can set up two different hurdles, point out the one you want him to jump, and have him do so. You can even get him to jump several hurdles, one after the other, by waving him on to the next after each jump. Just be sure not to always set up the hurdles in the same places. Eventually he should jump any hurdle you select; wherever he is, your pet should be able to follow your point to see what you want him to jump.

After your pet has proved himself inside with your standard hurdles, you can take him outside—but only if your dog is trained off the leash. If not, you must confine your activities to an enclosed yard, garden, or dog run. In any case, when first outside your dog should be confined by his leash. This way you can correct him immediately, so that he doesn't get into the habit of doing anything wrong.

Off the leash, a dog may jump on command but then may just keep on going. This is why when he reached the other side of the hurdle indoors, you should have commanded your pet to sit or lie down to keep him under control. Outside he's likely to forget to stay and take off to freedom; the leash will keep him under control at first until he learns. However, remind him when he is almost ready to land, but still in midair: Call out the command you want him to perform once he gets over. This way when he lands he'll know what to do—sit, come, lie down, jump, or whatever.

Outside there are any number of hurdles and objects for him to jump over. Garbage cans are city favorites, as are park benches. In fact, if you are in the park frequently, benches are great for teaching larger breeds to jump. Start with the leash on, and have your dog stay on your left side while you both face the seat side of the bench. Stay close to the end of the bench so that while your dog has to jump over it, you can walk past the end. Run toward the bench and order your dog to jump. If he refuses, jerk him over. When he goes over on command without a jerk, take the leash off and work without it. Proceed in the same manner you would if you were indoors. If you find your pet is reluctant to perform outside, go through the training from the very early stages, the way you did indoors.

Over an Open Bar or Stick

Hold a thick, straight stick or broom handle in your right hand. Put your pet on a leash and hold it with your left hand. Placing your dog by your side, position the stick squarely in front of him, about a foot or so off the ground. Jam the other end against a tree or wall to be sure it remains perfectly steady and completely level. Give the command "jump." If he does, praise him profusely. Chances are he won't, however. Jerk your dog over with your left hand, saying "jump" as he is actually going over. Slacken the leash as soon as he lands, so he isn't made uncomfortable. Then when he obeys in one direction, turn around and do it in the opposite. This exercise will teach your pet that when you say "jump," you mean exactly that—even if there *is* a way for him to go underneath.

Once a dog jumps readily, you will be able to try it without putting on a leash. But for now, just hold the stick level, while at the same time giving a jerk on the leash and saying "jump." This should trick him into going over alone. As your dog becomes accustomed to jumping, gradually raise the stick higher.

When you are sure of your dog, remove the leash and work him without one. Soon you will be able to substitute other jumping objects and simply be able to thrust out an arm or leg, tell your dog to jump, and have him sail over it. When finished with this training he will also jump over bar hurdles, and not duck under them.

Many dogs may be reluctant when first working this command, so go slowly—he'll soon learn it's just another object to be jumped. If your dog thinks that the stick is a toy and tries to grab it with his mouth, don't jerk it away: This will only encourage him to play. Keep him on a taut leash. Hold the stick firmly and slap the side of his muzzle so he is forced to take his mouth away.

If your dog knows the command but is lazy and refuses to jump cleanly, he needs correcting and reworking. To make him pick up his feet more quickly, tap him on the front legs with the stick. Raising the stick slightly when he is on the way over will force him to raise his back feet higher so as to clear the stick completely. Be sure to make corrections when your pet is on a leash so that he cannot duck away, but also be sure your reprimands are not severe enough to discourage him from jumping.

Broad Jumping

This command means having your dog jump clear across a fairly wide area, such as a narrow stream or a low, wide hurdle. The actual jump requires forward momentum as opposed to an upward thrust. This means a longer takeoff; a running start is needed here to give your dog the speed to carry him forward through the air. Think of it in terms of the broad jump in track events. Naturally the length of the jump your dog can achieve will vary according to his size. To start, a leash is needed for control. Hold the leash with both hands as you do when walking your dog. Keep your dog on your left side, with your right hand holding the loop at the end of the leash and your left hand near the dog's collar.

With your dog on a leash by your side, approach the obstacle and give the command to jump. If possible, both you and your dog should then go over the obstacle together. Otherwise, select something you can easily sidestep while your dog leaps across it. If your dog is reluctant, jerk the leash upward and forward to get him over. Stretch your left arm out as far as you can while still holding the leash so as to support your dog's weight. When you are both on the opposite side, praise your dog and give him a treat.

Walk forward with him beside you for a short distance, then turn around and repeat the jump in the opposite direction. Once your dog is jumping freely with no support from your pressure on the leash, don't go over with him, but sidestep the jump while your dog goes over alone. Simply jerk the leash to help your dog get started.

Once he's going over, let the leash out through the palm of your left hand and hold the leash out from your body to keep the dog under control. Be sure to give enough slack for your dog to go over without any encumbrances. If the leash is not entirely loose when your dog lands on the opposite side, he may be thrown off his feet and become reluctant to jump again. When he reaches the other side, tell your dog to sit, stand, or stay so he learns not to just keep going. Praise him for correct responses.

Once he's proficient on the leash, try him without. Make your dog sit and stay about six feet in front of the jump while you stand beside or near it. Command your dog to jump. When he lands on the other side, tell him to sit, come, or lie down. Next stand a couple of feet away and then try from various positions. If he is proficient, praise him; if not, go back and rework your dog.

Your dog may refuse the broad jump, not wait for the command, run around rather than over it, or walk over rather than jumping. The way to eliminate the problems and to get perfection is to systematically work your dog and ask for correct behavior from the start. If your pet anticipates your command, leave him in a sitting position in front of the jump while you take a position at the side of the jump as if going to give the command. But instead of commanding your dog, walk back to him several times. This way your dog won't know when he is going to be commanded, and will be less likely to anticipate. To correct a dog that takes off in the other direction as soon as he lands, quickly give the command "sit" or "come." Teach your pet not to cut corners by being exacting with him when teaching him on the leash. A dog who attempts to walk across the jump needs to be nudged up into the air by rapping him on the feet.

To stop problems your best bet is to go back to early stages and work from there, making sure he is perfect throughout each step of the training.

Jumping Through

A dog that has been trained to jump *over* and *across* will readily learn to jump *through*—especially if he already knows how to jump a stick or bar hurdle, and is already familiar with the concept of going over a suspended barrier rather than ducking under it.

For the first few lessons keep your dog on a leash, even if he's well trained. Use a hoop or other aperture for your dog to jump through. Leave your pet in a sitting position while you go to the full length of the leash. Hold the hoop in your left hand and the leash in your right. Command your dog to jump whatever you have selected, and snap the leash forward quickly to bring your dog through the center of the aperture.

Once he's through, immediately praise and reward your dog. After a few lessons your dog should obey the command instantly without a leash. If he refuses to jump, however, pull him through the opening. If necessary, hold the hoop or other aperture to be jumped close to the floor and raise it gradually.

To teach your pet to work without a leash from a distance, start him only a few feet from the hurdle. Keep working him close until he obeys your command to jump immediately. This is one of those tricks that everyone loves, because even though it is basically simple, it looks complicated. Just be sure to match the aperture to the size of your pet, or he might get stuck midway.

Retrieving

Your dog's jaws are designed to hold and carry, comparable to our hands in usage. All dogs have the ability to retrieve and carry, but some have more of a natural talent. These dogs seem to chase and pick up everything. The only problem is that these natural retrievers are not always proficient at carrying things that they don't necessarily like to retrieve. A dog is considered trained in retrieving when he goes to get what he is told, not only his favorite toys.

"Take," "Hold," and "Drop"

Before your pet can learn how to retrieve accurately, he must first know how to take, hold, carry, and drop. In retrieving, therefore, the logical first step is to teach your dog these tasks. Even a dog who isn't trained to retrieve can use these commands. It makes a great trick to have your dog carry a magazine, newspaper, or small brown shopping bag. Once they learn this feat, dogs really enjoy it—perhaps because it attracts so much admiring attention and praise. Usually a dog carrying something in his mouth will prance around proudly.

The most obvious starting point is to simply get your pet to hold something in his mouth without spitting it out. To start off, ask your dog to hold something for which he has a particular liking, such as a rawhide bone or a toy. A stick or a rolled-up magazine or newspaper taped at either end are also good choices. Just be sure it is easy and comfortable for your dog to hold, and adjusted to fit his size. Don't use something such as a glove or other object that he could associate with your possessions, or he may start chewing on them. In fact, your pet should learn not to mouth or chew anything he

157

is carrying. When a dog begins to chew on what he is holding, reprimand him with a sharp rap.

With your selected object close by, place your dog in front of you. Make him sit before giving the command. If you feel your dog is likely to make a fuss when you place something in his mouth, put his leash on him and slip it under your foot. This will hold him in place but leave your hands free.

Offer the object to your pet and tell him "take." If he takes it and holds it, praise him profusely. If he objects, insist that he take it: Hold the object against his mouth and repeat "take." If he doesn't, place your free hand over your dog's muzzle. Exert pressure close behind the incisors on each side of the jaw with your thumb and middle finger.

This will make your dog open his mouth. When he does, quickly slip the object in. Then immediately release the pressure, and switch to holding his muzzle closed so that he can't spit it out. Say "hold" while holding his mouth closed and stroking him encouragingly, so that he keeps it in his mouth for a short while. After a few moments, release your hold on the muzzle and tell your dog "drop it." Because of the circumstances, he should spit it out immediately. If not, take it out of his mouth gently. Don't exert force to remove it by pulling or twisting it out. The intense training for "drop it" comes later.

If your dog absolutely refuses to open his mouth to take the object and puts up a fight—or if, once it's in, he tries to claw it out—you must insist. If you lack the perseverance to hold out until your pet gives up the struggle, you will never train him. If he has his leash on and you're standing on it, he cannot get away no matter how hard he tries. If necessary, keep exerting pressure on your dog's jowls to get them open— or conversely, firmly but gently pressing your dog's jaws together to make him hold onto the object. You must make sure your dog takes the object and doesn't spit it out until told to do so. Therefore, when your dog stops struggling, have him sit down quietly with the object in his mouth. Hold him for a few moments before telling him "drop it" and taking the object out of his mouth; then praise him.

In teaching, however, be sure that you don't give your dog lessons in "hold" and "drop" too closely together. These are two opposing actions and must not be associated, or your dog may never learn either command properly. Try to instill the "hold" and "carry" commands before working the "drop" command too emphatically. At first, assist your dog to drop the object when told to do so rather than forcing him to let go.

Once your dog sits quietly with something in his mouth while you hold it closed, try to get him to hold it without your help. Build up to this point by first holding your hand ready on his muzzle, but exerting no pressure. This way if your dog shows an inclination to let the object drop, you can quickly close your hand around his muzzle.

Once he is good at this stage and holds the article for a few moments until told to drop it, go one short step further. Instead of holding your hand around his muzzle, simply slip your hand under his chin, ready to catch the object if he drops it before you take it out. If he does, put it back in his mouth. Keep telling him "hold it" until he does.

Remember that one or two minutes of training at a time is fine. Just make sure the lesson ends with him doing what you want, and not the other way around. Even if you have to do everything yourself, end the lesson by making sure he has held the object in his mouth for a few moments. Then when you're ready, open his mouth and take it out. Signal that the lesson is finally over by giving your dog his special release word and signal.

After he will take and hold when asked, your dog is ready to learn to actually reach out on his own volition to take the article you're offering rather than have you open his mouth and place it in there. That is the real meaning of the "take it" command. It may take quite a few tries before this happens, but it will if you persist.

Hold the object to be taken in front of your dog's nose and tell him "take it" the way you did when you opened his mouth and placed it in. If he does nothing, put your hand around his muzzle as if you were about to squeeze, but don't. This should be enough of a reminder to persuade him to take it. If not, squeeze his muzzle slightly. Gradually eliminate the use of your hand over his muzzle until he readily takes the offered article.

Next, before your dog will pick up an article from the ground (as he must in retrieving), he must learn to reach forward by himself to take it when asked. Place your dog in the heel position. Make him sit, hold him on a short leash, and hold the article to be taken about four inches from his nose. Give him the command "take it." If your dog doesn't reach for it, put his leash on—if it isn't already on—and jerk hard in the direction of the article as a nudge to get him going. Every time your dog reaches for the article, let go of it, but don't be in a hurry to take your hand away. Keep your hand close to his muzzle momentarily to give your dog the impression that if he fails to hold it by himself, you might hold his mouth closed with the article in it. Gradually move the object to be taken farther away from his mouth until he will reach and even step forward to take it from a few feet ahead of his nose.

Once he reaches to take it readily from a distance and is steady holding it in his mouth, teach your dog the "drop it" command. Once your pet will drop what he is holding every time he is told to do so and is proficient in taking and holding, you control the basic retrieving actions. At first your pet was probably only too willing to let go of whatever article he was holding as soon as your hand was removed from his muzzle, so you merely had to put your hand under his mouth to catch it. However, a dog who knows how to take and hold without you physically helping him will hold the object more tenaciously; you have taught him to do so and indicated approval when he did. To counter this, you have to teach your pet that when told "drop it," letting go is the correct thing for him to do.

Never pull the article out of your dog's mouth; make your dog let go by himself. After your pet has held the chosen object for a few moments, command "drop it." If he doesn't, don't grab at the article or fight your dog by pulling against him; instead just pry his jaws apart while you gently remove the article. Put your two fingers back behind the object he is holding and quietly spread your fingers apart. This will pry open his mouth and cause the article to drop out. Hold your other hand open under his muzzle so that when you force the object out of your pet's mouth, it falls into your hand. Once he lets go, praise your pet by stroking him approvingly. If he is stubborn about letting go, command "drop it"; when he refuses, flick him in the end of the nose with your finger until he does. Or slap him on the side of the muzzle with a blow equal to his stubbornness and size. Just be sure not to let your pet decide when to drop the object—that's your job.

In the early stages of training your dog to retrieve, do not insist on perfect obedience or special little refinements. Don't demand he sit before retrieving, or go to the heel position after bringing the object back. Work your pet easily and casually. The most important thing is to get your dog to go out, pick up the requested object, and bring it back. Later, when he is proficient, you can be more demanding.

This doesn't mean letting your dog get away with not listening, however. Be adamant and insist that your dog do what you ask. Even if he doesn't want to do it, you must carry through. If your pet will retrieve only what he likes and refuses all other items, you'll never have a trained retriever.

Therefore, start off the training easy, as if playing a game to get your pet on the right track. But once he knows what it is all about, you have to come down hard on him if he refuses to listen. Your dog must know that you expect him to work, but as for all elective training such as this, the degree of perfection you want from your dog is up to you.

Carrying

After teaching your pet the absolute essentials of simply taking the object from your hand and holding it in his mouth until told to drop it, you're ready to expand his manipulation of these basics. Your dog has to learn to actually do things, rather than just sitting, while holding something in his mouth. While carrying objects, your dog should heel, stay, and come, obeying just about all the other obedience commands he has been taught.

First teach him to take, hold, and drop the article while in motion. Put your dog on a leash and walk him around. Halt at intervals, and make your dog take and then drop an article. This will get him used to the idea that your command to hold an article can come at any time, even when he's walking.

Next have your dog hold something while he is actually in motion. Hold him on a short leash and sit him down in front of you. Giving him something to hold, place your hand underneath and around his muzzle as a support to remind your pet to keep hold of the article. Keep it there while you start to walk him forward slowly. As he responds, gradually release your grip on him until your hand is only resting under his mouth. Finally, your dog should carry it without any support. After this, walk your dog in an at-heel position, keeping the leash slack. Your dog should carry as he walks along, and should continue to hold the article when he sits until told to drop it.

Each step of the way, be generous with praise for deeds well done. Later test your pet's progress by having him hold the article while he remains in a sit-stay position as you walk away. Then, after a short time, call him to come to you. Don't allow him to drop the article until you tell him to do so and take it from him. If asked, your dog should even "drop it" when moving.

Picking Something Up Off the Ground

In order to go out to retrieve, your pet has to learn to take an article off the ground without you handing it to him. Sit your dog in front of you and hold the article to be retrieved close to the ground just ahead of him. (Make sure it is something he can pick up easily and not have to struggle to get his mouth around.) If your dog shows no interest, jerk the leash until he does. Once he takes it from your hand when held close to the ground, actually place the article on the ground just ahead of him and tell him "take it." If you insist he comply, soon he should pick up any article you drop on the ground. If your dog is stubborn about picking up, a series of snaps on the leash will sometimes work where one snap failed. You could even drag the article in question along ahead of your dog and give a number of short jerks on the leash while pointing to the article and telling him "take it." Your dog thus learns that you pointing to an article and telling him "take it" means for him to pick it up, hold, and carry it until you tell him to drop it. When your pet is good, praise him profusely and make him think he is doing something wonderful. Your dog needs this kind of reinforcement to understand that "take it" means taking whatever from wherever you ask him.

During this latter part of training use an assortment of articles, not just one or two. Otherwise your dog will learn to hold just those few articles and will be restricted. Have him hold articles made of different materials such as wood, leather, and paper. But do so only after you are positive he's so well trained that he would never chew anything. This familiarity with various objects and textures will prepare your pet for more advanced retrieving work, such as seeking out lost articles and scent discrimination. Use the words "take it" whenever you give anything to your dog, even a cookie. This will ensure he understands the command.

Once your dog is taking articles from the ground on command, it's time to get him interested in running after the same articles. Drop a stick on the ground a few feet in front of him. Point to it and give the command "take it." If he won't fetch, attach the leash and jerk him to the stick, then pull his head down until he picks it up. If he won't, force it into his mouth and praise him when he does take it. This forced retrieving should be over quickly, but it is often necessary. If your dog sees you give up when he refuses to work, you'll never get him to do the job.

If your dog shows any inclination to play with the article you use for training, take advantage of this. Keep your dog on a leash, but give him plenty of freedom. Tempt him with the object to be picked up and get your dog just interested enough to make a grab for it. When he does, let him take it immediately, and at the same time say "take it" so that he associates the command with the action.

You may have to assist by slipping the article into his mouth, but your dog should be given as much praise as though he had made all the effort. For practice, place your dog in front of and facing you, then walk backward while telling him to come. Wiggle the article in front of him close to the ground until he takes it. Next walk slowly, dragging the article along the ground ahead of him until ready, then tell him to take it. When he reaches for the article, let go and praise him. In the meantime, you should keep moving forward so that your dog learns to go toward the object to pick it up.

Basic Retrieving

Retrieving means your dog must go a distance away from you, pick up any article in his mouth by himself, return it to you, and then drop it when told. You're in control when your dog performs this whole sequence of actions at your command, rather than when he feels like it. Your pet should already know each step of the command separately; now these elements have to be linked together to form the chain action of retrieving.

Start by keeping your dog on a slack leash and giving him something to carry in his mouth. Let him go out to the full length of the leash and make him come when called a few times while holding the article in his mouth, and then have him drop it when he gets to you. This will get him used to returning to you while holding the article, and dropping it into your hand or in front of you when asked.

Next you have to get him to walk out away from you and pick up the article to be returned, then come back to you with it. To do this, leave your dog's leash on and make him sit. Toss out the article to be retrieved four or five feet in front of your pet. Tell him "fetch it" or "go get it" and move toward the object with your dog. If he won't pick it up, put it into his mouth after giving him every opportunity to do so of his own accord. Once he has it in his mouth, quickly move forward away from your dog so he's again at the full length of the leash. Call your pet to you and make him come, reeling him in if necessary. Then when he is in front of you, tell him "drop it" and take the object away from him. (Later, when he is proficient, you can teach him to sit in front of you for a few moments before relinquishing the article.) Continue this while gradually allowing him to execute the maneuver without your help until your dog goes out readily by himself and brings back the requested object from the end of the leash distance. During this training, throw the object to be retrieved in a number of different directions so that your dog understands to go anywhere you ask.

After he is retrieving readily when told to do so, take your dog's leash off and work him without one. Have your dog sit down by you and then toss the article out a few feet. Tell him "go get it" or "fetch." (Having taught him "go" as described in Off-the-Leash Training can be invaluable here if you want true control.) In the beginning you may have to encourage him by going out with him at least partway, perhaps even all the way. When he picks the article up, quickly move back to the spot from where you threw it and call "come." Upon his return to you, tell him to sit, then command him to drop it.

Praise your pet profusely for obeying, and end the lesson there. If he flubs at any point, intercept and correct immediately. Even walk him through it if necessary. When he's good in the next lessons, gradually increase the distance you throw the article. Keep working until your dog retrieves whenever he hears the command.

If you have problems teaching your dog to retrieve at a distance, use a long leash as an aid—fifteen feet is usually enough—and work it as with a short one. You can also use a fishing rod and reel to help you teach your dog retrieving from a distance. Attach a favorite toy to about twenty feet of fishing line. Cast it out and flutter it around to get your dog interested enough to go over to it. Usually a toy bouncing around on the end of a rod and line will excite a dog, but if yours shows no interest, try another article that's really enticing. When he picks it up, call him over to you, reeling him in as he comes. When he gets there, tell him "drop it." Praising him with gusto when he does—whether with your assistance or not—will whet your pet's appetite for retrieving.

Problems in Retrieving

To calm your dog down and bring him under control, the relaxed attitude of early training must eventually give way to more intense work. Therefore, gradually make him wait longer before letting him go out to retrieve. If you don't, your dog may anticipate and rush out even before the object is thrown. If he does, put your dog on a leash and make him stay by your side when you throw the object out. Do this several times without ordering your dog after it. If he attempts to go out after it, jerk the leash back. He has to learn to retrieve only when told.

If your dog has the exact opposite problem, he probably goes through the act of retrieving, but in slow motion. Making a real game out of it might tempt him to start after the article more enthusiastically. First throw the article, then run after it yourself and pick it up and throw it again. Your dog may soon realize that he must go after it immediately if he wants to get there before you do. But in doing this, be careful you don't end up with a dog who sits staring at you while you retrieve. If your pet shows no interest in competing with you, stop.

To give him more forceful incentive, hold a rolled-up leash or some other object in your hand and throw it calmly at or behind him to get him going out to the article. Keep doing this until he finally goes, then call him back to you with lavish enthusiasm to let him know you are pleased. If your dog goes for the article easily enough but brings it back at a snail's pace, go out and drag him to you. Otherwise, have another person throw something or make a loud noise behind him to send him toward you. (A tidbit might help tempt him back as a final resort.)

If your dog throws the retrieved article down in front of you, as if to tell *you* to pick it up, he's not completing the job properly. To get your dog over this habit of dropping the article as soon as he reaches you, tell him to sit and stay the moment he arrives or even a second before. Quickly reach over to put your hand around his muzzle. Then when ready, ask him to drop it—and this means placing it in your hand or dropping it in front of you *after* you request it. This should stop your dog from dropping the object prematurely. Repeat over and over to encourage your dog to deliver the object in the proper manner. If he gets to the point where he sits in front of you but then drops the article, give a quick ''stay'' to make sure he keeps a firm hold on the object. Then to teach him patience, make him sit and hold it for longer than he would normally before telling him to drop it.

When the leash is off, you'll have to control your dog by voice and hand commands. However, many dogs work strictly on instinct and don't pay any attention. This means you have no means of correcting mistakes and relapses when off the leash—and to correct this lack of knowledge you have to go through a whole exercise. First command your dog to stay by your side while you throw the object out. Then to get your dog to go out for it, tell him ''fetch'' or ''go get it.'' Just as (or before) your dog picks up the object, tell him ''take it'' and quickly say ''come.'' Make your dog sit in front of you after he gets back. When ready to take the article, tell him ''drop it.''

Get into the habit of using these commands. They can always be dropped when your dog no longer needs them, but they help keep him under control when first teaching retrieving. Additionally, they allow you to call out a reminder if need be. While teaching voice commands, be sure to work on the hand signals too. This is the opportune time to get him used to following your hand directions. After you have your dog sit and stay, put your hand in front of his nose, command ''fetch,'' and point in the direction in which the article was thrown. This way, even if he doesn't see it thrown, he at least knows in which direction it went.

Retrieving in Water

You can't teach a dog to swim; he'll just jump in and learn. You, however, can give him the right opportunities. Select a body of shallow water that's not too cold or dirty. Wade in a few feet yourself and call, coax, and cajole your dog into the water.

Some dogs love water and will jump in with glee, but most are unsure at first and will run up and down the water's edge, looking for a way to reach you without going in. Even if he wades out a short distance, he may not get up the nerve to take the plunge. If he does refuse to go in, you may have to resort to using the leash. Simply put his leash on and walk him into the water. Continue working him on the leash until he will go in when you tell him to do so. When he does go into the water, start off the actual retrieving-in-water exercise.

Throw a stick into very shallow water where your dog has to wade to only about halfway up his legs. Command your dog "fetch" or "go get it" and point toward the stick. If he does so, praise him profusely. If not, put his leash on, walk him into the water to the stick, and put it into his mouth. After he does it with ease this way, remove the leash and work him without it. At first be sure your pet only has to wade in to retrieve the article. Later, when he is secure in the command, take your dog into deeper water.

Using a fishing rod and line will sometimes save the day with this trick. Tie a toy instead of a hook to the end of the line. Show the toy to your pet, and flip it out into the water. Drag it through the water to get your dog excited enough to chase it. Once he's doing this, take the toy off the line and tie it to the stick or other object you want retrieved, and throw it out for him. Now he should fetch with enthusiasm. Later, you should eliminate the toy and just throw the stick for him to fetch.

Retrieving Over Hurdles

Only when your dog retrieves perfectly in open terrain, has been taught to jump over an obstacle on command, and is proficient in the ''go'' command (sending him away from you to a specific destination) is he ready for this training. Use a low, solid hurdle at first and have him jump it a few times. Show him the object you want him to get, and let him play with it. Put him on a leash and take him in front of the jump. Throw the object to be retrieved just over to the other side, and tell your dog to jump. When the dog goes over, let him go alone while you remain. Hold the leash slack so it doesn't interfere with the jump. Once he is on the other side, point to the object and say ''take it.'' When he picks it up, call ''come.'' Move back slightly from the hurdle and jerk him over. After your dog finishes the return jump and is in front of you, tell him to drop the article.

The leash should always be ready to make corrections: Jerk him when necessary. Once he can retrieve when ordered from right in front of the hurdle, go on to directing him from a distance.

Attach a long line to him rather than a leash, and back up so you are both four to five feet away from the hurdle. Command your pet to jump it, and once he is over, tell him ''take it.'' When he picks up the article, call out ''come.''

Constant repetition of this will teach your dog to leap over the obstacle and come back to you. Once dependable, your dog should be worked free. But when you first remove the leash, stand near the jump so he's not tempted to run around. As he works with ease, gradually move farther back. Your control is through voice and hand commands, and you should command him every step of the way at first. Later you can drop the extra commands and simply throw the article out to the other side of the hurdle, ask your pet to go get it and point.

If your dog does everything right but returns without jumping the hurdle, stand near the jump and throw something on the ground in front of him just as he comes around the jump. Then take him back to your original command spot and make him do it over again. If your dog goes over the hurdle but then just stands there with the object in his mouth as if unsure, even after being called back, use the same techniques you did any time he refused to come when called.

Two Dogs Retrieving

Possessiveness of objects can extend to any situation, any place, and against all competition. In the park a ball or stick can become a major possession. If two dogs go for it and collide, a fight might get started.

If you have two dogs, you must teach one to back off and not to pick a fight when the other has the stick. Your dog must learn to honor another dog's catch and not try to grab it. Do this by stopping the aggressive one. If your pets play in a communal dog run, you might have to teach all so they can learn to play together in peace.

To prevent such problems and to teach your dog to play, you and the other owner should go to separate spots about fifty feet apart with your backs to each other. You should both throw a stick out for your respective dog. Each of you should then gradually turn toward the other, each time throwing the sticks closer to one another until both are approximately in the center of the fifty-foot divide between you. Both dogs will eventually be standing together. At this point, only one of you should throw a stick so that both dogs go for it. But because they are used to both having separate sticks, the dog that gets there first should take the stick and go back to his owner. However, if there is a squabble, reprimand them thoroughly. Any outbreak of real fighting or possessiveness should be handled as suggested in "Controlling Aggression."

Discriminating Among Objects

After your dog has learned to retrieve, you can teach him to select one specific object from among several. Scent discrimination is the way this is done most easily. Later you may be able to teach your dog to pick up signals indicating which article you want; but scent discrimination is generally the most common method of detection, and is the one with which all discrimination starts. Size, familiarity, and hue recognition can all come later.

Many people think this trick is accomplished by putting a really good smell (such as sardine oil) on the article you want your dog to select. This will work, of course, but it's best to play it straight and train your dog to use his nose to distinguish one ordinary scent from another.

Compared to humans, the dullest canine nose is exquisitely sensitive. These animals make predominant use of their noses, since their sense of smell is the keenest of their senses. The upper part of the dog's nasal cavity possesses a large area of olfactory mucous membrane having many smell receptors. The nose is constructed in such a way that every inhalation and exhalation causes all the air to pass directly over these nerve endings. In addition, a second smell organ, the vomeronasal, is situated in the roof of the mouth behind the front teeth. This remarkable olfactory ability allows a dog to track and locate specific objects or individuals, detect minute traces of scent, and discriminate between two similar odors so well that a dog can be trained to tell the difference between twins. Some even claim that receptors in a dog's nose enable it to sense warm objects—perhaps explaining why St. Bernards are able to detect a living man under the snow.

There are differences in the attraction that various scents hold for a dog, however. Odors of animal origin are especially enticing, though a dog can tell the difference between organic musk and artificial musk. For some reason, dogs are extremely sensitive to acidic odors such as those found in salts, sulphuric acid, and vinegar. In fact, a dog can smell one part acid diluted in one million parts of distilled water. Conflicting smells do not mask odors. Training only enhances a dog's ability to analyze complex mixtures of different odors, and it is this analytical capacity that permits dogs to identify people on the basis of body odor. Therefore, your dog can be taught to recognize corresponding scents so that if you give him an odor to sniff, he will be able to pick an object out of a pile with the same smell on it.

The preliminary work for this trick is to have your dog retrieve his special toy or bone from among two or three articles. Your dog will probably recognize his own belonging, especially if it is the most tempting of the articles offered. So place one of his toys in the midst of some others. When he picks his out to play with it, praise him profusely. When your dog selects one special article from others, he is using his nose to recognize a particular smell. Praise him when he does. This will reinforce his use of smell to recognize his belongings. Once he does so readily, have him transfer this ability over to selecting objects with familiar smells on them from among those with strange smells.

The idea is to teach your pet to retrieve the object that corresponds to whatever scent he is given at the start, not just to run out and get the nearest article and bring it back gleefully. Your dog must distinguish one smell from another, sniffing at all the articles in order to be able to discriminate accurately, because he has to find the single article with the right smell and bring it back as soon as he finds it. At the beginning, therefore, make sure you scent only one article.

Start by using two or three similar (preferably identical) articles, one of which has your scent on it and the others not. This ensures that your dog will recognize the right one by scent alone. Pieces of a stick cut to a few inches in length or even rawhide bones are fine. Handle one a lot, but be sure never to touch the others so that they are free of your odor. Carry them with tongs or have someone else handle them.

Place one or two of the identical articles a short distance from you. Hold the selected article in front of your dog's nose for a while, so he gets a good whiff. Then tell your dog to take, hold, and drop the article.

After he does this, toss it out near the others. Tell your dog "fetch" or "go get it." If your dog picks up the wrong article, tell him "no"; wait to see if he drops it and goes to the right one. When he does, call him to you quickly and when he's by your side, praise him.

If he fails, repeat the entire command. This time, however, instead of throwing the article out next to the others, throw it halfway between you and the other objects so it's the most obvious. When he picks it up and brings it to you, praise him enthusiastically. Gradually toss it closer to the other objects until your dog has to pick it out from among the several.

If you cannot control your dog or if he refuses to respond, put him on a slack leash. Have all the articles piled close together, making sure not to touch the sterile articles except with tongs. Take your dog to the pile, throw the one you handled with the others, then tell him to take it. If he momentarily sniffs at the others, say nothing. But when he touches the right one, quickly say "good dog" to help make him feel secure about taking it.

If he attempts to pick up an unscented article, jerk the leash hard, say "no" quietly, and gently pull him away. This will make your dog realize he has done wrong. If you aren't fast enough and your dog picks up the wrong article, tell him to drop it, and pull his jaws apart until it falls out. Just be sure not to touch the sterile article yourself and add your odor to it. Again ask him to take it, and repeat until he takes the right one.

If he refuses within about three minutes, finish the lesson by shoving the correct article into his mouth and praising him for taking it. When he gets the idea of selecting the correct article, give him more and more freedom on the leash until he can retrieve at the full length of it by himself. Once he retrieves the right article on a regular basis, try him without a leash and control him by voice and hand signals. Do this by working as you would for plain retrieving.

As your dog becomes proficient at selecting the scented article, add more unscented articles to the pile from which he must select. However, don't give him more than five or six and still expect your pet to bring back the right one. Too many can be confusing. To be sure your pet doesn't become accustomed to only one spot, occasionally change the position of the scented article. Partially hide it at times, or place it a slight distance from the others to encourage your dog to hunt for the article if he doesn't find it immediately. Don't make it easy for your dog, because he won't always be working under ideal control conditions. Therefore, add some twists—such as putting out a circular assortment to see if he can find the right object.

When he gets proficient at retrieving one type of article, go on to others—then on to an assortment rather than similar or identical items. Gather up a varied collection of articles made from different materials. Keep one of each as the scent article, and handle the others only with tongs. No matter what assortment you use, be sure that you touch only one article—all others must be untouched.

Once your dog picks out your odor, he can be extended to include any number of others. Have a friend give your dog his hand to smell. Then have him handle an article to put his smell on it. Your friend should then give the article to your dog to hold for a few moments and have him drop it. He should then pick up the article he touched and put it with the other odorless ones, being sure not to get his odor on any of them. Send your dog out and have him retrieve the one item he was just shown. If he balks, take him through the steps outlined and make him take it. (Just be sure *you* can correctly discriminate which article is the right one.)

At any point in this training, if your dog seems to come to a standstill and is making no progress, go back and review. Make sure neither of you is making a mistake. If your dog runs out and just stands there without picking up the article, it's probably due to poor training in retrieving and scent discrimination. You might have been too severe: Your pet is now afraid to pick up anything in case it is the wrong article.

This dog has to be encouraged and praised. Handle a

frightened dog by putting his leash on, but not using it for anything but gentle guidance. There should be no harsh words, only encouragement. Praise profusely when he's right, and give only a quiet but definite "no" when wrong. Review from the beginning and build confidence slowly.

A stubborn dog that never learned the early lessons well needs to have a leash put on him and have it snapped hard as a correction for refusing to obey. He should be handled firmly. Mistakes usually mean that your dog needs to go back to "kindergarten" for a while until the lesson sinks in.

Seeking Lost or Hidden Articles

When a dog can retrieve by recognizing scents, he is ready to learn to seek lost articles, an exercise that needs a combination of both skills. Start off by having your dog retrieve a special toy in play. Later hide this favored item so that he must use his nose to find it. This will give your dog the idea of searching for the article you want—which is what the command is all about. Now change the command from "take it" to "look for it." This expression indicates to your dog that he must hunt, rather than expect to find the article to be retrieved in plain sight.

At first use some item your dog likes; leave it where it is not difficult to see. Additionally, teach your dog to seek hidden articles all around your home so as to train him to cover a reasonable area. Give names to these familiar articles your dog is seeking. This will teach him to distinguish such frequently used objects as "ball," "leash," or "paper." Give your dog the command to go find a definite article, and have him seek it.

When your dog is fairly proficient in this exercise, take him outside. Later add difficulties. For example, do the exercise

175

where the grass is taller. Throw the article out and give the command for him to go get it. He knows it's there because he saw you throw it, but he can find it only if he smells it out.

To teach your dog to backtrack and search for a lost article, take a favorite toy that both you and your pet have handled a lot. Walk along with your dog and discreetly drop it without him seeing you do so. Then stop a step or so farther on, point to where you dropped the article, and give your dog the command "look for it."

Go with him until he finds the object. After a few times of assisting him he will realize what you want and will soon search by himself, following the scent trail you and he have left behind. When he does, increase the distance you ask him to go and search.

If your dog is stubborn and won't go by himself, walk him on a leash and hold the article in your hand. Drop it, making sure your dog sees it. Walk about five or ten feet more, make an about-face turn, tell your dog to go look for it, and release him. If he doesn't do it, even at this short distance, he obviously doesn't understand retrieving and needs a complete review. Put your dog on a leash and walk him toward the article, point to it, and demand he take it. Make him pick it up and hold it, then go out to the end of the leash and call your pet to come so as to make him bring the article to you.

After a few lessons like this he should get the idea. Then once again go to the first steps in searching and seeking back. When he's proficient at seeking back, drop the article and instead of walking away in a straight line, add turns. At first just single left- or right-hand turns are fine, then add a number of different turns. Additionally, work in different places, and each time drop the item a little farther away.

Trailing and Tracking

In trailing and tracking, a dog smells out specific people and traces them down. This skill could be very useful in helping a lost dog find his way home, or it can simply allow him to hunt out a friend or guest for fun. At the same time it hones his best sense instrument—his nose—which in turn enables him to function better at certain other tasks.

Since your dog must follow the path made by an object or a person disturbing the ground in passing, it is not a good exercise for short-nosed dogs like a bulldog or pug who can't reach the ground conveniently. A dog can work by sniffing in the air, but he'll be less accurate.

The time of day influences the conditions for tracking. In the late afternoon and early evening the air is heavy and the dew begins to fall, thus holding the scent close to the ground. Early morning before sunrise also fosters these conditions. Once the sun is out, the moisture evaporates and scenting becomes difficult, with the hottest part of the day being the most unrewarding. Heavy rainfall will temporarily lessen the smell, but once the rain stops the smell is still there. High winds can disperse odor and cause problems; a dog can still track when going with or against the wind, but problems arise with crosswinds. If the wind is hitting an embankment, cliff, or trees, it may rebound and cause problems. A strong odor will overpower a scent. Running water and leaves blown about cause trail scents to shift and be broken. And it is hard when coming to a stream, as the odor gets to drift up and down slightly so the dog has to search.

There is no basis in fact to the belief that simply having an object or body float about above the ground will allow odor to drift to the ground. A body actually has to make contact to leave an odor. However, a dog can trail a person who has traveled over an area in a car by following the car's trail.

177

To learn tracking, your dog must be controlled by a harness or regular collar and a light line, twenty or so feet long. This is basically a game of hide and seek in which someone hides and your dog finds him, so you really need a friend whom your dog likes to help with the training. Have your friend walk off in a straight line into the distance. When he or she gets out of sight, give your dog a smell of one of your friend's belongings and tell him "go look." Then let your dog out on the leash to hunt for your friend. Follow your dog at the full length of the leash, but control him to be sure that he doesn't run off. When he locates the person, both you and the object of his tracking should praise the dog profusely and give him some tidbit as a reward.

Do a few simple exercises like this with different people, over and over until your dog gets the idea. You must keep changing assistants, and you too should hide once in a while; have a friend hold the leash while your dog tracks you. This gets him used to looking for lots of different people, including yourself.

Once he's proficient at finding someone he is tracking along a straight line, have the trail made harder. The person being sought should make a right turn, then a left turn, and then several different turns before your dog starts tracking.

If he loses the trail, take him back to where he was correct and start again from there. If you think he has lost the trail, don't urge him forward: Speed is not as important here as accuracy. Eventually when he gets off the leash, your dog will tend to be less sure of himself when looking for the trail, so be thorough now. He must be proficient on the leash before you can remove it.

Once your dog is acclimatized to working on the line, take it off and work him free. Again start by having the person being tracked walk a straight line only a short distance so that your dog finds him readily. (You have to watch exactly where the person goes so you can help your dog if there's any problem.) Hold him in place until the person laying the trail has been out of sight for a few moments. Then tell your dog "go seek." Once he is proficient at searching in a straight line, proceed with turns as you did when he was on the line. Be sure to have your friend hold your dog while you go out and hide. Then have him send the dog out to find you—perhaps the most important tracking your dog can do.

In these complicated training procedures you need firm patience to hold out until the dog gives in—do not necessarily get rough, just quietly and definitely win each battle so the dog will acknowledge you as the victor. Do not, however, become so enthusiastic that you train your dog all day and never give him a moment's peace. Training a dog constantly will produce the same result as nagging. Except for regular training periods, dogs should be allowed to relax and be natural—providing of course they are being well mannered. Just be sure your dog is happy at the close of the training period, so give your dog something pleasant to remember.

Seven

PREVENTING AND ELIMINATING BAD HABITS

The Purpose of
Negative Training

Unfortunately dogs are not always the perfect creatures we masters might like them to be. A pet-dominated family can be miserable, and any dog can become a household terror. No one wants a dog who chews up your antique armoire or eats up your favorite Boston fern. And if you don't train your dog, you can make enemies. If your dog misbehaves, *you* may blame the dog, but everyone else will blame you.

When a dog is taken into your home, he must be taught to respect the rights and feelings of the humans he associates with. He has to learn he can't rip up the house, bully everyone into a corner, or annoy your friends. Not everyone is crazy about animals, and so he has to be trained not to dig up your neighbors' lawns or chase their cars. Barking is not fair to neighbors, nor are piles of feces on the floor when visitors arrive, nor are attacks on postal employees or delivery persons. Guests don't want to be jumped on by a noisy dog; car chasing can be dangerous to everyone, and dogs jumping around in a car are equally dangerous. You have to keep your dog on your own property, and when he is left alone there, he should be reliable.

People complain that their dog barks endlessly, chews the rug, or snaps at their mothers-in-law. Before the dog will stop such upsetting, destructive behavior, he has to associate something unpleasant with that activity. But when negative training is explained, "I couldn't be cruel to an animal!" is often the response. These same people, however, do not hesitate to request that you find a new home for their animal, or a place where they can leave him—even if the final result is the dog being put to sleep. It is really kinder to train a dog with a little bit of preventive medicine.

All dogs have the potential to develop bad habits, and unfortunately, some of the natural tendencies and basic instincts—which can be very undesirable under the restricted conditions of urban life—can also be difficult to inhibit.

Once you let a lot of problems build up, you will really have your work cut out for you. Therefore, starting off on the right foot is important to you as well as to your pet.

If you already have your dos and don'ts list prepared, decide also where you want and don't want him to be in your home. To start teaching your pet what you *don't* want him to do, go through a watchful session with him. Giving your dog rules during this session will make for a happier, more secure pet. Once he knows what is expected of him and what he can and cannot do, your dog will feel more at ease. This initial training will serve to start him off as a good member of your house. This session shouldn't take more than ten to fifteen minutes. You should have only two during the first day or so, being sure to keep them well separated from any positive lessons. Take the leash off your dog and allow him to wander around, but don't take your eyes off him. If your dog does something wrong, make it clear that you don't want him to continue. A negative, unpleasant action is the only thing that will discourage your pet. Petting your dog and explaining why misbehavior is unwanted will have no effect. A friend took her dog over to the bed which he had recently destroyed, and explained why he shouldn't keep on digging and scratching it to shreds. To add punch to the explanation, she gave her pet a cookie to show him that if he didn't touch the bed again, he'd get a treat as a reward. Our friend then left for the day, only to return that evening to find her other bed ripped to pieces! The dog greeted her happily, led her over to the newly destroyed bed, then sat down—drooling, awaiting another treat. He thought he had been given the treat as encouragement for chewing!

If your dog looks ready to climb on the furniture, tell him to get down and give him a little tap. Stop any mad running around immediately. Since a dog will usually sniff and then lick before he starts to chew, try to catch him in the sniffing-and-licking stage. Sit with a little magazine nearby, and if he goes over to nuzzle the plants or furniture, throw your magazine at or near him and say nothing.

When correcting your pet for a misdeed, it's best to catch him in the act. Generally a dog can only associate the activity of the moment with the correction. However, no matter whether your dog is caught in the act or not, you must correct your dog every time he makes a mistake—even if you discover it a few hours later. If you do have to punish your dog after the fact, always be sure he understands *why* the punishment is being given. Your pet must make the association between the unpleasant reprimand and his evil deed. If there is a separation of time between the misbehavior and the punishment, your pet may become confused. Be sure to remind your pet, simply by pulling him over to the spot where the damage was done. Even if the misbehavior occurs in front of people, you have to correct your pet no matter what the reaction of the onlookers. If not, your pet will think that all he has to do is misbehave when you are not around or when there is an audience.

The Word "No"

"No" means just what it says. There really is no formal way to teach it to your dog—and there's no need to. "No" is a word people use continuously when their dogs do something wrong, and your pet will pick it up naturally. However, just to make sure your dog completely understands its full impact, connect the word "no" with something unpleasant, so that your pet thinks of "no" as a preface to something more substantial. If he steals food from the table, slap him on the nose or flank and tell him "no." Next time, the word will remind him of the slap.

However, keep in mind that the effectiveness of the word "no" is quickly used up. If you say it too often, eventually it doesn't mean anything. Therefore, it's often better not to use the word "no"—simply reprimand your pet physically. Save the word "no" only for *temporary* compliance: Use it for the particular times when you don't want your dog to do something that's normally allowed. To stop him, say "no" simply to express disapproval, rather than as an effective method of negative training. What creates a permanent prohibition on the action is disciplining your pet without saying anything. Therefore, for any habit you want to stop permanently, don't bother to use the word "no." Don't say a word, just reprimand your pet.

Direct Physical Reprimands

To be effective, corrections have to be administered with enough severity to leave no doubt in your dog's mind that you are displeased. Half-hearted, almost teasing punishment is not only ineffective, it can be harmful—it can make your dog more disobedient, even mean, just to test how far he can go before you stop him decisively. Better to make the correction sure and fast, getting it over quickly. Just be sure never to punish your dog while you're in a temper, or you're likely to flail out with no direction. Stay calm and act methodically. You must be explicit about why your pet is being reprimanded so he understands not to do it again.

Direct physical action is what a mother dog uses with her puppies and what adult dogs use in their interactions with each other. A mother dog can't explain to one of her pups why he should or shouldn't do something. She nudges, snaps, and slaps him into place. In teaching, an animal is used to direct, physical, bodily action; therefore, you must bring yourself to exert the reprimand. Some training methods advocate hanging a dog by the neck on a leash, but this is especially cruel since it garrotes the animal.

If you have a delicate little animal, pick him up by the shoulders and shake him. This is the way bitches punish their young, and pack leaders admonish inferiors. When you must slap your pet, the fleshy part of the rump is an ideal place. Use your discretion about the severity of the reprimand. You must not be overly emphatic in your correction, but it must be definite for it to be effective. A short, sudden touch, and that's it. Just be careful that you don't hit out wildly, perhaps hitting your dog in a sensitive place or making him hand-shy. Your dog will try to avoid your swinging hand by wriggling or running away. Hold your pet firmly with one hand, aim properly, and slap with the other. As a reprimand instead of—

or in addition to—a slap or other direct corrective measure, use Tabasco sauce. Administer a small quantity of Tabasco sauce full strength to your dog's gums when he does wrong, and leave it at that.

The forcefulness of corrections made should depend upon you and your dog's disposition. You must know when to stop, because otherwise the correction will be detrimental. Be kind with a shy pup, but firm with one that has a willful nature. If a dog is shy or nervous, negative training should be approached gently at first, and with much less severity than with an outgoing, feisty dog that needs more severe treatment.

The Rubber Arm Technique

You will be able to exert tremendous control over your pet if you can establish that you can reach him anywhere—and this is what the Rubber Arm technique allows you to do. To correct or train a dog from a distance, simply throw an article at him or on the floor next to him. He will smell the object, recognize your body odor on it, and thus realize that you can reach him no matter where he is. Throwing an object next to your pet simply startles him. Direct contact is generally the most effective use of the Rubber Arm technique, since it inflicts a certain amount of discomfort. No matter which system you select, however, just keep in mind that to be effective, the object must have some impact. You must toss it emphatically enough to make your dog feel its presence.

In the Rubber Arm technique, your choice of object to throw should depend on the size of your dog, how far away you are, and whether you want it to hit your dog or just land on the floor beside him. A short piece of chain (no more than two or three links), a tin can filled with a few pennies, your house keys, or a small magazine of *Reader's Digest* size are all possible choices. Throwing things that make a real clatter near your pet are especially effective because dogs are easily startled by sudden noises. But an object intended to hit your pet should be softer, while still having a certain amount of mass.

Executed and used properly and appropriately, the Rubber Arm technique is one of the most important aspects in training. When your dog is misbehaving, don't say anything—just throw the object at him. That's all there is to it. If the act is performed with the proper force, your pet will either stop what he's doing or start paying attention to you. Throw your Rubber Arm object every time he does what he's not supposed to, or is not listening, and he will soon learn.

When you aren't around, use a booby trap. If you want your dog to stay out of a particular room, balance a light plastic bucket atop a door that has been left ajar, so that it falls when the door is pushed open. When your dog walks through the doorway, it will fall on or near him. If your dog climbs up on a couch where you don't want him to go, simply put an obstruction such as clean wire screening on the cushions. This should be annoyingly uncomfortable for your pet when he jumps up, and thus discourage him. These basic tricks, plus in-person reinforcement of the lessons when you are in, will soon teach your pet to stop the unwanted behavior at all times.

Once you start working with your pet, it won't be long before you will be thinking up your own traps. Just be sure that whatever traps you set up will not hurt your dog in any way. (For example, a mousetrap can injure his nose or paw.) They should merely startle or make it uncomfortable enough to keep your dog from continuing his behavior without being harmful. It's the surprise *and* the knowledge that his action has caused the unpleasant result that stop your dog, not necessarily the pain.

Jumping Up on Furniture

There is a distinct disadvantage to having dogs on your sofa or bed: Hairs that can irritate human skin impregnate the upholstery and sheets, and dirty paw marks soil the clean material. Additionally, if your pet is allowed up on furniture at your home, he will take the same privilege when visiting in another person's home. Sharing your bed with your dog can be especially exasperating. Small dogs don't believe that a pillow is only a human headrest; for them it makes a perfect bed. Some large dogs spread out to get comfortable and tend to take over the bed, leaving you in one tiny corner or even on the floor. Dogs who burrow know that the warmest spot is under the blanket, and work their way through until they get there. Other dogs try to scrape and dig out a hollow in sheets to sleep in—a task in which they sometimes succeed. Snugglers keep close enough to feel your presence, making it hard for you to roll over. Nightwalkers make brief trips to check out that the house is secure from intruders, and often take their shortcuts across you. Some people don't want a dog on the furniture at all; others let their pets up on everything. Most people are divided in their feelings, however. They don't mind their dogs going up on a certain chair or sofa, but have special items they don't want their pets to soil. Some people even have specific *parts* of a piece of furniture they don't mind their pets on: For example, the foot of the bed is fine, but the pillow is not.

A friend had a dog who used to lean his hindquarters against the couch so it looked as if he were sitting on the sofa like a person. The habit was so amusing that our friend never corrected it. However, when his owner purchased a new white couch and the dog's special ''seat'' spots turned a dirty gray, the little quirk was no longer so amusing. Take a lesson from this: Before deciding to allow your pet up on your furniture, make sure that you'll want him to stay there. No matter what your feelings, it's best to teach a dog to stay off everything at first, then later give him permission to go up where and when you want.

When correcting your pet, you must be absolutely consistent. If something is permitted one day, your dog naturally assumes it is all right to do it again. You can't scold your pet one day for doing or not doing something, and the next ignore the very same action. A dog that understands what is and is not allowed is happier and more secure.

It doesn't take long for a bad habit to develop. Therefore, be firm over not allowing him to lie on chairs and beds. These traits might not seem offensive at the outset, but they will eventually. Don't let your dog do things that you don't want to continue. If you are not firm and consistent, most dogs are smart enough to take advantage of you. Push him down or chase him off every time he gets up. Start this teaching process immediately, even with a tiny puppy. A pup thinks that because you cuddle him on your lap when you are sitting on the couch, that it's all right for him to go up there anytime he wants, whether you are around or not. You have to teach him that this is not the case and that he is unwelcome on the furniture *unless* you call him up or are holding him. As a substitute for the plush cushions, give your pet a personal place of his own to lie on, such as a basket or mat. Every dog needs a place he considers his own property where he can be completely comfortable. Make sure he is out of the way of household traffic, but still situated where he can be close to the family and see what is going on in the house.

Once your pet knows he's not supposed to be up on the furniture but goes up anyway, be insistent and correct him firmly for doing so. Besides chasing him down, correct him with a slap or employ the Rubber Arm technique. It is often hard to catch your pet in the act; when you are out, your dog sneaks up on the furniture, only to slither off again when he hears you return. Therefore, booby traps are one of the best solutions to this bad habit.

Place a small piece of a dowel stick, a pencil, or a large spool of thread under one leg of the piece of furniture in question so that it is elevated ever so slightly on one side. (Never prop it up high enough to allow your dog to get underneath—always keep your dog's size in mind.) Be sure it is precariously propped and will topple easily. As a further precaution, drape some cloth over the furniture to keep entry under it impossible for your dog and also to discourage nosing at the prop. When the dog jumps up on the furniture, the prop should break or become dislodged, causing the piece of furniture to fall back down with a mild thud. This should unsettle your pet enough to stop him from jumping on it, because a dog won't climb on anything that he feels isn't stable and secure. You could also temporarily affix the four wheels off a pair of roller skates or a skateboard under a small piece of furniture. When your dog jumps up, the piece will slide beneath him, and your dog will most likely get off.

Another type of booby trap is designed to make the furniture itself uncomfortable to your dog, and thus discourage him from using it. Set up the bottom of a board or window screen across the piece of furniture he likes to climb on, balanced as if it were a lean-to. Make sure it's not balanced securely, but will slide or fall down when your dog jumps up on the furniture. Your dog may keep off in the future if you put something up on the furniture that will make a noise or be annoying to him. Removing the soft cushions may work; or place noisemakers such as cellophane, tissue paper, or toys that squawk under the cushions.

Scratching or Digging at Furniture

To make furniture more comfortable, dogs will instinctively scratch and dig with their feet and nails. In the wild this is a normal part of the shelter-building behavior of dogs preparing themselves a lair or den. Before your dog lies down on furniture, he may also indulge in the same behavior to try to get to the source of your smell, which has penetrated into the furniture upholstery. The scratching doesn't stop once the dog is comfortable, however; eventually it becomes something to do in itself. Your dog may get so engrossed in what he's doing that he just keeps ripping up your furniture.

The best solution to this problem, of course, is to teach your dog never to go up on the furniture in the first place. If you don't want to take that privilege away, however, place some screening over your dog's favorite digging spot, which will make it uncomfortable for him. Other obstructions can also be helpful. Catching him in the act and using a direct physical reprimand is more effective, of course. Use the same techniques used to stop a dog that barks. Pretend you have gone out, then sneak back to catch him scratching. If you persist, your dog will soon come to understand that being allowed to sleep on furniture does not give him permission to rip it to shreds. If he can't learn to stop, take away the privilege of going up on furniture. He has to learn that the price of sharing your comfortable place to sit or sleep upon is not scratching.

Digging Under Plants and Eating Them

Digging at the earth around the base of plants is another habit that dogs develop. If your dog likes to dig inside flowerpots indoors, cut out a disk of screening or chicken wire to fit inside the pot. Cut out one or more circles to fit around the plant's trunk or stems and bury the screening just under the soil. Now when he goes to dig at the earth, your dog will catch his nails or teeth in it, making it uncomfortable for him, and he will stop. Putting an unpleasant smell or flavor in the soil can also be helpful if he digs in it with his nose. You could even sprinkle some fine black pepper, vinegar, or bitter apple into the topsoil after first making him dislike it by holding it in his nose. You can use any number of repellent smells, but first you must be sure they can't harm either your dog or your plant.

Since digging comes naturally to dogs, you may find that your dog may start digging up the outside garden to bury bones—or just for pleasure. If you catch him in the act, reprimand him severely. Here, you can use more than a Rubber Arm technique; turn the garden hose on him. You may have to wait for hours to catch your pet in the act, but this is effective if you plan your action, set him up, and let him have it. To reinforce this—or if you can never catch him and he constantly returns to one particular spot—bury some screening or chicken wire under the earth as you would with indoor plants. This will annoy your dog when he starts scratching and will keep him away from there. Sprinkling an unpleasant substance on the soil will also repel him.

Though basically carnivorous, dogs like to ingest grass and select plants as good natural chew items. Sometimes dogs don't even eat the plants, they just maul them by brushing against them with their bodies, or dig at the dirt around the base of the plant. If you find your pet nibbling plants, first try for the obvious solution and simply add fresh vegetables to his diet. An addicted dog who can't resist eating your plants could possibly be lacking the roughage and vitamins they contain. However, it is more likely that you'll have to use more forceful corrective measures to stop your plant-eating pet.

When you catch your pet near your plants, first reprimand him physically. Then rub some vinegar, lemon juice, or bitter apple full strength on his gums. Once you've made him hate the stuff, dilute the same substance with water in a spray bottle and spray the plant with this mixture, making sure your pet sees you doing it. Next time he goes back to the plant, the smell should be enough to remind him of having the unpleasant substance rubbed full strength on his gums. This should deter him, especially if backed up by direct reprimands when you catch him in the act. Do not spray any substance *at* your dog which could get into his eyes. Just rub it into his gums full strength.

Chewing

On walking into some homes, you would think that the resident dog was trying his best to destroy the place. Corners of rugs and cushions are chewed, wearing apparel is torn, legs and arms of tables and sofas are all half eaten. Chewing is a major destructive habit that needs prompt decisive action. Chewing is an all-too-common problem because a dog's mouth performs the same function as our hands in exploratory behavior. It is especially prevalent among young dogs who, in exploring their environment, tend to gnaw and eat a lot of unusual things in order to find out what they are. Growing dogs also chew to strengthen their jaws and teeth, especially at four to five months when they are teething; at this time they must gnaw on something to loosen their temporary teeth so they can fall out and make room for others. This urge is usually outgrown by eight to ten months of age, but by that time tremendous damage can be done to your household possessions. Besides, if allowed to continue into adulthood, chewing may well become a habit pleasurable unto itself. A real chewer will sink his teeth into anything within reach, and rarely will he stop spontaneously. You have to be the one to insist that he do so.

Once you know the reason why your dog is chewing, you'll be better able to cope with the problem. Boredom, anger and spite at being left alone, even medical problems, can cause your dog to chew. Therefore, if your dog suddenly starts chewing—or is an insatiable chewer and absolutely refuses to stop no matter what you do—investigate all the possibilities. Sometimes simply taking away the cause can cure the habit, but generally the cure requires a combination of methods.

Sometimes there are mitigating circumstances for a dog's misbehavior: He might chew because he is teething, but unfortunately, indulging in ways that are natural in the wild may not be acceptable in your home. Chewing wood is fine when it's a tree limb, but not when it's the leg of your dining room table. Scraping and digging for a den are okay in the dirt of the forest, but are not appreciated on your eiderdown quilt or in your prize garden.

Ironically, overfeeding is a major cause of chewing. When your pet is fed incorrectly, he needs to relieve himself more frequently. But since the first thing a dog learns is not to break house-training, your dog will look for something to occupy himself and keep his mind off his urge to relieve himself. Chewing is a perfect solution. To counteract this, feed your pet the correct amount of food and the type that agrees with him. Knowingly or unknowingly, owners frequently reinforce and even encourage the formation of bad habits. When their dogs lick at chairs, pull on shoes, take socks, or bring the leashes out they ignore it. They then wonder why the dogs eventually chew or possessively hoard these items. To prevent your dog from gnawing your possessions, give him a suitable substitute he can chew to satisfy his oral cravings.

Rawhide bones and solid, hard rubber balls are good choices. Encourage your pet to chew on these to the exclusion of everything else. Don't give him anything that can be harmful if ingested, such as soft rubber toys. And be sure not to give him anything that he could later generalize to include your possessions. For example, never give your pet an old shoe or discarded glove. Later he may not stop to distinguish between his old one and the new pair you just bought. Giving your dog bones from the butcher can be dangerous if they can splinter or are small enough to get lodged in the throat. (Small fragments of bone can become impacted in the large intestine of older dogs and cause serious constipation.) If you must give him one, make it a heavy thigh or shank bone that you have thoroughly boiled to remove all the grease, thus making it almost sterile. If you don't take this precaution, the grease stains will get into your floor and furnishings, encouraging your pet to chew at those spots.

A dog who chews out of spite or anger has no excuse and needs to be corrected harshly. There is no way to explain to a dog that you have to go out to shop or work and can't always be with him. Simply confining your dog in a separate room for a while each day while you stay in another will demonstrate to him that at times he will be alone without your company. Every once in a while check him to see if he is up to any mischief. If he's being good, praise him; if he is doing something he shouldn't, punish him. After this he may be on guard, not knowing whether you are there or not. However, confinement generally needs additional methods to ensure compliance. If your dog is really obnoxiously spiteful, direct harsh reprimands are needed.

No matter what the cause, a dog must be reprimanded for any misbehavior. The standard negative training methods are, again, the corrective measures used for controlling bad habits. Of course it's best to prevent a chewing habit from ever starting, but once it's begun you must be firm and use definite measures to stop the behavior. Don't allow yourself to cement the habit further by being lax in your corrections.

Before a dog starts to chew on furniture, he will usually show some interest in it by smelling or licking it. This is how he finds out what he likes. Whenever you catch him in the licking stage, throw a magazine or leash down next to him. Don't say anything, just startle him. He will immediately associate something unpleasant with the chewing of forbidden objects. A few lessons should be enough to teach him what he can and cannot chew—or even touch.

When you have to reprimand your dog for doing damage, be consistent. Don't let him get away with *any* chewing. If you actually find him dining off anything, don't nag! Correct him quickly and immediately; let him know right from the start that you don't want him to continue chewing. Disciplining your dog with a slap or with any of various Rubber Arm techniques when you catch him in the act is equally helpful.

If you return home to find that your dog has been busy chewing up the place, you can still reprimand him. But first you have to remind him of his misdeed so he knows why he's being corrected.

Never call your pet if you intend to punish him, or else every time you call he will think he is going to be punished again and will never come. When you want to administer a correction, go to your pet and get him. Don't use your dog's name to admonish him, or—again—he will associate it with punishment. (In fact, don't threaten your dog at all, just make the correction. If you talk to your pet, it'll give you time to think of excuses why you should go easy on him. Remember, if you fail to correct your dog for one reason or another, you'll end up ruining him.)

Take your dog by the collar or scruff of the neck, lead him over to the object in question, and punish him. Don't be kind. Your dog must learn that your favorite Persian rug and antique French armoire are just as valuable to you as your Salvation Army couch.

Finely ground black pepper can be especially effective in preventing chewing, because it leaves a reminder when the dog returns to continue his destructive behavior. Pour it full strength into the palm of your hand and hold it to your dog's nose to make him hate it. Then put it on the objects he chews or mouths and hold your dog's nose to them while you count to twenty, then give him a good spanking. When he approaches the treated object after this, the smell of the pepper should be enough of a reminder of the previous unpleasant experience and should act as a real deterrent. Since the pepper is only a dry powder, it can be removed easily and won't damage your belongings. Use this same pepper on all chewed items. Just be sure to leave them coated with the pepper for a while as a reminder until your pet is properly trained.

Booby Traps

When you are not around, the only thing that really *teaches* your dog not to chew (rather than just remind him) is a booby trap. A correction should be explicitly connected in your dog's mind with the undesirable action, so booby traps are a perfect solution for halting many of your dog's bad habits. As any owner knows, most destructive damage such as chewing is done when no one's around, and traps have the great advantage of catching your pet in the act whether you're home or not. It is your dog's own actions that activate the punishment. Therefore the reprimand is instantaneous, and he feels responsible for the correction. But more than this, because your smell lingers on the booby trap from when you set it up, your dog will associate it with your authority—your presence is felt at all times.

All booby traps should be startling, but harmless. For example, to stop a dog that likes to jump up and pull things down to chew, balance a piece of cardboard atop a shelf or on the edge of a table. On the cardboard, put some tin cans, light chains, foil pans, or anything else that makes noise, and dangle a few tempting strings down from the shelf you have constructed. To the strings attach some of your pet's favorite (but forbidden) chewing items, such as a sock or slipper. When your dog runs over to seize any of the tempting dangling items, the shelf and its noisy burden will fall down. This should scare him enough to make him run away, and he will be reluctant to pull down any more items.

While you are not around, use preventive confinement to keep your dog under control until the habit is forgotten. Then when you think he's cured, test him by using the standard trick: leaving your dog free in the house while you go outside and wait at the door. Keep your Rubber Arm object close at hand. Return unexpectedly, and if your animal is acting destructively, administer appropriate discipline. Otherwise, have a friend walk your dog while you hide in the house. Your friend should then return, drop off your dog, and leave. Secretly watch your dog, and the minute he goes for anything forbidden, unload with your Rubber Arm.

Clothing Fetishes

Some dogs love to take their owner's clothing out of closets— or better still, out of clothing hampers, where the garments are especially dirty and well worn. Your scent gives the dog an impression of security. Unfortunately, most dogs aren't content to just sleep on your clothing—they have to lick, nibble, and scratch at them too. If you are around, employ the standard correction methods. If not, sprinkle some finely ground black pepper on the clothing (after first making your dog hate the stuff by holding it to his nose for about fifteen seconds). This way, your scent is obliterated by an unpleasant odor.

You could also try booby-trapping him: Fill a can half full with pebbles or pennies and attach a string to it. Then to the end of the string tie his favorite article of clothing and balance the can on a closet shelf. When he pulls on the clothing, the can will tumble down on him. Or balance a light plastic bucket atop your slightly ajar closet door. When your dog noses the door open, the bucket will fall, keeping him away in the future. A dog who opens the clothing hamper to pull things out can be discouraged by attaching a pebble-filled can with string to an article of clothing. As your dog pulls out the clothing, the can will clatter along with it. Booby-trap a freestanding hamper as you would a garbage can (see Food-Related Problems).

Teaching Your Pet to Behave Himself Alone

There will be times when your dog has to be left alone. You are not going to be sitting at home by his side constantly, and the sooner he learns to cope with this fact of life, the better. He has to learn to accept his solitude. Unless there is something specific to do, such as going for a walk, a dog will usually just lie down and sleep. So don't feel guilty about leaving your pet alone. Your guilt can cause you to overlook your dog's small misdemeanors, which in turn can lead to much more undesirable behavior.

During this time alone, your pet will tend to get into all sorts of mischief. Your dog may whine or bark and scratch or gnaw at the floor or wall where he is restrained. This may be out of boredom, loneliness, or just bad temper, but no matter what the reason, he should be stopped. Give your pet some toys to ensure that he has something to occupy his time. This will help relieve the boredom that can lead to chewing your belongings and will also help him forget his urge to relieve himself if need be. To prevent these toys from being pushed out of your pet's reach while he is confined, get a heavy rubber ring or doughnut-shaped rawhide chew. Tie this to a heavy cord or chain, attached in turn to a stationary object such as the eye hook to which his confinement chain is attached. Then to help eliminate your pet's scratching at the floor and walls, make sure he has something to sleep on.

To teach your pet to remain alone, start off by leaving him separated alone in one room while you're in another. Make sure he is comfortable and has a couple of playthings. If he's confined, be sure the equipment is adjusted correctly. The minute he starts to whine or bark, rap loudly on the door and tell your dog "no" or "quiet." This should make him let up—at least momentarily. Wait to see if he starts again; when he does, give him the same treatment.

If your dog is a real nuisance, go into the room and *quietly* give him a slap on the rump or a shake. To have even more of an impact, use your Rubber Arm technique as a corrective measure. Simply open the door and toss something at or near him, then walk out without saying a word. Use the same technique to correct your dog if he scratches or chews. However, in this case it is advisable to leave something chewable around as a temptation. Then wait, and after he has been alone for a few minutes and all seems suspiciously quiet, open the door suddenly to see if anything is being touched. If it is, throw your Rubber Arm object. Sometimes a good test of your dog's reliability is to leave him in another room overnight to see how he behaves.

Once your pet will stay quietly and does not indulge in any undesirable behavior when he is in one room and you're in another, go one step further. Go outside the front door and wait to see what happens. If your pet misbehaves, use the same methods of treatment as you did before. Once he's good, go away for fifteen minutes or so and sneak back quietly to see if you catch him in the act. Gradually increase the time spent away until your dog remains perfectly behaved.

Food-Related Problems: Taking Food from Strangers

Food is so basic to a dog's life that it can spawn all sorts of problems. Stopping these bad habits will help avoid many upset stomachs and may even prevent poisoning if your dog ingests something he shouldn't.

Taking food from strangers should be discouraged unless you give your pet permission. To teach him not to accept food offered him by persons other than yourself and your family, hold him on a leash and have another person approach with a piece of meat or other tidbit in his hand. As your dog reaches for the food, reprimand him harshly. You could even have the person offering the food give the correction, but the dog has to know *you* don't want him to take it. After a few such lessons, leave your dog alone with a stranger while you observe from a hiding place. Have your helper tempt your dog with a morsel. If well trained, your dog will turn away. But if he goes for it, unload with your Rubber Arm equipment. Just be careful that you stop after instilling just the right amount of wariness in your dog. If you go too far, he may learn to fear people.

Begging

Begging for food while you are eating at the table or whenever you go into the kitchen can be one of the most annoying canine habits. It can even develop to the point where he follows guests around at parties, looking for any crumbs they might drop. Never feed your dog when he whimpers for food, but wait until he has stopped. If you give in, he'll soon learn that he can get his way with just a little whining. When he comes nosing around, don't feed your animal off your plate from the table. If you must feed your pet, save scraps on one side of your plate, and feed them to him in the kitchen—not from the table. This way your dog knows he will get something and so doesn't need to mope sad-eyed around the table.

The dog who steals food left on the table or out of people's hands needs to be corrected. When your dog is young, simply start off by saying "no" each time he reaches for anything. If he actually touches food, reprimand him with a sharp slap. If you see him sneaking something on the other side of the room, startle him by throwing a magazine or other such article. To teach him not to steal when no one is around, go into another room and leave the dog alone with the opportunity to steal. Leave some tempting morsels around, conveniently placed and easily accessible. Observe your dog without him knowing, and the minute he goes for the food, toss something at him. Persistent stealing should be met with increasingly severe reprimands.

Picking Up Food in the Street

Dogs' sense of pleasure is not the same as ours, but runs mostly to the olfactory delights of sniffing and licking at carrion and other strong-smelling materials that we might find repulsive.

But foraging in gutters and picking up food in the street is a terrible habit that can be dangerous for your dog. The food could be rotten, may be poisoned, or might contain a bone that can get caught in his throat. Pups are especially prone to picking up things they shouldn't—it's part of their investigatory behavior; but no matter what their age, all dogs are tempted by a possibly appetizing tidbit. To teach your dog to resist temptation in the street, command "no" and sharply jerk him away every time he starts to take something in his mouth or even sniffs at it. You could also give him a slap on the rump. Or, as your dog lowers his head to investigate the food, kick it out from under his nose by scruffing your foot along the ground and pushing it out of his way. If your pet consistently walks with his nose glued to the ground, ready to grab at anything he comes across, teach him to keep his head up by hitting his nose with a sliding glance of your foot. If your dog runs free of the leash, throw something hard at him when he goes sniffing around items that attract his attention.

Garbage Rifling

Garbage rifling could lead to gastric torsion, commonly called bloat, in larger dogs that gorge themselves, but it can get any dog into trouble. If you see your dog moving around erratically and uncomfortably after eating, and if he seems to have gas he can't relieve, starts to retch foam, or starts to expand slightly around the middle, get him to a veterinarian. His stomach may well blow up like a balloon, rupturing his intestines, and he will die. If your dog goes into the garbage, he can also cut his nose on empty cans and other sharp objects, and ingest any number of harmful items. If you catch your dog, employ the standard direct reprimands or the Rubber Arm technique. However, dogs usually rifle garbage at night, or at least when you are out. As a booby trap, place long, blown-up balloons (conveniently covered with an enticing gravy) to tempt your dog just under the cover or drooping out of the can. When he goes to touch them he may well sink his teeth in, thus bursting the balloons. This should frighten him away pretty fast. Bursting a couple of balloons near your dog first may discourage him so that the sight of the balloons alone will keep him away until he forgets the habit. Another solution is to sprinkle the garbage with black pepper or Tabasco sauce. However, the draw of the garbage can is so enticing to dogs that the temptation always exists. Therefore, you should keep it tightly covered at all times, especially at night, and empty it promptly. Immediately discard bones and meat or even their wrappers that are being thrown out. No dog can be completely trustworthy where food is concerned.

Drinking Out of the Toilet

Many larger dogs develop this habit, which for one reason or another is not always desirable. If you use a deodorizer it won't be good for your dog. If you don't use one your dog may get too much liquid, or you might just find it distasteful. To stop the habit, prop the seat of the toilet open with two or three unsharpened pencils or small dowels distributed evenly around under the seat. When your dog goes to drink, he will dislodge the sticks or pencils and the seat will slam down, frightening him off.

Feces-Eating

Eating dirt, sand, wood, and even their own feces and droppings of other animals is often connected with boredom. This most disagreeable problem is common in caged or otherwise closely confined dogs. (It can also be caused by a dog trying to hide the evidence of his breaking training.) Nutritional deficiency is believed to be another possible cause. The dog supposedly is trying to obtain certain B vitamins formed by bacteria in fresh feces. No matter what the reason, however, this disgusting habit needs to be curbed.

Relieve your dog's boredom by exercising him and supplying him with toys to occupy his attention. If you feel he could possibly be nutritionally deprived, a little fresh raw liver could help in supplying the required additives. Never allow a dog with this habit to relieve himself on paper in the house, to avoid temptation. To discourage this habit, your veterinarian can give you a substance to feed to your pet that will give his stools an unpleasant (to him!) taste. Red pepper or something equally nasty poured on your pet's stool also should deter him. Of course you should never neglect the tried-and-true direct correction method.

Eight

CONTROLLING AGGRESSION

The Natural Scheme
of Aggression

Aggressiveness is not in itself a completely negative trait. It's normal for your dog to display a certain amount of self-assertion, but an overly aggressive dog is a most undesirable commodity.

Dogs are not naturally vicious as a species. They save their aggressive behavior for eliminating enemies and intruders, capturing food, or establishing dominance to form a stable social structure within their pack. Overt aggressiveness takes either of two forms: hunting behavior or fighting. The hunter's inner motives are essentially different from those of the fighter. The overall outward actions may appear similar, but the differences become apparent if you look closely. A dog about to catch a good meal has an excited, anticipatory stance, while a dog ready to fight growls and lays his ears back defensively.

It's perfectly normal for an animal to assert his dominance. Through these actions he learns to whom he is subordinate, and who he dominates. For dogs, it is important to form a hierarchy that indicates what position in a group each animal takes. Usually bickering and fighting is to establish separate rank orders among each sex, though the dominant female usually also dominates most of the males. No dog is completely relaxed until his social relationship is established. Even a sexual display such as mounting is used as an indication of dominant aggressive action. In fact, it is one of the earliest signs of impending aggression, and is also used as the ultimate coup de grâce of possession. Your dog's mounting of other dogs, people, children, or objects is not sexy but aggressive and should be discouraged immediately. Getting away with mounting simply encourages your dog to go on to the next step—possessive ownership.

As a rule, dogs in the wild have efficient hunting and killing instincts, as well regulated and carefully controlled as their social relationships. They also have extremely reliable killing inhibitions. Rarely will a male attack a female or a young puppy; if he does, something may be drastically wrong. The male's inhibition against biting bitches is chemically produced, whereas his indulgence toward pups seems to be elicited by their behavior—if an approaching adult seems at all threatening, a puppy throws himself on his back, presents his naked belly, and passes a couple of drops of urine which the adult promptly sniffs. This allows the dog to recognize that it is a puppy. If the puppy or female is annoying or attacking, an adult dog may display his teeth, but won't use them other than in a quick, threatening snap. Even when a real fight erupts between rivals, it stops as soon as the animal being pursued is chased off or rolls over submissively.

In your home, unfortunately, the genetically controlled instincts and patterns are often disrupted in some way—perhaps because of our social structure. Even natural forms of aggressive behavior have to be kept under control in order for a dog to live amicably with you, and any out-of-control aggressiveness can present an especially disturbing problem.

Normal Aggressive Signals

Other than the barkless African basenji, dogs have a whole vocal repertoire of barks, howls, growls, and whines that are directly associated with body language. These noises have no messages really akin to words, but are rather warning signals or sounds that reinforce a certain emotional state.

All species have a system of communication, but the more social the animal, the more elaborate the silent sign language. Because of their highly social nature, dogs are especially aware of subtle movements and changes of postures. They watch the way you move and stand, whether you are tense or relaxed, fidgety and anxious or confident and smooth moving.

A dog's variety of special postures and behavioral patterns stimulate other members of the same species to respond. These various signals regulate social distance, either to keep others away or to invite closer encounters. To increase distance, a dog will stare and snarl; while tail wagging, submissive grinning, and standing in a low position indicates willingness to meet. Other signals also instigate group actions or reactions. Thus intense sniffing around will attract another dog, and running with a toy or bone will attract a following.

As part of an overt, friendly greeting, a dog barks excitedly, wags his tail high, and comes bounding to you. When soliciting play, dogs will sit and stare at each other, watching for the slightest move, and will then bound at each other as if by prearranged signal. The tail is held high and wagging, while the front end is lowered so that the dog seems bowed down. He alternately raises his forepaws or may leap backward and run off, inviting you or another dog to give chase.

To seem more threatening to others a dog effects a general enlargement of the body: The shoulder and rump hackles are raised, along with the ridge down the center of the back. The neck is arched, and the head held high. The dog stands tight and tall, seeming to walk on tiptoes, with every muscle tensed, ready for action.

On the other hand, a dog who wants to make up tends to avoid eye contact and makes himself appear less imposing by lowering his body to the ground. The tail is held low, often between the hind legs, and may be wagging. Sometimes the ears are flattened down against the head, and he gives a submissive grin.

A dog's tail is the part that most people look to as an indication of mood. It is extremely expressive, but its motions can often be deceptive. When excited, a dog wags his tail in an upright position; but when held at different angles and wagged at different speeds and distances, the tail can indicate either aggression or friendliness. A tail held high and almost vertically, wagged stiffly and quickly, is an aggressive signal; an excited tail is high too, and wagged happily to and fro. A very erect tail wagged slowly is a sign of a dominant attitude; while a tail held low and wagging rapidly is associated with subordination and/or the offering of friendship.

Facial expressions—especially changes in the mouth area—are another clear indication of mood. When greeting in a friendly manner, humans smile or laugh. Some dogs grin in a kind of half smile: The mouth and lips lift upward at the corners, and the tongue lolls out between half-open jaws. But interestingly, dogs seem to use this expression with people only, not with other dogs. Perhaps the gesture is in mimicry of us. This "grin" must be differentiated from the submissive grin or normal social smile that dogs use when greeting a social superior. In this gesture, the lips are retracted horizontally and the teeth are not bared.

When a dog gives a direct stare and a snarl, with lips pulled horizontally forward and upward to expose the teeth, it is of course an aggressive gesture. The ears and corners of the mouth are also backward and downward. This means to watch out.

An animal's major drives are often in conflict with each other, so his body may often reflect more than one mood at any given time. For example, a dog who is eager to investigate something, but uncertain or fearful of the consequences, will express both emotions simultaneously, reflecting the conflict going on in the animal's mind. If the dog doesn't know how to cope with the situation, quick reversals of expression occur. Being torn between flight and fight, fear and aggression, is usually the reason for a dog displaying ambivalent behavior. Such a situation can be very touchy. If a more intense display occurs when you move closer to a dog, watch out. On the other hand, if the tail drops a little and the animal shifts slightly backward, he may be bluffing. Sometimes a dog who wants to be friendly but defend his territory at the same time may wag his tail in a low, submissive greeting while his hackles are still up and his facial expression still aggressive. The fear biter does so out of both fear and aggression, and if you are concentrating on the wrong part of the body, you may not get the message. When looking for messages from your dog, look at the overall body stance first, then go into details.

Triggers of Aggression

Sometimes it seems that an aggressive action occurs suddenly, for no apparent cause. Intensive, crowded living conditions may make an animal more suspicious and defensive. These pent-up frustrations may seemingly discharge out of the blue. But there always has to be a trigger of some sort to set off the aggressive reaction, even though it may not be apparent.

An obvious instance is the dog who is possessive of his belongings, territory, or companion. This type of dog may be docile until there arises an actual threat to his ownership. The presence of this challenging person or animal initiates an aggressive guarding of whatever the dog considers to be his. In some dogs, human intervention has adjusted the normal, ritualistic expected triggers of aggressive behavior so that a dog reacts to things that normally would not bother him. In this way, the creation of various breeds has produced certain dogs with more feisty or aggressive natures. In certain dogs, in fact, the natural controlling inhibitions have somehow been eliminated. In a fight, therefore, a weaker dog may continue to resist until he is nearly dead, or the stronger may continue to attack even after his adversary has surrendered. In this case, the trigger initiating the aggressiveness is no longer the threat that would once have been necessary: It is simply the presence of the other animal that keeps each one going.

Sometimes there's absolutely no way of predicting what will set a dog off. Changes in a routine and set circumstances can cause an aggressive reaction—either fearful or antagonistic. Some dogs may react badly to somebody who doesn't show the signs he normally associates with people. Animals build up special expectations of the world, and any changes that differ from these expectations are upsetting. The unusual motions or odors connected with mental retardation, nervousness, schizophrenia, or a physical impairment (such as a limp) can all act as triggers. Some dogs even react badly to

211

minor unfamiliarities in their own owners. Because of this, if you wear unusual clothing or appear drastically different, a dog may suddenly attack or at least be warily antagonistic. Dogs have even been known to attack when their owners fall accidentally—possibly because the dog no longer recognizes the owner rolling on the ground. Or it could be that a dog's dominance and leadership drives make him seize this chance to be superior.

This is also true of fellow dogs: One pair of sisters from a litter lived together for years and appeared to be the best of friends. Then one got a twig stuck in her mouth so she couldn't close it. Her sister promptly proceeded to attack her. This should be a lesson for you: Act as normally as possible with a dog, especially if you expect or sense aggression. A dog can tell if an individual is afraid and will take full advantage to bully and browbeat him.

STOPPING UNWANTED AGGRESSION
Causes of Undesirable Aggression

Uninformed and unsuspecting owners allow uncontrolled, vicious dogs through halfhearted leadership, and actually encourage it in other ways. Some people find it amusing when a little dog growls and barks, or reassuring when large dogs do so. Unfortunately, encouraging what you consider to be cute snapping or snarling will only teach your pup to grow into a dog who bites. The flattering thought of a puppy who comes to your aid when anyone approaches you or your family will not be so reassuring when your full-grown dog takes a chunk out of a neighbor. At maturity, a dog who's been raised too permissively may begin to take advantage of you.

Teasing is one method used to train a dog to attack. Unfortunately, unsuspecting people often use this method to make their dogs aggressive. Sometimes the owner doesn't even realize what's happening; perhaps a jealous child or a neighbor annoys your dog when you're not around. A teased dog may learn to be a vicious animal. Make sure no one grabs bones and toys away from your puppy for the fun of it. He should not have to growl and chase other dogs or people away from his food. A tug-of-war over a toy is in effect a form of teasing that teaches your dog the power of his teeth, and should not be encouraged unless your dog understands it's only a game and you are in complete control. A dog who is kept enclosed in a yard or confined consistently in a small area should be protected from people who would throw things to incite him or run around just out of reach, taunting him. All of these teasing games can cause your pet to become nasty.

Perhaps the most prevalent (and so disconcertingly unintentional) aggressiveness training is done by owners who believe they are actually reprimanding their pets. Whenever a dog hears a noise, sees something unusual, or spots another animal, he may growl and bark. On hearing this, the owner may pat him and say "good dog" to calm him down. Actually this "good dog" encouragement is a good way to teach a dog to bark and growl. The dog, thinking this is what is wanted, may eventually go on to more pronounced forms of aggression. What you should actually do is slap the dog or reprimand him in some way for his undesirable behavior.

During a puppy's formative months, many owners make mistakes that cause long-lasting problems. They play extremely roughly with their pets, sometimes even putting on gloves so the animal can continue to bite without hurting them. They seem to be unaware that one day the dog, depending on size and breed, will have a bite with a pressure ranging up to eight hundred pounds per square inch. They mistakenly believe that this roughhousing is what a puppy would do with other dogs. However, if your dog played too roughly with his playmates, they'd let him have it. Pups play-fight with each other, and in this way learn self-control and how to regulate the strength of their bite so as to develop a soft mouth. In fact, it is by play during puppyhood that a dog develops skills in hunting, prey chasing, and killing. Animals raised in isolation or removed from the litter too young often do not know how to use this kind of behavior appropriately, and can misdirect and misuse it.

Only your decisive leadership can give your dog the secure feeling that you're going to take care of everything, and that he doesn't have to worry about the job of leading and protecting you.

If you don't take on the task of being the ultimate boss in your household immediately and definitely, your dog may well try to take charge, threatening and attacking visitors, even bullying and biting you if you don't do as he wishes. You have to be the leader, and your dog—whether male or female—should be disciplined when he gets aggressive. The only time any show of aggressiveness should be permissible is when you can control it through proper guard training (which is covered later, as a trick). But this can be done only after your dog is thoroughly controlled through basic obedience training.

General Ways of Coping with an Aggressive Dog

Scientists have discovered that if the amygdala, a group of nerves in a region of the forebrain, is destroyed, the aggressive urge is eliminated. But this extreme step is not the ideal solution. Tranquilizers your veterinarian prescribes can suppress—but not change—behavior.

Aggressive males can sometimes be helped with castration, which eliminates the hormones that spur on male rivalry and territorial aggression. The only time castration is really reliable, however, is before the testicles start producing testosterone. It has been proven one hundred percent effective only if done before the second week, though good success has been achieved when performed at three to five months of age. But in older adult dogs, castration has at best a fifty-fifty chance of making an aggressive dog more docile; even then, training and discipline are still needed. (It will of course eliminate fights over sexual possession, but that is only one manifestation of aggression.) Castration is not effective in changing an older dog's aggressive behavior, however, if the habit is really engrained. As a rule, if training doesn't dent your dog's behavior, castration probably won't help either. Teaching your pet to keep his aggressive urges under control is what is needed.

As with most canine problems, prevention is the best cure. Males are most likely to become aggressive, but that doesn't mean females can't too. A dog with a propensity to be scrappy will often show this tendency when young, and this is one time you cannot afford to be lenient. Your reprimand can't hurt half as much as the damage even a small dog can do to a person or another animal.

Obedience training is the best first step in controlling and preventing aggression. It shows your dog that you, not he, are the boss in your home and leader of the pack. In this way, the control you establish over your pet will keep him out of trouble. If your dog is trained and has learned to respect you, he should heed your warning or command not to indulge in obnoxious behavior—especially if it's accompanied by a slap. So to prevent a problem from developing, you should watch for any early warning signs and be firm in your treatment. Be aware that such actions as leg lifting, mounting, growling, and possessiveness are all signs of aggression. If you ignore them, your pet's aggression may get so far out of hand that he takes over your home and bullies you into a corner. Therefore, get to work on solving this problem when it's still in its early stages.

From the outset, your dog has to learn to control himself. Play with your dog, but don't play roughly. Teach him that he cannot use his mouth for nipping, even playfully. Every time he bites at a piece of clothing or at your hand, give him a slight tap and tell him "no." If you don't, he can develop a biting habit.

When your puppy playfully nips at your hands and fingers with his sharp milk teeth, give him feedback that this is wrong by reprimanding him in return. When he nips, don't pull your hand out of his mouth—pulling against his teeth will scrape your hand and break your skin. Hold your hand in his mouth, but slap the side of his muzzle sharply with your free hand until he lets go and backs away. Be sure to slap him only on the *side*. Don't slap him underneath or on top of the muzzle, or you'll

215

drive his teeth into your hand. Make sure that your dog is the one that backs off; this will teach him to respect you.

A cardinal rule in dog ownership is that any dog who snaps or shows signs of aggression must be severely curbed immediately. Associating something unpleasant with the aggressive behavior is the only way to reverse this trend. You need to handle sternly any early signs of aggression. A growl should be met with a hard snap on the leash, a smack on the rump, or something thrown at him. Ignored, growling can lead to nipping and biting. Don't let your dog think he can scare you. Stand your ground and assert your dominance. If you insist, he will back down.

Success depends on the dog's age, how engrained the habit is—and how scared *you* are, and how willing you are to work. Every time your dog makes an aggressive move, throw a Rubber Arm object at him, hard, or give him a good kick in the rump. The reprimands have to be severe. In his agitated, aggressive state, your dog's adrenaline is flowing so he feels little pain.

Excessive Barking

Barking is so natural to dogs that you should not completely suppress the action, but rather control it. It is good to have a dog that barks to warn of the approach of strangers or when something unusual happens, but the dog should stop immediately when told. You don't want a dog that flies into a frenzy of yapping every time a stranger passes outside. Some are even inclined to bark every time the doorbell or phone rings. Other dogs bark only at specific objects or noises, but any dog who has a tendency to excessive, unnecessary barking should be controlled.

No one type of personality of dog tends to bark; any dog can become a barker. Dominant dogs may bark out of aggressive territorial possessiveness, while a shy, timid dog may bark to achieve self-assurance. Some dogs do it just for the fun of it; others may be reflecting their owners' nervousness.

And a dog that feels lonely and deserted when left alone can develop the habit of barking, whining, crying, and howling.

No matter what type of dog, what the reason, or what form the barking takes, you must stop all barking firmly and decisively. Leaving the dog to "bark it out" in the hopes that he will eventually tire of his own accord is only wishful thinking. There is an electronic collar that gives your pet a shock when he barks; another sets off a piercing whistle. (However, it can be triggered by another dog's bark, and some people misuse it by imitating a bark whenever they want to punish their dogs.) Catching the habit in its early stages is by far the best way to curb it. Once well established in an adult animal, barking may require a lot of work and time to control. In fact, an avowed barker can be a real chore to stop.

When correcting a barking dog, the first thing you should do is look for the cause. It is rare, but sometimes there's a logical reason that completely absolves your pet. For example, one dog barked and barked all day long when his owner was away, but didn't make a sound when she was home. Repeated complaints by the neighbors were followed by threats of eviction. She tried every solution imaginable, but nothing helped. Finally she used detective procedures, pretending to be out but really hiding, and found that a disgruntled neighbor—out of revenge for a few loud parties—was knocking on the ceiling of his apartment below to keep her dog barking.

Having an outside instigation for barking is highly unusual, however. Generally your dog is the responsible party, and direct corrective action toward him is the cure. If you're around when he first starts to bark, grab his muzzle firmly and squeeze. Tell him "quiet" in a firm, quiet voice. If this has no effect, give him a good shake or slap as a correction. Otherwise throw something at him in the Rubber Arm technique. If the dog continues to bark, cuff him on the nose and say "no" again to impress on him to heed the command. If he is on a leash, jerk it hard to keep him quiet. If a dog is corrected every time he barks, and the negative associations are proper, your dog will soon learn.

Mostly your dog will bark when no one's home to correct him, and so will just keep on barking. Therefore, start training him to stay alone quietly while you're still home. Close your dog in one room while you stay in another. Turn up the radio to mask your own sounds. The minute he starts barking, rap on the door loudly, saying nothing. This will stop him at least momentarily. If he starts up again a few minutes later, go into the room and correct him in person. Either slap him or use the Rubber Arm technique: Simply open the door quickly and toss a magazine or some other article at or near him. Make sure you're definite and deliberate in executing the correction. It is better to give one good reprimand at the very start and stop the barking fast.

This will work for dogs with a newly formed barking habit. But dogs catch on rapidly to tricks, so if your dog is an entrenched barker, it won't take him long to realize you're out there somewhere. Once he catches on, he will bark only when you actually leave the house. To fool him into thinking you have left completely, you've got to be cunning. If he suspects you are there, he will keep silent until he feels sure you've really gone.

To trick your dog, open the front door and then slam it shut as if you've left, but stay quietly inside. Sneak back and stand outside the door of the room where your dog is confined and wait. At the first sound from him, rap sharply on the door. Hang around. If he continues to bark, go in and reprimand him. Next give your pet the freedom of the house, while you leave completely. Only instead of going away, hang around outside. The minute he makes a sound, rap on the front door, or quickly open it and throw a Rubber Arm object at him without saying a word.

If he persists even with this treatment, enlist the aid of a friend. Have him walk your pet while you hide in a closet or secrete yourself somewhere else in your home. Turn on a radio as a distraction. Then have your friend drop your dog off and leave. Once alone, your dog will probably start barking. Wait until he does, then quickly jump out and throw something at him using the Rubber Arm technique—making sure it connects. It's obvious that he needs severe treatment to stop his vocalization.

What if your dog barks only at specific things, such as the telephone ringing? Set your dog up by having a friend call you about five times in a row. Every time your dog barks, throw something hard at him. Simply sit reading or watching

TV with your throwing object in your hand, and unload it on him without any warning when he starts up. To control this while you are out, hide as you would for generalized barking; when he barks, let your dog have it. Follow this procedure for anything that seems to trigger barking.

To train a dog to stay by himself and not bark, patience is sometimes needed—especially if you have allowed the barking habit to get out of hand. The first thing dogs learn about barking is not to do it when you are there, and they're smart enough to stay quiet even if they just suspect your presence. It can therefore be a long time before you catch him. But catching him in the act and punishing him immediately is the only way to really do the job. He must never know whether you are around or not.

Overpossessiveness

It's no fun having a dog who growls, snarls, or snaps at anyone who approaches when he is eating or playing with his toys. Prevent your dog from becoming overpossessive by taking his toys away from him, removing his food, and adjusting his bed every once in a while. This should be enough to prevent possessiveness from starting, and to teach him all about sharing. Don't tease him by quickly grabbing at his belongings; that will make him nervous and snappy. And make sure children steer clear of his eating area, because he may think of them as rivals for his food. Tell children not to annoy him, and reprimand him for making any nasty moves. Some dogs consider one small area such as their sleeping places the ultimate safety spot, and become so overprotective of it that they will attack anyone who comes near. The moment your pet manifests such behavior, reprimand him harshly. Make sure your dog realizes that others can approach that spot, but at the same time be sure no one annoys him there. Every dog is entitled to feel secure and comfortable and to have a little privacy.

If your dog shows any resentment at giving up what he's

holding, stop him the first time it happens. Take hold of the object requested and insist that your dog let go. If he does, praise him; wait a moment and give the object back. If he refuses and even growls when you reach for whatever he's holding, don't grab at it or jerk your hand away. Instead take hold of it, and give him a sharp rap on the side of the muzzle to make him let go. If necessary, pry your dog's mouth open and take the article out. If he adamantly refuses, throw something hard at him to make him drop the object. You must make him let go or his possessiveness will become increasingly worse every time someone goes near what he thinks is rightfully his. If your dog gets away with a snarl the first time, the next time he may actually bite since he feels he has already warned you to steer clear. Once you have taught your dog to let you take things away from him, expand the lesson to include at least other members of your family. To be sure your dog gets the idea that his possessions are not sacred, have different members of the family gently interrupt his feeding or play from time to time.

Besides relinquishing objects on demand, your dog should learn to accept things in a gentle manner. Give him a biscuit or rawhide bone. If he reaches out and takes it quietly, let him have the object immediately and praise him. If he grabs it and tries to take half of your hand with it, don't jerk back. If you quickly withdraw your hand, your dog is likely to retaliate by making a countergrab. Don't let him grab it away; hold on to the object while remaining perfectly still, and remind him to be gentle.

Territorial Defense

The drive to defend what he considers his territory is one of the major causes of canine aggression. It is a matter of survival for a wild dog to defend his den or sleeping place against intruders. It is natural for a dog to defend his home ground against intruders, especially dogs of the same sex. In nature, animals respect each other's territory principally through fear.

Even a mini poodle may be able to drive away a St. Bernard if it enters his property. Male dogs are usually the most aggressive about their home territory: This strong protective instinct develops as the dog matures, and is probably related to sexual maturity. However, you will usually see signs of aggression, perhaps subtle, well before then.

Some especially defensive dogs develop a resentment toward any animal or human visitor. A dog who is constantly restricted to a small area over a long period of time and never allowed freedom can develop abnormally intense territorial instincts. These dogs develop a pattern of noisy barking and aggressiveness. The dog will bark as a stranger approaches, but will back away if the visitor gets too close. If the stranger backs away, the dog will give chase. In this way a person approaching a chained dog will frequently be met with barking, lunging, and even attempts to bite. There is no way to prevent this other than not to restrict your dog permanently in close quarters. But never allow any teasing of a chained or penned dog; it will make him more defensively aggressive.

Another dog will pick out specific intruders to react to—a mailman, a delivery person, a passing dog—perhaps because he knows these are going to enter his personal territory. He will make a big thing out of the intrusion—barking, threatening, sometimes even attacking. If you think this habit is cute or clever, you won't be able to stop it. Despite your halfhearted commands for him to stop, your dog will sense that he is really pleasing you. If you express real disapproval, most dogs will desist. To stop this problem, your dog must be reprimanded physically either by direct action or the Rubber Arm technique. Enlist a visitor's help: having him reprimand your dog by throwing some Rubber Arm object at him is most effective. But ultimately your dog must understand that it is *you* who disapproves. Additionally, have the person your dog has chosen as a target give your dog some tidbit of food every time he arrives. After you notice progress, have the visitor give your dog a treat only on a random basis, so the animal knows that there's always a possibility of getting a treat if he continues his good behavior. If a dog takes a particular dislike to someone who must enter your home or property, try having that person in for coffee and a chat, so that the person joins what the dog considers the acceptable inner circle.

Charging at Doors and Windows

Whenever anyone passes, rings the bell, or enters your home, some dogs charge doors and windows with a fury. This can be disconcerting at the least. If you are in when this happens, and you catch him in the act, use a direct reprimand such as a slap, or throw something using the Rubber Arm method. You could even set him up by having a friend or family member ring the bell or bang on the window. When the dog charges the door, let him have it with your Rubber Arm aid. Or go outside yourself and ring the bell. When you hear your dog charging, quickly open the door and throw something heavy in front of him—like the telephone directory of a major city.

Even if you have managed to control this behavior while you're at home, a really errant animal will usually start again when you are not around. To handle this, have a friend walk your pet while you hide somewhere in your home near the door or window he tends to charge at. Be sure to have an appropriate Rubber Arm object with you. After a few minutes your friend should drop your pet back home, then leave, only to return a couple of minutes later to ring the bell or knock on the window. When your dog makes his move, quickly jump out of your hiding place and throw something at him.

Aim carefully, because you won't get too many opportunities to surprise your dog in this way! It won't be long before he gets smart enough to check out every hiding place in your home to see if you're still around. However, if you can manage to really surprise him in the act a few times, he'll never know whether you're in or not. That in itself should be enough to stop him.

To reinforce your personal, direct training, use booby traps to prevent your pet from charging the door and windows. This way your pet will be corrected whether you are there or not. A good trap is to blow up some balloons and hang them against whatever your pet tends to charge. When he leaps up, he will burst the balloons, or at least be surprised by their presence. This works especially well if you blow up one or two first and burst them near him. You can also stretch a string across the door or window in question, then take another string and tie it to this one so they are perpendicular to each other. Attach the other end of the second string to something such as a book that you balance atop the narrow ledge above the door or window frame. Then when your dog hits the horizontal string, it will pull on the vertical one, causing the balanced object to fall and startle him.

In this same context, jam a couple of large tongue depressors into the crack above the door where it meets the frame. They will form a platform on which you can balance a book or some lightweight but potentially noisy aluminum broiling pans. When your dog hits against the door, it will cause enough of a shock to bring down the pans. Select whatever traps suit your dog's size and nature and use them separately or in combination. Just be sure to use things that cannot hurt your pet, only startle him enough to discourage repetition of the act. And don't let your dog see you set up the trap.

The Body Language of a Biter

You should be able to recognize an unfriendly animal so as to correct him in time—or if necessary, to protect yourself. Dogs are not always as friendly as most people expect them to be, and you can annoy dogs into growling and nipping simply by approaching them. Fortunately almost every dog will warn you or signal his intentions in some way. A tail held high and almost vertically, wagged stiffly and quickly, is an aggressive signal. The dog may then stare directly and steadily at you, and snarl by pulling his lips backward and upward to show his teeth, at the same time drawing his ears backward and downward.

Often the elements of fear and aggression can be seen simultaneously in a dog's body language. This happens most often when major drives are in conflict with each other: You see the desire to investigate something or be friendly, but at the same time the uncertainty or fear of the consequences. The dog doesn't know how to cope with the situation, and outward actions express the conflict in the animal's mind.

This kind of ambivalent behavior is seen oftentimes when you pass a dog who wants to be friendly, but at the same time wants to defend his territory. This situation can be very touchy, because it can easily turn either way. Just be sure to observe carefully. If you move closer to the dog and he gets more tense and takes on a more aggressive stance, watch out. On the other hand, if he relaxes slightly and his attitude is friendlier, he is usually bluffing.

If you are attacked by a dog and have no adequate defense, stand stock-still. Many dogs will attack only a moving object, and most police dogs are trained to attack until the person stops moving. If you get bitten by an unknown or suspect animal, hold the dog and have officials or a veterinarian check on its health and ensure it is rabies-free. Cleanse the wound thoroughly and promptly with soap or detergent solution, and see a physician, since you may need inoculations.

If a normally docile and friendly dog suddenly bites for no apparent reason, he could be in pain or something could be wrong with him. Check with a veterinarian. To get an injured, biting dog to the veterinarian (or simply to control one) muzzle him temporarily so that your dog can't open his mouth to snap, but will be able to breathe. Use a length of gauze bandage, one to one-and-a-half inches wide. Cross it around the muzzle, knotting it in the middle while leaving equal lengths of bandage free. Wind it around the mouth two or three times with a final knot under the jaw. Then take the loose ends back and tie a knot just behind the ears. Once it's on, watch your dog. If your dog starts to vomit or appears to be having problems, remove it immediately.

Basically, there are two types of biters: fear biters and antagonistic biters. But a biter is a biter, no matter what the reason; and whichever type he is, you must stop your dog at the first signs. The major responsibility for biting dogs lies squarely on the shoulders of their owners, who make excuses for their pets and refuse to exert adequate physical force to discipline the animal until it's too late.

Antagonistic Biting

Antagonistic biting doesn't just happen; it usually builds up over months or years, starting with growling and other simple bullying actions. A dog who indulges in unprovoked biting is not a good pet; the stress he brings on the family takes the joy out of having him. There are no quick, sure cures for a biting dog—all the remedies take time. Any signs of aggressiveness toward you should be stopped immediately. Slap him hard, give him a boot in the rump, throw something at him hard to let your pet know you can and will fight back. A biting dog is unwelcome and dangerous, so be adamant about correcting him.

Frequently a dog will bite to "protect" his owner. In a household with two or more owners, the dog will often pick on one or more of them, usually because he looks upon himself as a higher-ranking member of the pack. To correct this, the dog has to be made to respect each family member equally. If all give him consistent daily lessons in basic obedience, he'll soon learn his place.

Additionally, each must discipline him for any aggression toward another. So when your dog barks and growls at others, it is you who must discipline him. A dog will never change his attitude unless the person he is protecting does the disciplining. Unfortunately too many people are flattered when a dog shows a guarding instinct. Then when he bites, they're sorry. Teach your dog to behave by putting him on a leash and having someone approach. If your dog shows any signs of meanness, reprimand him sharply—and physically.

Fear Biting

With a fear biter, it's his defensiveness and fear of being hurt that pose the problem. He's only looking to avoid the danger his deluded mind anticipates from every source. This trait may begin as an extreme wariness of large, noisy, or unusual objects, and progress to overt aggression as he matures. Don't praise or try to comfort this type of dog when he shows fear; this only reinforces the reaction. In fact, make sure he knows the behavior is not wanted. If there is no reason to fear, don't allow your pet to put on an irrational show. The creation of an unchanging environment is nearly impossible, so you will have to be alert at all times. There will always be new things cropping up that will cause the nervous, fearful aggression. If your pet doesn't outgrow his fear reactions, he may need to be constantly muzzled; if truly neurotic, he may need to be destroyed.

Most dogs are not really naturally unpleasant, they've just learned that with bullying they can get their own way. If your pet has a family history of aggressiveness, however, you might have your work cut out for you. A dog with a really engrained habit may have to be muzzled until he is used to being handled. In fact, sometimes you may even have to give up: A truly vicious dog can only tentatively be trained to behave. An incorrigibly nasty dog that cannot be trained no matter how harshly he is reprimanded will have to be constantly watched. If your dog's behavior cannot be controlled by training, another home might be the answer. And unless you are the cause of his behavior, even this solution of another home is useless. The pattern of biting will probably continue in his new environment, so be sure the new owner is aware of the problems.

If there are young children or elderly people who may be in danger, and if the problem is incurable, constant muzzling or ultimately euthanasia (having your pet destroyed) may be the only solutions. You could also give him to an attack school where he will remain alive, but you won't know what happens to him. Before giving up, however, give training a good try. Often it was your fault that the behavior started, and so it is your responsibility to correct it. With work, aggression can generally be stopped. Few dogs are incorrigibly vicious, especially once you impress upon them that aggression will bring about a really painful reprimand as a direct result. Better to train harshly than to have him destroyed.

Chasing Cars, Children, or Bicycles

Not all dogs chase cars, but if yours shows interest in this dangerous sport, discourage it at once. He will either harry the local drivers or get himself run over (cars do kill, a fact of which most dogs are unaware). The first time your dog shows the least interest in chasing cars, get into your own auto with a friend. Have your friend drive slowly away, tempting your dog to chase. But do not call your dog's name or actually say "come." When he gives chase, have your friend stop the car suddenly, jump out, and reprimand him.

If you can't get someone else to help, use this procedure by yourself. However, for most methods of teaching your dog not to chase cars, you usually need two people—one to drive the car slowly while the other pelts the chasing dog with various Rubber Arm aids. Use short lengths of chain, empty beer cans, a bucket of water, a squirt gun filled with lemon juice, or anything else that will be severe and shocking enough to discourage chasing. (This kind of treatment should make him realize that cars fight back.) To make him realize that *you* don't want him to chase, hide and wait for him to start chasing a car. When he does, jump out and throw something at him from behind.

If your dog chases bikes, it's the rider who should resort to throwing things at him. This is easier than having you hide and reprimand him thoroughly when he goes to chase, either directly or by the Rubber Arm technique. But make sure the bike riders have your permission; you don't want neighborhood children declaring open season on your pet. Chasing children is quite common, and your dog may even pick out a specific child to harass. Even if the dog has no intention of hurting anyone, this can be really frightening to a child. To correct this behavior, hold the dog on a leash and have children run around. Meanwhile, keep your dog by your side and check him from chasing by reprimanding him harshly every time he makes a move. Don't hesitate! If you do, one day your dog may injure a child—intentionally or not.

In all cases of chasing, you can correct the problem if you are around. The minute the dog starts out after something—be it a car, jogger, bike, child, or whatever—pick up a handy object and throw it at him hard enough so your dog knows chasing is not permitted. It can be helpful, too, if you enlist the aid of the person being chased to reprimand your pet. However, make sure the person involved is careful to do it quickly and get it over with. If the reprimands are too halfhearted and teasing, your dog may well intensify his pursuit rather than retreat.

Chasing and Fighting Cats

Cats have long been reputed to be the archenemies of dogs, and judging by the behavior of some dogs, the myth might contain a grain of truth. In actuality, however, cats and dogs rarely hate each other naturally. A dog generally chases a cat simply because the cat runs away. When this happens, the dog follows his natural chasing instinct. After a while the chasing becomes an engrained habit, triggered by just the sight of the cat. Unless your dog receives some kind of discipline, he will continue what he considers fun.

Do not spare the rod here, because it's not just the cat who could get hurt. One good scratch from a cornered cat can destroy your dog's eyesight. If a cat stands his ground, a smart dog will retreat; but a young dog is unaware that sharp claws are hidden under those furry paws. So the severity of your correction should be strong enough to teach your dog to leave cats alone. Every time he starts out after a cat, reprimand him harshly by employing some Rubber Arm technique or turning a garden hose on him. But you have to be vigilant. Even the most obedient dog may not be able to resist the pleasure of the chase, whose lure overrides the thought of the pain to come.

Dogs and cats can be trained to get along together. Reprimands and constant familiarity can make everything easier. Even if your dog hates cats, with enough discouragement he will learn to stop chasing—but it takes time. Some incorrigibles need a few good hosings-down. Set your cat-chasing dog up; sit outside with a garden hose handy and wait for a cat to saunter by. When your dog starts to go after it, let him have it full strength.

Once a cat and dog fight is in progress, things are happening fast, so do not put your hand in. Instead, pour water over the pair, throw something at them, beat them off each other—but move quickly before any serious damage can be done.

If your dog has moved up from chasing to actually killing cats or small animals, he has to be treated with more intense methods.

Chasing and Killing Small Animals

Hunger is not necessarily the basis for hunting behavior. Even well-fed dogs will go through the motions of smelling, seeking, chasing, biting, and shaking to death with equal enthusiasm. A passionate hunter cannot be cured with abundant feeding, but there is no reason to let a dog continue killing for the sheer fun of it.

No chasing or killing should be encouraged as amusing. There is always the possibility that your pet could get bitten by the animal he's hunting and contract rabies. Even cow chasing isn't a sport to be encouraged. Bovines maintain a group herd reaction, held over from when they protected themselves from the wild carnivores that hunted them. Thus they may group together to chase a dog and sometimes even trample him.

To stop your dog's chasing habit, take a fishing pole and line or a stick with a string tied to one end. Get a reasonable facsimile of the animal your dog likes to chase and tie it to the other end of the line. Drag this decoy along the ground and tempt your dog with it, but do not say a word. When your dog jumps on it and picks it up in his mouth to shake and kill, throw something at him hard, using the Rubber Arm technique. Keep it up until he stops chasing the decoy. Just be careful to make the decoy closely resemble the animals he likes to kill so that you do not discourage his retrieving tricks. Additionally, be sure to keep this lesson well separated from any lessons training him to retrieve and carry.

If your pet actually brings you gifts of dead groundhogs or rabbits, you have to tell him in no uncertain terms that these are not gifts you want—even though he thinks he's doing something fantastic by bringing you food. To stop him, make him associate the carcass with something unpleasant. Season the dead animal with a heavy dose of Tabasco and pepper. Put it to your dog's nose, let him smell it, and reprimand him severely at the same time. Don't spare the rod.

Sometimes it is difficult to deter the hunting addiction. If your dog's a real killer, don't be fooled into thinking he did a miraculous about-face without any reprimands from you just because you see him inviting to play a small animal that he would normally kill. Dogs sometimes use play-soliciting behavior (known as tolling) as a ploy to lure their prey into closer range. This is usually done on open ground, because if openly stalked the prey becomes alarmed and runs for cover. Most people seeing this think the dog is playing and don't realize what's happening until it is too late.

The Social Reasons
for Dogfights

Testing for social status is normal in dogs. If there is no clear leadership in a group of dogs, conflict may break out until one is established. This aggression may be overt; or it may be so subtle that you're unaware of what is happening because the bullying occurs when you are not around. In any group of dogs, the best promoter of peace is a clear pecking order. But for this order to remain stable, the group has to stay constant. Bringing in or removing one member of a group will disrupt the status and necessitate its reestablishment. An animal that has not learned his place shows no respect for authority or social order, and shows no mercy to subordinates. This is why fights often occur when new pets are brought into the home or put in with others who have formed a social circle, such as dogs who normally run together in the park. Most often newcomers are eventually assimilated into the group, but some tightly knit groups will not easily open up for a newcomer—especially if he poses a threat to the more dominant dogs.

With beagles and some other breeds, the social hierarchy is not obvious; while other breeds have a clear, sharply defined one. Terriers are so competitive they cannot tolerate the close proximity of other dogs that might be a threat of any kind. Only a very small social grouping is possible with these breeds; they will allow no threatening newcomers and will constantly bicker amongst themselves. With this type of dog, the only time peace reigns is usually when the dogs have been housed together from an early age or when they are a mated pair. Because ranking is established early, these preacquainted dogs may squabble, but rarely get involved in injurious fighting unless extraordinary circumstances prevail.

Whenever conflict begins in a group, the aggression tends to travel down the line: Top Dog bites Number Two, who in turn bites Number Three, and so on. The poor bottom member may receive the redirected aggression of most of the other members, so that several may turn on him at once. And if you have two dogs of one sex and one of the other, one of the same-sexed pair is likely to be left out or even picked upon. This hierarchical positioning is seen most dramatically at feeding time, a prime fighting time. Dogs low on the totem pole may not even get to eat unless you control the situation: Teach them all to share, give each his own dish, and then supervise.

Fighting and Sexuality

One main cause of fighting is a dog's sexual drive. This natural (and highly volatile) hormonal force is seen most acutely when there is a female in heat around. A male dog may become aggressive toward strangers who he thinks might interfere with his possession of the female.

After the actual mating, a previously normal dog may start exerting dominance. However, it is the violent rivalry among male dogs over who is going to mate with whom that causes the worst problem. If more than one male is present around a female in heat, there will undoubtedly be a fight for sexual possession. This uncontrollable urge will pit even the best of pals against each other. At this time, a dachshund may well take on a Great Dane. On the distaff side, a female in heat may also fight with other females to establish a dominant sexual partnership for herself; she wants no competition.

Recognizing—and Preventing—
an Impending Fight

Some dogs are forever seeking fights with other dogs, but this problem doesn't usually become seriously engrained until the animal is two to three years old. You should be able to observe early signs of such a propensity in your dog and begin corrective reprimands before it's too late. Some precociously pugnacious pups grow into nasty dogs who are never completely reliable and have to be watched constantly.

A dog who has never seen or associated with other dogs is another problem. At first he may be unpleasant toward them from anger or fear, and it may take a while for you to teach him to accept others. Thus any time that two dogs get together, a dogfight may occur: though a well-trained dog is less likely to fight with another animal. Watch for early signs of antagonistic behavior between your dog and others, and be prepared to stop it immediately.

When your dog approaches another, watch their body language. They will display behavior as described under Normal Aggressive Signals if trouble is impending. If your pet and a strange dog approach each other in this fashion, watch out: A fight could follow. Two dogs following each other around a tree or fire hydrant, each lifting his leg as he goes to urinate over the other's marker, are also showing aggressive behavior.

You should be able to observe trouble brewing. Don't be fooled into thinking your dog is all tensed up ready to play. A friendly dog has a looser attitude; his tail swings wide, and he walks with his body low.

Every time your dog looks as if he is going to fight, stop him immediately, before he can get into it. An obedience-trained dog is a boon in this situation. If he obeys, the authority of your voice should control him under all circumstances. Thus when you see signs of aggression, you should

233

be able to forestall a fight by calling him off—but it won't always be possible. If your dog is on a leash and he lunges at other dogs, barking ferociously, jerk him back severely. And as simultaneously as you can, flip the end of the leash sharply across his rump, or give him a slap or kick. If he is free, throw something at him hard and make sure you hit and hurt him.

A couple of these reprimands will make him think twice before acting, and will teach him to stay away from other dogs. Just be sure your corrections are severe from the start. You must hit your dog hard at this time. He is so tense from his pent-up drives that ordinary treatment is useless; his adrenaline is pumping so fast that he is numb to mere discomfort.

Breaking Up a Dogfight

A fight in progress is entirely different from one that's just brewing or threatening. A ferocious full-blown fight can start in a split second; once in progress, the pace is fast and furious. Flailing bodies, bared fangs, snapping jaws, the snarling and growling all blur together with lightning speed. To stop the action, you must act rapidly—and surely.

There are all sorts of theories about how to break up a dogfight, but the basic (and correct) goal is to get them to back away from each other—to distract or scare the dogs into forgetting about each other. To avoid being bitten, keep your hands away from the dogs' mouths. Dogs in a fight don't stop to think whose flesh they're biting. Besides it doesn't do any good to try to pull apart two dogs while they still have their teeth sunk in each other. In a fight, a dog tries to get a good hold on his opponent to pin him and make him submit or—failing this—to shake him and break his neck. Therefore, yanking one will make both hang on harder than ever, and the skin will become lacerated and torn as you drag them apart. You must do something that makes them forget each other so that they let go and back off by themselves.

Of the methods of breaking up a fight in progress, the more practical are: 1. Douse the offending pair with water from a hose (if possible), or at least a bucketful or more.

2. If both are on a leash, choke the more aggressive of the two. When he lets go, pull them off each other. (However, if your dog is on a leash and is attacked, chase the other dog off; because if you hold your dog in a fight, he will be defenseless and will get hurt.)

3. Inflict pain so severe that the aggressor will let go. A good kick across the rear is sometimes all that's necessary. Females are usually easier to handle, so you could try grabbing them on the fleshy part of the legs and pinching hard to make them release their hold.

When males fight, it's more serious and you have to apply more severe force. If your dog is fairly well trained, concentrate on beating off the other dog with a stick and calling yours back to you. Of course, if your dog is the aggressive instigator, you'll have to beat yours back. When breaking up the fight, just take care that one or both of the dogs don't turn on you. After the dogs are apart, take them away—and keep them away—from each other to prevent the fight from starting up again.

Your own dog may have a specific place where he picks fights, or there may be another animal he constantly confronts. For instance, when a dog passes your home, it often makes your dog feel that his territory is being threatened, and he will attack. To counteract this, stop him by setting up a trap for him. Keep a powerful garden hose or several buckets of water handy. When a dog passes and yours makes any aggressive moves, turn on the water full force. Keep a large number of throwing objects handy inside, and pelt the dogs with them forcefully.

POSITIVE AGGRESSIVE TRAINING
"Speak"

This is one command that is better not taught unless thoroughly controlled. If you constantly give your pet treats for barking, you may be encouraging barking and yapping—which in turn can become a real problem that requires much corrective training. Make sure you teach him controlled speaking, or barking on command only. Don't allow him to begin barking for its own sake, or to use this as the first step in aggression.

If you can make your dog bark on a given signal, however, it can be a great trick that can also help your security. The mere barking of a dog is often enough to make an undesirable person back off. And if either you or your dog are ever injured, he can signal where he is or you are by barking. If your dog's lost or has been accidentally locked up somewhere, he will respond to your command to bark—even at a distance. But if your training is lax and your dog isn't properly controlled, he may become a nuisance and bark constantly. In the process of learning to speak on command, therefore, your dog should also learn when not to speak. Indiscriminate barking is easy to encourage; the hard part is getting him to stop on command.

By far the easiest way to start off the training is simply to encourage your pet every time he barks. Every time you hear your dog bark, tell him "speak" or "bark," whatever word you want to use as a signal. The hand signal you use is up to you, but the standard one is to hold out your hand and move it up and down slightly. At the start, whenever he barks of his own volition, give your selected voice command and hand signal. To reinforce the barking, give him a treat every once in a while. This way he'll start to associate his bark with your command and signal.

If you take advantage of all the available opportunities to

make your dog connect barking with the command, he will. Some dogs bark at the slightest provocation, while others are slow to become aroused. A yappy dog naturally learns to speak more quickly than a quiet one—he may also take more working later when it comes to controlling him.

After a while, try getting your dog to bark by giving the appropriate command and signal. If he does bark, praise him profusely. If not, keep working. Once your dog does connect the bark with the command and signal—so that he barks when given them alone, without having the action initiated by some other stimulus—try commanding him from a short distance away, then gradually from a greater one. Ask him to bark when and where he least expects it, such as when running around in play. Soon he will learn to obey at any time, and under all conditions.

Once you teach your dog to bark on command, you must train him to stop when told. Signal your dog to stop barking by holding your left hand waist high with the open palm facing downward, and move the wrist in a short horizontal side-to-side motion. At the same time you command him by saying "quiet," "stop," or "enough." If necessary, stop him forcefully by jerking on the leash or slapping him when he doesn't stop. Praise when he does.

Guard Training

Some dogs that have been selectively bred and trained to fight and kill show no mercy. Generally, however, dogs will display their teeth but not use them—but no one else knows your dog won't use his teeth when he threatens them; and in guard training this is exactly the type of behavior you want.

The number of owners who want their dogs trained to attack is startling; perhaps they are unaware of the ramifications. Many "guard dogs" which people purchase at astronomical amounts of money have been confined, chained, teased, and starved to get them to bite and attack. Some are even trained to take the initiative. This type of dog is like a loaded revolver, and may go off unexpectedly. Dogs kept as pets should not be trained to attack, because an attack-trained dog is not really a reliable pet. For an amateur to attempt such a responsibility is foolhardy. You could ruin your dog, and even end up with a couple of lawsuits on your hands. When the objective is to teach dogs to protect and guard property and attack on command, a little knowledge is dangerous under the best conditions and could be disastrous.

It may be amusing and even flattering to the vanity if a dog barks when a person is near, or growls when he guards his personal property. Unfortunately, if you encourage him, it may get out of hand and lead to problems once it gets past being a game. A dog's natural instinct is to watch over those he loves; this should be sufficient protection in the home and is infinitely safer for children. It is understandable if you want a dog to warn the household of the approach of a stranger. But a dog should not be allowed to bark and growl, much less attack, of his own volition. Dogs that are not controlled and have no bite inhibitions should not be guard trained. Aggressive dogs should be corrected and controlled, not encouraged.

How It's Done for the Movies

If a film dog were trained to be really vicious, it could be very touchy for most people involved in making movies and commercials. What directors usually do is fake it by using a friendly dog that has been taught to look nasty and bark a lot. If you take a careful look at dogs on the screen, you would most probably see by their body language what is really going on. The dissonance between the front and back shows an ambivalent behavior; from the wagging tail you will see that they are really playing.

Dogs who seem to be snarling are often made to look that way by wrapping special rubber bands around the upper muzzle, drawing the lips back to display a glaring set of teeth. The dog can then jump at someone with impunity, because there is no ferocity behind the look.

Different ploys are used for more exotic scenes. For instance, in one movie a wild, even rabid dog had to bark viciously from behind a screen door. Fakery wasn't good enough for the director, who wanted the real thing. But the only thing that made the dog starring in the movie look angry enough was the presence of another large male dog.

For this scene, the dog was secured tightly behind the screen door on a chain which was not seen on screen. Another large male dog was then placed behind the camera, out of reach. The sight of this other dog drove the chained "star" wild, and he ranted, foamed, and fumed to perfection. Remember when guard training: Don't teach your pet to *be* vicious—just to look it.

In the way of protection training the only thing any owner needs is for a dog to be a guard. A guard dog is one that will do *only* that. On command, he will give a warning bark, growl, and/or show his teeth in a threatening gesture, but is never allowed to go beyond this threat. If trained to be on the alert, however, a dog is not really dangerous, because he has not received sufficient intensified training to make him so. Your dog must be completely under control at all times, and must understand this training is a response to a command like any other obedience training: That is, he must perform it as a trick, and not as an expression of aggression. You cannot train your dog to guard unless he's thoroughly obedience trained and completely under control. If not (and especially if you are overly permissive), guard-training your dog could spell trouble. If your dog is to be given some assertive aggression training, even as a trick, he must be dominated or he'll dominate you.

Which Dogs to Train and Which Not

Not every dog has the temperament to do guard work. Some breeds are easier to guard train than others because of inbred genetic factors. Both overly aggressive and timid dogs are unsuitable. On the other hand, a dog to be guard trained needs to be a little spunky. A naturally reserved dog is easier to train than one that is overly friendly. A dog may fail because he is too well socialized. Some dogs have a tremendous inhibition against attacking superiors, including humans; though if an owner is threatened or in danger a dog may rally to his assistance, perhaps in reminiscence of defending the pack or group.

Forget the nervous, intolerant dog that is distrustful of strangers, unusual objects, or abnormal situations. On the other hand, some dogs with pendulous ears or curly locks look too cute to be taken seriously. Bear in mind that certain (toy poodles and Pekingese) dogs never look truly aggressive no matter what they do, while German shepherds and Dobermans just naturally scare people without having to make a sound or attempting to look mean. Size itself can be an important factor, as a friend who was mugged found out when his attackers weren't scared off despite his mini dachshund's good bark. A small dog can be effective in causing a commotion, but isn't suited for all work. Larger dogs with plenty of "hardware" to display are most effective in face-to-face confrontations.

You can test your pet if you want to see his suitability for guard training. Set up an aggressive-play situation between you and your pet. Wiggle a short, strong strip of a heavy material on the ground in front of your dog to rate his degree of response: no response; a weak response where the dog soon loses interest and nibbles; a moderate response where the dog bites, pulls, growls, and shakes his head violently.

Shout and slap your hand on the ground to see how the dog reacts. Does he recover readily from the threat? Is he timid, remaining frozen afterward, or does he remain completely unperturbed? Does he stop, but then resume the game, or is the pup completely scared?

Let go to see if the pup stops and waits for you to resume playing. If he runs off, "killing" the object, check to see if he will readily surrender it when you go get it, or whether he is overpossessive.

The Warning Bark

Teaching your dog to bark is one of the main ingredients in guard training. If your dog will bark a warning at your command, whoever he's barking at will assume that your dog will do anything else you ask. However, barking can be an effective deterrent only if done at the appropriate time. It must look to anyone who is threatening you as if an excellent working aggressive relationship exists between you and your dog. So be sure to vigorously train your dog to start and stop barking on command.

To test that your dog knows how to do this, put him on a leash. First give the command and signal for your dog to bark, then tell him to stop barking. Your dog should obey both commands. To reiterate: Give a slight up-and-down motion of your hand accompanied by whatever word you have selected for him to bark, and to quiet him, wave your hand and tell him "enough." If he doesn't obey, review his training in the "speak" trick.

Guarding Territory

This is one time you don't need a huge dog, because your pet is usually hidden behind closed doors and no one can see his size. His barking alone is usually sufficient to chase off anyone hanging around for illicit purposes, who wants to attract as little attention as possible. Just keep in mind that if your small dog doesn't manage to keep out an intruder, he may get hurt or stolen. Teach him not to put up a defense, but to run and hide in a place where he won't be found. Once your dog has been taught to bark on command he can readily learn to vocalize when there is anything unusual going on around your home or property. If he doesn't have this accomplishment down, however, teach it as outlined under Positive Aggressive Training: "Speak."

Just be sure to control the times when he barks. There has to be a specific reason for him to do so, or he may end up barking at the drop of a pin, or for the sake of barking. You want to sharpen your dog only to the point where he's on guard against the unusual and will bark at threatening people or situations. Therefore, when your dog barks at the door or at strange noises that could indicate a problem, encourage him. Actually order him to bark when you feel it's appropriate for him to do so. On the other hand, quiet him if he overreacts. And don't encourage barking whenever the elevator or a car goes by.

Once your pet has learned to bark and growl to protect you on command, transfer what he's learned to guarding an object. Place your pet beside his favorite toy and tell him "watch it." When he does, and barks and/or growls, give him a treat. Then say "okay," "enough," or whatever his release word is, and lean down to remove (or just touch) the object he has been guarding. Your pet has to learn that he must stop guarding when told by you to do so. Accomplish this by always touching the object once he's finished, so he doesn't get any ideas about guarding on his own volition. This is just another obedience lesson, and your pet must not generalize to protecting anything he wants for himself. Therefore, discourage any indication of this kind of behavior developing. If he barks and guards when told, however, praise him profusely, and do be sure he continues until you tell him to stop. To prevent bribery, teach your pet to refuse food from strangers. He may eat a piece of poisoned or doped meat thrown in the yard— with disastrous results. Teach your dog not to take food from people or in the street, and train twice as hard.

To be impressed, some people need to be shown a little nastiness of expression and demeanor in addition to barking. Teaching your dog to growl, snarl, and show his teeth is only a small controlled step beyond barking on command. A certain amount of teasing is the only way to get this type of training done, but you must be constantly on the alert to see at what point you must let up. You don't want to give your dog more training than is needed and make him difficult to handle.

Put your dog on a leash. Stand in a corner with him where he can't back away or move out, keeping him on your left side. Have someone—a stranger to your dog, if possible—act as an antagonist. He should cover his face to affect a menacing look, and walk slowly toward your dog with a stick or an umbrella held in a threatening way.

This will frighten your pet, and he won't know what to do. At this point you should tell your pet "watch him," "kill," or whatever word you select to make your dog display mock-nastiness. (Often half the effectiveness of this command is the implication of the signal word you give, such as "kill," "draw blood," or "castrate him"; you can add to the total effect by choosing the right word!)

The stranger then has to agitate your dog in some way to get him going. Have him hit the stick on the ground next to your pet. You may even have to have him actually tap or nudge your dog with the stick several times at the chest area— not to hurt him, but simply to annoy. Continue with this procedure until your pet makes a noise. Eventually your dog will make some sound, whether out of fright or just plain annoyance. The minute he does bark or growl, the person should drop the implement immediately and quickly run away, feigning fright. When this occurs, praise your dog lavishly to

243

encourage him and then walk him away from the corner. The agitator should then go back and pick up his stick or umbrella while you and your pet are out of sight, and walk away with it. You and your dog should again walk back to the corner and repeat the whole procedure. Each time your dog barks and growls, the agitator should run away. Your dog will soon see what is happening; because he feels his barking is causing the person to flee, he'll bark more readily and more strongly each time.

When you feel your dog understands what's happening, have the agitator stand in front of your dog without picking up his hands or touching him. Give the selected verbal command the way you did every time he barked or growled in the past. If your dog responds, the antagonist should quickly turn and walk away, as if frightened. Then praise your dog profusely. When you feel he has barked or growled enough, stop him by saying "quiet" or "enough," and giving the appropriate signal as you did when teaching him to bark or speak.

Next, your antagonist should stand in front of your dog while you say nothing. This way, your dog learns to do nothing except when told to do so. If he barks or growls without your command, say "no" and correct him. Your dog is to growl only on command, and make this clear in no uncertain terms.

Nine

ADAPTING YOUR DOG TO A HUMAN ENVIRONMENT

Why It Is Important

What wild dog ever had to worry about traveling in a car or airplane? Where would he ever be subjected to such household hazards as electrical wires or poisonous cleaning fluids? Why would he have to worry about constantly meeting strangers and adhering to an arbitrarily established code of social decorum? In his hunts in the open, he would wander around a specified range that, however large in area, would not vary. And his means of transportation would be his own four legs. Nature itself would have equipped him to cope with the environment, any dangers would at least be within the powers of his reasoning to comprehend or his instincts to deal with. He would live within the confines of a closely knit pack; and strangers would be met with caution or hostility, unless of the same species and obviously no threat.

Nature has given your dog certain physical and emotional attributes that let him fit an environment and life-style quite alien to ours. These capabilities are more attuned to survival in the great outdoors, and it's your responsibility to teach him to survive within the confines of human society.

Accident Prevention

One person we know let his dog run loose in the house while he was painting the porch floor. Sure enough, the dog soon trucked on over to his water dish in the corner, leaving a charming footprint trail. The animal didn't know what the "wet paint" sign meant. Take this as a lesson. Somehow your dog will find a way to climb the wall if it's the one that you are painting.

Certain basic dos and don'ts can make your home and surroundings far more amiable for your dog. Your world is full of potential hazards for an animal: Simply taking a few protective measures can help ensure his safety. Many an emergency veterinary visit arose because of an accident that a little simple forethought could have avoided. A fishbone in the throat, a tennis ball or corn cob lodged in the stomach, a needle stuck in the skin, or paint on the pads of the feet are all common. You can't keep your home a sterile environment, of course, but you should realize your dog has an insatiable curiosity and loves to investigate objects of all kinds. Many dogs chew and swallow things. This habit can be curbed with training, but it is ultimately the owner's responsibility to keep tempting objects away. Inquisitive dogs may ingest such things as candy-coated pills or prescription drugs, which can cause havoc, as can many of the temptingly smelly household products with their poisoning potential. And if you don't see your dog's little toy Granny gave him, and he is throwing up, assume he's swallowed it.

Since the mouth is a dog's major investigatory tool, teaching your pet not to chew as outlined in the section on bad habits can prevent many unfortunate incidents. In fact, one of the best ways to combat accidents is to never let your dog get away with any bad habits that could eventually become harmful to him. Common sense should tell you what they are. For instance, take a bottle of Tabasco sauce, let your dog taste it undiluted, and then daub electric wires with it. (If a dog does electrocute himself, don't touch him until the current is turned off—especially since he often urinates, leaving a conductor puddle. Then give artificial respiration and call a veterinarian.) The same holds true of any other dangerous object. In fact, don't even wait for situations to occur, but set them up. Put an electric fan on the floor and let the dog see you playing with it. His curiosity will bring him over. Never call him, just tempt him. When he does start sniffing at the fan, give him a good whack and tell him "no." You might think this is a bit harsh, since you actually enticed him to do it, but just think of what the blades could do to his nose if he went to investigate the fan when turned on.

Since a dog can easily swallow things in the excitement of play, give him sensible toys—rawhide chew bones or hard rubber balls. Toys with sharp edges or pieces that can be broken off and swallowed are inadvisable. Squeak toys are also poor choices: Not only are they easily chewed to pieces and the squeaker easily swallowed, but your pet will invariably want to play with them at three A.M. when everyone is fast asleep.

Many people ignore seemingly self-evident safeguards, thus causing unnecessary hazards for their pets. Dogs should be carried onto escalators. If your dog walks on one, his paws can get stuck and his toes get caught and torn—he could even lose a foot. Many a small dog has had his knuckles broken by passing feet—especially high-heeled ones. Almost all animals are terrified of standing on gratings because they feel a kind of insecurity, as if suspended in midair. And at the same time, they sense the danger of catching their paws in the metalwork and breaking their knuckles. Do not allow your dog to run into an elevator ahead of you, but teach him to wait until told to enter. If you do allow him to rush in, you could lose him when the elevator doors close with only him inside.

A dog's leash is often the source of unexpected problems. When out with your pet, be sure to watch where both he and the leash are at all times. If the end of the leash gets stuck in a closing elevator door, the leash could strangle him as the elevator begins to move. If you let the leash drop and allow your pet to drag it around, it can easily catch onto objects and entangle him.

Tying your dog up on his leash can lead to all sorts of trouble, too. The first rule is never to tie him up with a choke collar, which can catch and garrote him. You should also never tie up your pet outside a store: He could be stolen or run over if a car backs up on him; or he could become overheated in the sun or chilled in the cold. Never tie your dog near a hot pipe or radiator, and if you must constrain him on a porch, be sure the leash is not long enough that he can fall off and hang himself.

Other potential canine hazards are not so obvious. For instance, when you go for a bicycle ride and take your dog along for the exercise, you may be doing him more harm than good. If your dog is running free beside you, he can adapt his own gait to move at a rhythm he finds comfortable. But if he is attached to your bike by a leash, he must keep up with your pace.

When holidays roll around, decorations need extra watching. For instance, Christmas can be a dangerous time for a dog. Trees with tinsel and ornaments can be tempting; your dog may jump up to grab at something and knock it down. Or he may eat some pine needles, holly, mistletoe, or other holiday plants that could poison or injure him. A child's new toys could also be dangerous; extra food lying around means overeating and possible stomach problems and disorders. Numerous visitors to the house can upset your pet. Therefore, be especially careful with your pet at this time to be sure he doesn't get into mischief—and be firm in your discipline. Teach him to stay away from possible dangers and watch for signs of misbehavior. Do this for all holidays, because each has a certain danger potential. Halloween pumpkins with lit candles in them can easily be tipped over by an unsuspecting dog—but he cannot escape by opening the door.

You must use your common sense to be aware of possible dangers. Either safeguard your pet by training him to avoid the problem, or protect him by your observation and intervention. Your pet's safety is your responsibility.

The Hyperactive Dog

Many overly active dogs are that way because they've had no training. Simply because they don't know what is expected from them, they are nervous and unsure. However, many have inherited hyperactivity and can't seem to keep still a second; while many others have caught the "hyper" syndrome of their environment.

Some breeds of dogs need more exercise than others, and that need may not depend entirely upon size. Some individual dogs have a high activity drive and need more exercise than others. If not exercised, these dogs may get into the habit of pacing. A full-grown dog in good health needs regular walks to keep fit. Even the smallest dogs should have a good run in the open air once a day or so—or if not a good run, at least a walk outdoors.

A dog who acquires his nervousness through contact with erratic owners can be cured only when you yourself calm down and treat him quietly and consistently. Again, this means training the dog in order to give him a set of rules. Let him know what is expected of him and how to behave in new situations. If you can't calm down, you will simply have to accept your pet as a reflection of yourself and put up with his behavior.

Inherently hyperactive dogs take to sustained pacing back and forth or weaving around rapidly to help satisfy their high activity drives. In addition, these high-strung dogs are often subject to overexcitement which can cause convulsions and epileptic fits. These dogs need to expend some of their energies through increased exercise. With this type of dog, extremely firm and vigilant basic obedience training and elimination of any bad habits are important. You have to force them to stay calm. For incorrigibles, tranquilizers are sometimes used the way they are for hyperactive children.

Dogs need to check out a new place before relaxing, but shouldn't be allowed to run madly around. If your dog does this he should be reprimanded. Make him sit for a moment so he can get a complete overview of new surroundings and thus feel secure enough to act calmly. Jumping madly around should be stopped, either by a slap or calm reassurance.

Running Outdoors

Some dogs can't resist the call of the great outdoors. As soon as the opportunity presents itself, they rush to get through open front doors, through car windows, out of elevators, and even off of boats. If this is the case with your dog, you must set up specific barriers that he isn't allowed to cross without your permission. And whenever he goes beyond those demarcation lines, you have to make it unpleasant for him.

If your dog likes to rush out the front door, for example,

you have to teach him not to cross the threshold. Leave the door open slightly and station yourself so that you are secretly on the other side. As soon as he comes out, throw something down hard in front of him—or, if necessary, on him. A cold bucket of water is extremely effective, if it can't damage anything or be too messy. An extra-loud, frightening thud from something such as the Manhattan Yellow Pages dropped in front of him is also useful. Another practical reprimand is a Rubber Arm aid such as a short, small piece of chain thrown right at him.

You have to get your dog to the point that unless you invite him outside, he feels more uncertain about what will greet him out there than he is tempted by unseen pleasures. When you do ask your pet to go outside, however, make certain that everything is wonderful so he feels absolutely secure. There must be no confusion in his mind. He must know that everything will be great outside when permission is given, but if he goes of his own accord the sky will fall in. The idea of this training is simply to teach him not to go without you, not to establish an inordinate fear of ever going out.

Apply these same techniques to teach your pet not to exit from any other aperture or cross any line without your permission. Don't let your pet jump out of car windows or he could be killed by a passing car. Be sure to pursue corrective measures vigilantly. Park your car in a secure area and leave the window open while you hide close by. As soon as your dog attempts to jump out, throw something substantial at him immediately. As an added precaution, do not leave any door, window, or other exit open temptingly—especially when you are not around. Windows should be left open just enough for him to get air, but not to get his body out.

Learning to Stay Clear of Cars

To a dog off the leash, one of the greatest dangers is cars. Dogs don't know cars are killers, and so don't take precautions against them. You have to teach your dog to fear and respect moving vehicles and give them a wide berth. First put him back on his leash and review the lesson of not stepping off the curb without you. Then go on to more definite car-avoidance training.

The best way to work this lesson is to commandeer a car, and enlist the aid of a friend who can drive. Select a deserted or at least not-too-busy street. Put on your dog's collar and leash and walk him by your side. Have your friend in the car approach slowly from behind you. When the car is a few feet away, have him blast the horn loudly. As soon as you hear the horn, jerk your dog's leash so that he's pulled sharply off to the side of the road. Repeat, going in the other direction. Keep working this way until your dog moves well off in the other direction without your assistance as soon as he hears the horn.

Once he does, gradually eliminate the blast of the horn. Keep working him until he moves off to the side of the road as soon as he hears the motor or sees the car coming. Once he is proficient on the leash, test him off—but do this only after he has all the basics of walking off the leash down pat, and has been well worked so that you feel he is trustworthy when free by your side.

If you cannot get a friend with a car to assist in this exercise, select a street that does not have too much traffic and has a low speed limit. Then simply proceed, keeping a constant vigil for oncoming traffic. You don't have the horn to warn your dog and thus set up a strong initial association; all you have is the sound of the approaching car. This is how guide dogs for the blind are trained. People often think these dogs cross the street at busy intersections because the light is green. Actually dogs are color blind: The guide dog judges when to cross the street by the flow of traffic.

Boundary Training

If you want to let your dog free but have him remain within a certain area, you have to show him what his limits are. Some dogs don't need much training to teach them to stay close to home, but the surest way to restrict your dog's boundaries is to keep him within a fenced-in garden. Have the fencing sunk a foot or so beneath the ground to prevent him from digging out. If there is no fence to constrain him, any dog can learn to take to the road, especially if there is another dog for company. You may have to pursue intensive training.

Your dog must be made to feel it's unsafe to leave the allotted premises by showing him that all kinds of unpleasantness will happen to him when he goes past his set boundary lines. Conversely, he should feel that staying on home ground is pleasant and secure. For this training you will definitely need some helpers, especially if the area is completely open or there are many exits. Have your helpers secrete themselves at intervals just outside the perimeters of the property, or at every exit. Each person should hold several good throwing objects for Rubber Arm use—rolled-up magazines, empty cardboard boxes, small pieces of chain, or house keys and key chains will do. The moment he starts off the property, whoever is closest to your dog should bombard him with whatever is available, and drive him back. No warning should be given; and the articles should be thrown with a great deal of force near him or, with less velocity, directly at him—being sure not to cause any injury.

Be careful that your dog doesn't generalize this training to include the times when you *want* to take him off the property. Therefore, every once in a while take him across the border with you and praise him, showing him it is good when you permit it. To test his proficiency, go through the same procedure you would for training him not to walk off the curb without you. Only here use the boundary lines you have established rather than the curb and street.

Socializing Your Dog

A happy pup will play and not just sit in a corner like a wallflower. Before entering your home his main contacts have been with one or both parents and littermates. Now you must establish a good rapport between your dog and people, especially family members and friends. The main ties your dog establishes will be with the members of your household plus your close friends and relatives. Some dogs are more friendly by nature, while others are more reserved. The highly developed social tendencies of dogs to interact with a small pack makes for easy involvement with family members. But your dog's relationships will usually not be too far-flung from home base unless you allow or encourage it.

Perhaps the ideal dog is one that is a little standoffish, but not hostile or terrified. If you cultivate this attitude on your dog's part, it may well help prevent an overly friendly animal from being stolen or making a pest of himself by running off to follow people, jumping all over them, or making annoyingly constant demands for attention. (It will also stop an unfriendly dog from running in fear at the sight of a newcomer or attacking in anger.)

If you have a basically friendly dog and let everyone he meets pet and cuddle him, he'll soon be running over to everyone, looking for attention. Whenever you run across a person who shows signs of being about to greet your pet, make your dog sit and stay by your side. Then allow his greeting to take place only after you give permission. Some people may get upset by this, but insist. This training will show your dog that he is to greet only those persons you permit. This will prevent your dog pulling you madly down the street to greet everyone he sees.

Jumping Up on People

Exuberantly friendly dogs that jump up on everyone to show their love can frighten children, irritate guests, and make general pests of themselves. Imagine how it feels to be rudely accosted by a strange dog, especially an exceptionally large one, trying to jump into your arms. Many people make the mistake of encouraging (or at least not correcting) jumping when their pups are little. They don't realize that cute and endearing behavior in a young pup can be a nuisance in an adult dog.

Ripped panty hose and clothing dirtied by muddy paws are the least of the problems you might encounter. One dog used to jump up and greet everyone he met in the street, including one particularly friendly elderly lady who encouraged him outrageously. One day, however, he did so on an icy sidewalk, and made her slip and fall. The woman ended up with a broken hip and the dog's owner with a lawsuit. Therefore, even if you allow your dog to jump on you, teach him not to do so with others.

Stopping this particular habit can be tricky and needs careful handling. You don't want to be so severe in your corrections that you make your dog shy of people. When training, take your pet's personality into consideration. If your dog tends to be nervous and frightens easily, be gentle at first. On the other hand, precocious types take more strict treatment to make an impression. In any case, you can't be squeamish when correcting him. When a dog is jumping up, his adrenaline is flowing in excitement; your reprimand has to be administered with enough force to jar him, or it will have no effect. You must leave no doubt in your dog's mind that jumping up is not a game. Be consistent in your corrections, and reprimand him each and every time he jumps up.

Every time your pup starts bouncing up on you, push him down. A small dog should be met with a sharp thrust of the hand so your palm hits him in the nose. If yours is a small-to medium-sized dog, grab his front paws and flip him gently over backward. It is an unpleasant experience for him to be tumbled on the floor because he loses his equilibrium and doesn't like the feeling of being temporarily out of control. For coping with a larger dog that jumps up, try treading lightly but firmly on his hind feet. Just be careful: For it to be an effective deterrent, you must step the moment your dog leaps. However, the feet of a dog hopping around madly in excitement are small targets; you have to be quick, accurate, and gentle, because a heavy shoe with a foot in it can damage your pet's paw.

A safer, surer method is to bring your knee up sharply against your dog's chest. Take a step forward on one foot, then bring your other knee up and forward. Simply raising your knee so that it bumps against the animal's chest is effective with some dogs, but most require that you exert more force to get the message home. Perform this maneuver quickly, so that by the time your dog regains his balance and is standing normally on all fours, you have both of your feet back on the floor.

Yet another method is to flip a folded magazine or newspaper on your dog's nose when he jumps up, then turn and walk away. Or you could throw something down on your dog's rump, per the Rubber Arm technique. If the correction is made properly and as simultaneously as possible with his jumping, your dog will associate the correction with the deed and stop jumping up.

One caution to heed in correcting your dog when he jumps up is not to say "down." If you must say something, say "no." "Down" is part of the lie-down command; if you make the mistake of associating that word with a correction, he may be reluctant to obey when you tell him to lie down, thinking he is going to be reprimanded. In addition, don't forget to praise your dog profusely once he's standing normally again.

To prevent your dog from jumping up on others, you could ask a few friends to make the corrections suggested whenever he jumps on them. If several people treat your dog this way, he will soon get the message that jumping up isn't wanted by anyone. Unfortunately, most people are either reluctant or incapable of correcting your dog effectively. Besides, your dog must understand that it is you who doesn't want him to jump up. You have to be the ultimate authority.

Every time your dog jumps up on someone else, use the Rubber Arm technique. Don't warn him by holding your throwing object threateningly; simply tuck it discreetly under your arm. When your dog goes to jump up on anyone, throw it near or at him, depending on how engrained the habit is.

Teaching a Dog Not to Go to Strangers

Many dogs are stolen when off the leash. Take precautions and teach your dog to stay away from strangers. Have him associate unpleasantness with anyone except you, people you are with, or others whom you give permission for him to greet. This means the Rubber Arm technique every time he goes over to someone when off the leash. If you don't want to throw anything, go over to him and reprimand him, then drag him away. You could even try to get some people to assist you by chasing him away whenever he goes over to them. This may sound harsh, especially if you want him to be friendly, but it could save you the heartache you would endure if he were to get stolen by one of those "friendly" people.

If you must allow him to be petted by strangers, do so only when you are close by and in control to give permission. Let him know that you have to say it is okay for him to approach someone by telling him so, and reprimanding him if it isn't.

Annoying Company

When guests are visiting your home, they are *your* friends, not his—and your dog has to respect them as such and not become annoying. Not that he can't greet them, but he has to understand that showers of excessive, unsolicited affection are unwanted. Conversely, he must learn that you won't tolerate a hostile attitude either.

When company is in your home, your dog should behave the way he would if they were not around. Teach him to lie down quietly and steer clear of guests unless they invite him to approach.

To satisfy his curiosity, allow a quick greeting when your company arrives and departs. However, hanging around and nuzzling people should be verboten. If you see your dog being a pest, try throwing a Rubber Arm object at or near him. If your dog keeps on bothering them, give him a slap and send him out of the room.

Besides learning to respect your friends when they visit you, your dog has to learn to be under control when visiting with you in a friend's home. He should stay by your side and not wander off to check out the house. When he goes to the park or dog run, that's the time for him to run with his pals. When you take him somewhere, keep him leashed. Simply keep jerking him back to your side every time he wanders, and push him into the down position.

On the other hand, a dog who's uncertain and nervous about contact with new people has to be taught to at least tolerate them. Even if you tend to be a loner and aren't overwhelmed with visitors, your pet will still eventually have to come into contact with a variety of different people during his normal day. A dog who shivers and quakes in the presence of strangers is upsetting and annoying. If your dog's reaction is to take fright, teach him not to panic. When people approach, don't allow him to run off to try to hide. Keep him close by your side and praise him for bravery in staying. Don't be overly insistent, just ease him into staying still and calm when people approach.

If your dog shows hostility toward new people, whether out of fright or anger, he should be reprimanded. He should then be made to stay quietly beside you, and forced to behave. Any persons approaching your pet should be warned of the danger. You could insist that your dog accept any greeting of which you approve, but the unpredictability of this type of dog dictates caution. Keep him on a leash and if nothing else, expect and insist upon civility. If he becomes a real problem, use the treatment recommended in the chapter on "Controlling Aggression."

Dogs and Children

Don't get a dog with the expectation that your children will care for him. No matter what your children's ages you can't expect them to take on the responsibilities of walking, feeding, and the other myriad details that come with pet ownership. Youngsters have short memories and forget easily. They are more concerned with baseball or other such activities. Twelve years old is about the youngest you can expect a child to take over the dog-related chores, but even then you will have to fill in when they're off doing the things children do. It's up to adults to consistently supervise the care of any pet in a household—without monopolizing the animal's affection, of course.

Children and dogs are not always the idyllic combination they are pictured to be. Not because they can't be, but simply because they have seldom been taught how to act with each other. It is generally the children who need the training. Many problems stem from the fact that pets are too often bought strictly as toys, and as such the children are never taught to respect them as living creatures. Small children like to pull and squeeze; some actually maul their pets. But when teethmarks are found on the child's arm, the dog is the one that is punished. However, it is usually the child that is at fault and needs training.

In one family, the parents bought dogs as playmate-companions for their two boys. To relieve arguments over whose dog it was they got one pet for each child. They couldn't understand why both the dogs took to one boy and not the other. But the answer was quite simple: The one boy was gentle and loving toward the dogs, while the other bossed them around and demanded their attention. A firm lecture on the proper care and treatment of animals was the solution. Children have to be taught not to tease, but to play nicely and treat their pets with respect. Constantly remind children that the dog is a play*mate,* not a play*thing;* and it will love them only if they are kind, thoughtful, and gentle with it. Look out for a jealous older child venting his spleen on the indulged new puppy. Your dog can easily become a scapegoat for redirected aggression of children frustrated by parental discipline.

You must insist that your child handle your dog properly. To start off, make sure your child knows the proper way to hold and carry a dog (a lesson that might not be wasted on adults either). The correct method is explained under Bringing a New Puppy Home in Chapter One: "Selecting and Caring for a New Dog." Before holding any animal, children should sit down because they may drop him if he starts to wriggle. Don't let very young children who don't understand grab at a dog. A larger dog should not be lifted at all; leaning over or sitting down to his level to pet him is more appropriate.

When first introducing your child and a new dog, do so slowly and supervise. In general, it's a simple process that happens quite naturally, but it is always best to watch. You can put a baby on the floor next to a puppy. Don't be afraid; the baby will be left intact, but do stick around. A dog catches on miraculously fast that children are his friends, as long as someone takes the time to introduce them properly. If you are worried, just be sure your nervousness is not picked up by either child or dog.

Don't leave children alone with your dog without first giving guidance in the correct way to play with him. Otherwise, your child could teach the dog to become wild. A young pup chasing madly around can be fun to watch, but a full-grown bull mastiff or Great Dane is not so amusing when he jumps and knocks people down. Your dog may run after children, playfully nipping or jumping at them without meaning any harm. Even if your child starts a game, the dog may not know when to stop, and someone might get accidentally hurt. It is up to you to keep reminding children how to handle your pet properly. Don't, however, be so overly cautious that you teach a child to fear dogs. Few dogs are hostile toward children. On the other hand, children rarely fear dogs unless taught to do so by the attitudes and warnings of parents or other authority figures. In fact, most adults who are afraid of dogs got that way because *their* parents were constantly warning that they would get bitten.

You and your children should know how to greet a new dog. When introducing yourself to a dog, present the back of your hand to its muzzle. A dog may snap at fingers, but will only sniff the back of the hand. Once he accepts that first introduction, he will usually allow the friendship to develop to the stroking stage.

When you already have a dog as an established resident member of your household, bringing a new baby home can cause some trying problems. More usually these fears are in the minds of the owners, but a dog who is used to getting an enormous amount of attention from his owners—even to being sole ruler of his household territory—can become upset. One dog became so upset about being pushed out of a central position that one day while the baby was in the playpen he jumped into the baby's empty crib. The parents misread the action as a sign of aggression, but it was only a cry for attention.

Generally, this all-too-common fear that the dog will react by being hostile toward the new child is completely unfounded; but if it isn't, you must stop the problem firmly at the first overt signs. Just be careful that you are not projecting your own nightmares into the situation. When the dog comes near the child, don't panic. Don't explain to him that he is not being forgotten, because the more attention the dog gets, the worse the situation will become. If you don't want him around the child, just quietly chase him away. Eventually dog and baby will become good friends. Most of the time when you hear of dogs being jealous of children, it's conjured up in the minds of the people telling the story. An animal *will* accept his environment.

As is true with older siblings in the household, jealous anger is usually vented against the parents and not the new baby. Thus your dog may react by doing spiteful, destructive things such as chewing the sofa. Or he may sulk, trying to make you feel guilty and pay him extra attention. Don't allow yourself to be pulled in. He should be reprimanded for misbehavior.

To prevent these problems from starting, don't allow your pet to feel hurt when a new baby puts in an appearance. Don't let him feel he's being pushed into the background, seeing some new creature receiving the care and attention that he thinks are rightfully his. Don't ignore your dog. When you are fussing over the baby, give the dog a pat too so he has the security of knowing that you still want him. However, don't overcompensate and be excessively oversympathetic with your dog. This is as bad as ignoring him completely. Don't worry; he'll soon accept the new arrival as if the baby were always there.

Jealousy: Loss of Central Position

Perhaps one of the major shocks any dog can receive in his lifetime is the realization that he is not the center of the universe. You—his owner—represent security to your dog, and he may think that the new arrival is interfering with his relationship with you. He may take on infantile attitudes such as clinging cloyingly to you. Ignoring him may force him to do things to attract attention or spite you. He may mess up in his training because he feels pushed into the background. If either of these reactions occur, don't let him continue. Treat him as normally as possible to reassure him that he is still an integral part of the family.

The arrival of a new spouse or roommate can be especially

traumatic. Your dog may take on a possessive attitude toward you. He may not let the new arrival into your home—and if he does, he may follow that person around or hang close to you, intimidating the new arrival by growling or making other threatening gestures. Here, *you* must correct your dog by reprimanding him for his aggressive behavior. If the offending animal isn't made to understand that you don't want him to possess you, the problem will progressively worsen.

You must give your new spouse or housemate every opportunity to work, feed, and walk your dog. Be insistent in helping—and yet not interfering in—the development of a relationship between them. Because it is flattering to cause such a rivalry, the owner often unintentionally encourages this overpossessiveness.

Often the bed is the focal point of this problem. If your dog is accustomed to sleeping on the bed with you alone, he may refuse to allow another person to share it. Be firm and reprimand your pet severely. Don't distract your pet by subterfuge and then ask your companion to rush for the bed. Your dog has to learn it is *your* bed, not his; and that he comes up only at your invitation. When he shows any signs of possessiveness, throw some Rubber Arm item at him or slap him hard—first you, and then immediately after, the newcomer. Just be sure whatever you do doesn't create a new problem. When a friend's new husband joined her in bed, her dog growled at him, and she threw something at the dog to correct him. The only thing she had close by were some carrots. The dog loved the carrot, and to this day our friend is throwing carrots for him.

Dogs and Other Pets

Bringing a new pet into the house can cause problems, whether of the same species or different. Two pets can be better than one, but they have to learn how to get along. Each has to respect the other's life-style and not interfere with it. Even if they never become great pals, they have to learn to leave each other alone at times; competition analogous to sibling rivalry in children can develop between pets. A new pet can be the brunt of bullying and punishment from the resident pet, who can also bring retribution for the new addition on the owner in various ways—ranging from sulking and not eating food to becoming disruptive in the house and breaking training. Jealousy can be a powerful force, and dogs are by nature selfish, unless participating in a coordinated group activity.

If you can, therefore, try to select dogs that are likely to grow to approximately the same size in order to ensure a harmonious relationship. If you already have an established dog, bringing in a younger animal is best. Few dogs will abuse a younger one, and in fact the older one may develop an almost parental attitude. It is also better to get an animal of the opposite sex since this eliminates social, territorial, and hierarchical rivalry.

Perhaps the best way to start off the relationship is to introduce the new and resident pets on neutral territory such as a friend's house where neither has been before. The resident pet will then not feel his home and security are being threatened, and will accept or at least tolerate the stranger. When you take your pets home after this initial meeting they will already know each other, and at least the initial step in the battle is already over. Don't give all of your attention to the new arrival, but rather share your time equally between old and new pets. Naturally anything new has a novelty factor that attracts your attention, so it's normal to be overly attentive toward the newcomer to the disadvantage of the standard resident. Often people do not even realize they are doing this, and so you must make a conscious effort to give equal attention to all. Giving more attention to the new pet will only make your pet feel his relationship with you—and consequently, his security—is being threatened, which can lead to difficulties.

Keep any newcomer to your home in a separate area for two or three days. All animals should be kept on leads during the first few hours of contact, and should be observed carefully. Remove toys or other items over which there could be squabbling. Be sure to feed your various pets out of separate bowls, and supervise them when together—a habit you might be wise to continue. Make sure the new pet does not pester or annoy the resident, and vice versa. The idea is to keep them controlled until they have accepted each other. On the other hand, you must not overinterfere with them and deny them the opportunity to become friends.

Allow the resident pet to dominate the new dog up to a point. It's natural for the dog to assert dominance over the new dog. To punish him for displaying superiority would be cruel, but if he starts to get rough, reprimand him. With time, you can teach all your pets to get along and accept each other, even if they are fierce enemies at first. Your insistence and their constant association will bring them to the realization that there is no other way. Your position as leader of your household is what makes this happen.

How to Recognize Emotional Problems

Dogs do develop emotional and psychosomatic disorders and phobias which manifest themselves in various forms of unusual and erratic behavior. Fortunately for you, dogs are not terribly complicated intellectually; they tend to accept things more readily, which helps limit the degree of emotional disorders they can develop. And dogs who do have definite emotional upsets can be dealt with once you realize how and why.

Just be careful you don't project your own complex emotions into a dog's actions. Since your dog's inner feelings are not open to direct inspection, all you can do is to infer when he is angry, frightened, jealous, or pleased. But you can never be absolutely sure that your dog's actions are identical to a human's. Investigating all the circumstances can help you better interpret your pet's actions correctly.

Both heredity and environment affect an animal's emotional stability. A propensity for timidity can be inherited, for example, but the environment influences whether this trait will develop or not. A timid pup may become shyer still with erratic, disturbing experiences, instead of achieving the confidence he could with a stable environment. Until maturity (at about a year and a half) your dog's temperament is not stabilized, and up to that time all sorts of things can change his personality. Even after then, a major fright or trauma can have a devastating effect. (Some emotional problems are the result of brain damage, but this isn't something you can do anything about.)

Your Dog's Background and Emotional Stability

The rearing a dog has had before you get him can affect him forever. Unfortunately, few pets come from a perfect environment. There will always be some problem that develops. But knowing what has happened to your pet in the past can help you understand the cause of present problems. Often, however, you will have to treat a problem symptomatically and try to make an educated guess as to what happened to cause it.

Problems can start so early in a pup's life that no one can have any control. Even your dog's mother and littermates can influence him: A mother who is nervous or who terrorizes her pups may make them nervous or aggressive. The only pup in a litter, with no siblings to play with, could have problems in personal relationships later in life. Any number of major or minor traumatic experiences that you will never know about can cause unusual reactions later.

If you can, try to get a dog that has been well socialized to people. If a dog passes thirteen weeks of age without having had human contact, he may not be able to relate well to people. If not handled with love in very early life, a dog may grow up to be less outgoing in personality, antisocial, and more easily upset. Dogs need experience with all kinds of people, other pets and situations. A dog that has been exposed to a varied environment will be easier to train and more temperamentally reliable. On the other hand, a dog that has not had the proper experiences as a pup may tend to avoid or be extremely upset by anything new. Dogs that have been caged or kenneled in isolation are especially prone to later emotional problems, becoming afraid of new places, situations, and people. Such a dog may be so used to staying alone that he finds his comfort and security in a special hiding spot. If he has been in constant contact with dogs, he may want to be only with them. Conversely, hand-raised pups who have never had contact with other dogs may not want to associate with other animals. They see themselves as different from them—in fact, as one of us. Similarly, puppies raised with cats may prefer them to dogs and humans. They may even pick up catlike behavior such as climbing.

How You Contribute to Emotional Problems

Once you actually have your pet, overindulging and overdomineering him are equally bad. Upon reaching sexual maturity, permissively raised pups often become difficult to handle because they have always been allowed to do as they want. On the other hand, too early and too relentless training may lead him to have overexcited, nervous reactions to the least little thing.

Your dog may reflect your personality as well. If you are high-strung and need tranquilizers to get through the day, your dog may react to your frenetic pace and become nervous himself.

Most dogs will react to a situation as they observe their owners do. Therefore, be sure your pet is not mirroring your own fears and dislikes. If you are afraid of thunder, for instance, your dog will be; and nervousness around certain people or new places can infect your pet.

Any traumatic experience, such as being too close to a loudspeaker, accidentally stepped on, attacked by another dog, or frightened by a large truck can bring on a generalized phobia about that situation. It can be so upsetting that your dog may refuse to go to any area that resembles the place where he was traumatized, or will at least show signs of fear. Thus an unpleasant journey as a pup might cause your dog to whine fearfully a few years later when he is put in a shipping crate or automobile. This fearful reaction to things similar to the original trauma might crop up at any time. Once a fear reaction has been established, it is extremely long-lasting.

In households with more than one owner, everyone has to get together and decide on one method of coping with the dog—and stick to it. Otherwise your dog can become so confused that he doesn't know how to react, or what's expected of him. A dog can sometimes become an emotional pawn between two owners, and if they can't come to an arrangement about working together with the dog instead of pulling from either end, the two of them should visit a psychologist to straighten out *their* problems. You have to stop using your dog as a tool for your own unresolved frustrations.

General Curative Approaches

Emotionally based problems should not be treated like bad habits. If you were to correct one as if it were just a bad habit, you would only be taking away a symptom; the problem will probably arise again in the form of a different symptom. Thus you may stop a dog from urinating when he's scared by thunder and lightning, but he may then start ripping up your home looking for somewhere to hide, or start nervously licking at himself. You have to eliminate the real cause—either literally, by physically removing a tangible trigger, or by unraveling the warped connection in your dog's mind.

Another problem with a phobia is that it tends to expand as your dog accumulates more and more things to be afraid of. A single phobia can be desensitized with reasonable success, but when it generalizes into many phobias—it is a different story. At this point, new phobias are likely to develop at any time and for any reason. To eliminate phobias, you need a combination of cures. Reprimands as used for bad habits may well be part of a primary cure, but generally they are used only in conjunction with others.

The best way to overcome a phobia in your dog is by associating something really pleasant with whatever upsets him. At the same time, show him there is nothing to fear or feel insecure about. The only way to solve most behavioral problems is repeated reconditioning so as to gradually get him to stop his adverse emotional reactions. With a major problem, you may have to chip away at it in very small pieces: Do not go too far at one time. And if there is a poor reaction to your treatment, stop it immediately.

Fear of Noises

Disruptions and loud noises can be particularly traumatic at first. Young pups have a tendency to give startled reactions to any sudden noise. A new noise breaking the silence causes drastic reactions. However, even without your help, most dogs will learn to accept normal disruptions. For instance, when an electric fan is turned on for the first time, your dog may jump; but if the noise continues, it soon just blends into the background and your dog doesn't notice it. It's the sudden, drastic changes occurring on a random basis that can cause problems.

Fear of a certain noise can develop at any time. For some reason, a particular noise may set off an adverse reaction in your pet. There's unfortunately little you can do to prevent the problem because you can't control every sound in your environment. All you can do is to try to expose your dog at an early age to as many noises as possible. When a new sound occurs, make your pet learn to wait and see exactly what it is before reacting.

To forestall this problem, be sure your pet does not get hurt or become drastically upset. If so, he may well develop a permanent fear of associated noises. As a pup, one dog had his paw closed in a slamming door. After that, any slamming door sent him into a panic. To correct this, each day over a period of weeks he was gingerly brought closer and closer to a closing door and was firmly—yet lovingly—encouraged to stay. When he did so, he was praised and treated with a tidbit. The idea is to teach your pet to cope with new situations by actually flinging him into the lion's den—but not to terrify him and thus cause an emotional trauma.

Thunder is perhaps the noise dogs most commonly despise, with firecrackers and fire engines close behind. If you don't cure your dog's problem, his fear reaction to a particular sound may spread and generalize to include all unusual sounds. If this happens, you have a heavy job on your hands. It's really annoying to walk down the street with a dog that jumps every time he hears a truck motor start up, a siren go off, or a garbage truck rattle by. Should this happen, do not pick your pet up and comfort him, or you may make a bad habit worse. At the same time, don't force him to face the offending noise. Overexposure can make matters worse or set your work back. Make him stay calm—and praise him when he is.

Once a real phobia has developed toward a particular noise, use more specific cures. One excellent solution is to make a tape recording of the abominated sound (or find records of various sound effects at your local record shop) and play it at various pleasant times during the day—like mealtime. Start off by playing the recording with the volume very low. As your dog appears to accept it, gradually raise the volume. Work until your dog can tolerate the sound at its normal rate of amplitude. (His love of food should keep him there.) Just make sure that the sound is not so unpleasant that all you succeed in doing is putting your dog off his food, and end up having to change his diet and mealtimes to get him to eat.

Done carefully, this acclimatizing treatment should solve your problem. Familiarity takes away the fear.

Once he realizes the noise didn't bother him at one specific time and place, he'll soon realize it won't hurt him any time. Start making the noise at different times and in different situations. If necessary, encourage him with kind words, petting, and tidbits. Just be sure you don't make it so pleasant for him that he cowers for more sympathy.

Your veterinarian might be able to prescribe a suitable tranquilizer that could help when you can control the conditions. But if you aren't around when the noise starts, you can't administer the medication. (Weather forecasting is not that accurate for those sudden summer thundershowers.) If you do use these tranquilizers as an aid, be sure the dose is sufficient to quiet your dog without making him uncoordinated. Use them correctly: The theory behind this solution is that under the right fear-relieving drug, your pet may learn to overcome the phobia. Unfortunately, it often simply means that your dog will gradually need more and more tranquilizers. Therefore, once your pet seems to have calmed down, gradually eliminate the drug. Use it just long enough to eliminate the dreadful fear.

The Shy Dog

An overly shy dog who can never be found because he's constantly hiding somewhere—even from his owner—is a nuisance, as is one that clings to you pathetically. Not only is this behavior annoying in itself, but it can cause additional problems. It's not normal for dogs to be antisocial. By nature they are pack animals, extremely social creatures who thrive on group activity. Whether they realize it or not, they need contact with others. In helping your dog overcome his antisocial quirk, you are doing him a favor. Constant isolation—even if voluntary—can be detrimental to your dog's health. Isolated dogs kept without human or animal contact have been known to die of loneliness. Laboratories even hire people to pet experimental dogs and keep them happy, or at least content. Besides, a dog who is shy of you and your friends may, if cornered and unable to escape, resort to a defensive-aggressive attack. Many fear biters are shy, unsocialized dogs.

To counteract this, give your dog lots of affection and handling. Do this even if he doesn't want it! Insist he allow you to handle him. No real, meaningful relationship can develop if your dog is not attached to you. A shy dog may never become an exuberant extrovert, but over a period of time he can be trained to stay with you and even permit strangers to touch him. But his confidence must be won before progress can be made—which can be a difficult task. These dogs are suspicious and wary; they seem to think that any person coming near them has some ulterior motive. Fear of the unknown, arising from lack of contact, is the cause of this reaction.

Some dogs are so nervous they actually quiver and shake when strangers are around. To stop this you have to convince your dog through firm, insistent reassurance that everything is fine. At first have strangers merely walk near your dog, but don't let them touch him. Once he stops spooking when a person gets close to him, let friends gradually reach out their hands *as if* to touch, but not actually do so. Later, when your dog remains calm as someone reaches toward him, have people gently touch your dog. Perhaps slip him a special treat at the same time to provide pleasure. If you are firm, you can gradually get your dog to permit strangers to touch him.

Be patient in this process; don't rush your pet. You can't drag him out, but must gently insist he come out of his shell. Pushing your dog into the middle of a crowded party will only make the condition worse instead of better. He may be so traumatized that you'll never convince him that the world isn't out to get him. At first work where there are only one or two people around, and do so only in familiar surroundings. Your dog feels comfortably secure in places such as your living room.

The Cowering, Submissive Dog

If your pet crawls along the ground toward you or your friends as though you were going to beat him when he gets there, it can make you feel terrible—especially when your dog rolls over and urinates a little in submission after he reaches you. This behavior needs to be normalized. You may not cure him completely, but hopefully you will achieve enough success that your pet won't make you feel like an ogre.

This behavior is usually a naturally inherited trait or an immature reaction, but can be the result of excessive punishment or overdomination, either by other dogs or people. Owners often cause it unintentionally. One of the most common training mistakes is to call a dog, then when he comes, punish him or do something unpleasant (such as giving him a pill).

Infantile submissive behaviors have been bred into dogs as a by-product of their deliberately cultivated propensity to view people as social superiors. (Some of these same animals may actually be dominant toward other dogs.) To make your dog less demonstrative in his show of submission, you must teach him that deference toward people does not need such a groveling display; it can be shown simply by behaving properly and obeying. Since he is crawling and cringing to please you, don't sympathetically pet your cringing, piddling dog in the hopes of bringing him out of it. Because he'll think you're praising him, this will only encourage the very behavior you want stopped. Instead, clap your hands. Startle him; do something to make him forget about submitting. If he sidles cringingly over to you, ignore him until his groveling is over, then pet him. And when petting him after he comes to you in a normal way, hold his head up and make him look up toward you to get him in the habit of keeping an upward posture rather than a cowering one.

Sometimes an overly submissive dog needs to be given confidence. In order to have him approach in a normal, confident manner, you have to boost his ego. Play a little game with him. Make little bluff attacks toward him, then quickly back away and run from him. Get him to come toward you as you go back. Soon he will be chasing you around and stepping out more confidently. (Just don't be overly enthusiastic in using this technique or it may give him so much courage that he becomes nasty.)

If your pet's oversubmissive display is the result of excessive punishment—either from you or a previous owner—stop the punishment and institute a lot of praise for deeds well done, especially for coming in a happy manner; and never allow anything unpleasant to happen to him at this time.

Fear of New Situations

If an animal is never allowed out of confinement, he will be reluctant to leave when given the opportunity. A similar phenomenon is reflected in the many dogs who have led such restricted lives that going to new environments upsets them to the extreme. Other dogs suddenly develop a naturally inherited wariness of unfamiliar places and surroundings; this trait emerges most often at four to five months of age. These dogs are abnormally fearful of unfamiliar objects; they may even react fearfully when their normal surroundings are altered, such as when you switch the furniture around. Instead of calmly investigating something new to see that everything's okay, this type of dog is more likely to panic, run off, and try to hide. The difficulty in coping with this foible is that there is always something new to contend with, so you can spend forever overcoming countless irrational fears.

Anything new causes a certain amount of confusion, so some reaction is normal. But your dog shouldn't run terrified into a corner or flail about every time something new happens.

Mobility is a way of life for most people today, and the family pet usually goes along too. He is taken to visit neighbors, on shopping trips, and to vacation in exotic places. You have to acclimatize your pet to innumerable different surroundings. When faced with the unknown, uncertainty can lead to misbehavior because your pet may be so upset that he relieves himself or runs around in a nervously irrational state. He has to be taught to behave no matter where you take him.

Teaching Your Dog
to Accept New Places

Start bringing your dog to new places at an early age so that he gets used to seeing his environment vary and won't become upset when it does. When in crowded places with him, firmly insist that he move briskly while at the same time reassuring him that he is secure. Your dog will soon understand there is nothing to fear. Upon entering a new place, always make your pet sit for a few minutes so he can survey the situation calmly. Then take him around to investigate under your supervision so he can be sure everything is okay.

When your dog reacts badly to sudden changes and annoying situations, don't become overly solicitous. Cuddling, cooing, and comforting your pet only encourages him to continue to freak out. Instead, firmly insist that your pet face the offending situation, while encouraging him with a reassuring pat to let him know you are with him.

To overcome this constant fear reaction, you have to make your pet face new places and changes squarely. Frequently take your dog to new surroundings with varying conditions. Don't be too demanding and drag him, but on the other hand don't stand back for too long, reassuring him that everything is all right. He must face whatever it is or he'll never get used to accepting the unknown calmly. When in a new place, don't allow your pet to tug and back away. Instead, hold him firmly in place on the leash and praise him when he remains calm. This will give him time to survey the situation and realize there's nothing to fear, and will teach him to follow the same procedure himself in the future. If you are insistent but show understanding and encouragement at the same time, your dog will learn a wait-and-see attitude: to examine everything carefully, then react with composure.

When visiting, don't allow your dog free to run around by

himself. In a store, always keep your pet beside you and not atop the counters, all over other customers, or rummaging through the goods. A sharp reprimand will keep him out of trouble. Restaurants that allow dogs do not want them to join you at the table. Teach your pet to stay under the table or quietly at your side by constantly pushing him back into place every time he moves.

A small dog can easily be taken everywhere you go without his presence ever being known. Carry him around in a tote bag, and teach him to stay in there, out of sight. Every time your dog pops his head out of the bag, push him back down. If you are persistent, he will soon learn to stay inside. Your job is to be sure that the bag is comfortable, well insulated, airy, and secure.

In moving to a new permanent or temporary residence, don't give your pet the immediate freedom of the new place. Allowing your dog to roam and do his own thing will surely result in mischief. You must ensure that he remembers his training and behaves himself. To make sure he remains trained when making the transition, don't hesitate to employ the constructive confinement technique whether during a hotel stay, an extended visit to Grandma's, or a move to a new home.

Psychosomatic Illnesses

Some dogs become so overly attached and dependent on their owners that they remain emotionally a perpetual pup. When this type of dog is separated from the owners for whatever reason, there can be adverse results. Refusal to eat, constipation, diarrhea, and general physical exhaustion may be the result of such emotional stress. Such overattached dogs may literally pine away, slowly deteriorating and perhaps even dying.

In this type of dog, separation from his owner creates a stress reaction that increases susceptibility to disease. Thus recovery after illness or surgery may be impaired if the dog is hospitalized. This type of dog should be sent to a kennel as little as possible; when sent, he should be given a homey atmosphere or he may become ill.

One trend of thought asserts that a great many of all illnesses are emotionally based. Some are, but first rule out the likelihood of a medical cause. Only then can you or your veterinarian assume the problems are emotional in nature. In all cases of sudden and unusual changes or illnesses, a veterinarian should check to see whether there is a medical basis to the problem.

Often people interpret a dog's behavior by assuming that he is showing his love through psychological ploys. This is more the exception than the rule, but he may well develop such a symptom if it's to his benefit to do so. Such ploys are usually designed exclusively to get sympathy. One friend's dog was perfectly able to use a leg that had been previously injured, but he persisted in limping around. Of course, treats and extra kindnesses were poured over him in sympathy. Then one day a really tempting tidbit was offered from several yards away and he quickly forgot the "pain" and bounded over for it. If you catch your dog in this kind of situation, turn off the sympathy and ignore him. When he realizes it's doing him no good, you'll soon see how fast he recovers.

Any change—a plane flight, a kennel stay, a visit to a new place, fear of a new sound, a bad reaction to strangers—can bring on a reaction in your dog. Stress, sustained excitement, and traumatic experiences can cause a number of psychosomatic disorders, from a wheezing asthmatic attack to hysterical paralysis. If your dog reacts in this way to a particular something, remove the cause and teach him to overcome his phobias by using the remedies indicated above. However, some psychosomatic problems with annoying but not dangerous manifestations are better off left alone: taking away a simple symptom could cause worse problems. For example, a dog that has diarrhea every other day with no medical basis may be relieving his nervousness. If this outlet is removed, the dog may develop more annoying and even dangerous problems.

Harmful Nervous Habits

Because your dog uses his mouth to fidget the way we would use our hands, the nervous idiosyncrasies he may develop are generally oral. They might start out as a reaction to some emotional disturbance such as a kennel stay, or in physical response to a long-standing itch or sore. With time, they just become something to do.

Some dogs suckle like a puppy on you, your possessions, or another pet, kneading with their forefeet. One theory holds that this is a sexually based form of masturbation; another claims it is the result of the dog removed too soon from his mother and the rest of his littermates. More probably it's just a way of relaxing and obtaining a feeling of security. Some people wouldn't even think of stopping a dog who displays such great affection by slobbering on their arm, but annoyingly persistent and excessive suckling may need curbing. Since suckling is a friendly act toward you, however, you must not be overly severe or forceful when stopping it, or you could alienate your dog. He's doing this to be close to you, so you don't want to discourage the motive, just the action. Push your dog away gently and when he refrains, pet him. If he persists, put an unpleasant substance (such as lemon juice) on your arm.

Do the same to a dog that is annoying another pet. You don't want to make them enemies, but you should stop him before the habit becomes annoying, especially if the suckler begins using his teeth.

If your pet is suckling on your possessions, however, stop it immediately by treating it as if it were a chewing habit.

Flea Biting, Licking, and Nibbling

These activities are a normal part of a dog's behavior, and dogs will do them when intensely excited at a greeting. They're also a natural grooming response brought on by your dog's social imperative to groom his companions. If you don't want your dog to groom you, push him gently away every time he starts to do it. Pet him only when he stops. If he persists, slap him. The constant licking of sheets or upholstery should be handled like chewing. Sprinkle some finely ground black pepper on the object being licked, hold your dog's nose to it, and let him get a good whiff. Or booby-trap the area by placing screening over it. Teaching your dog to stay away from whatever it is he loves to lick and nibble will keep him away from temptation.

Lick Granuloma

This reasonably common but potentially dangerous oral fixation often develops into self-mutilation. A dog may start licking at his own body for any number of reasons, but licking can become so obsessive that dogs develop a positive mania for it. If your dog suddenly starts licking at one particular spot on the skin—frequently between his toes or other spots around the foot area—check to see if there is a skin irritation that needs veterinary attention. If you find a cut, don't think that licking will heal wounds as many people believe. If anything, persistent licking can damage the cuts further. No matter what he is licking, discourage him. Try trimming the hair around the area and rubbing on some harmless but foul-tasting stuff such as Tabasco sauce or lemon juice. (Mixing it with Vaseline may make it easier to apply.) Or better still, get a special smelly salve from your veterinarian. Try bandaging the area for a day or so to get him to forget it.

Just keep in mind that to cure your dog, you must make him forget the spot he is already working on, and also make sure he doesn't find a new one. Mindless licking can often result in self-mutilation, so you must be firm with your dog. Slap him hard when you catch him in the act. Put an Elizabethan collar around his neck so he can't get at the licking spot. This special cone-shaped collar, made up of two half circles of cardboard or plastic laced together, is designed to prevent an animal from getting his head around to his body. By simply forcing him to forget the action for a while, you might make him stop it.

However, our studies have shown that one of the major causes of lick granulomas is improper feeding—or more specifically, overfeeding and incorrect diet. The dog's been taught not to relieve himself in the house and not to chew anything. Therefore, when he is agonizing because he ate too much, he goes to work on himself rather than do anything he's been taught not to do. Simply following the recommendations in food and feeding will help him. Cut his intake to the correct amount, and get him on a food that doesn't cause him to drink too much because it's salty or too dry.

Scratching

Scratching at a specific spot can be equally as bad as constant licking. The dog keeps digging his nails into one particular area and rips the skin. The same type of treatment applicable to self-licking applies here. You could also put booties on your dog's feet so he can't open the skin with his nails, and keep the nails trimmed short until he stops scratching.

Drooling

Drooling is a normal feature with certain breeds of dogs. If such is the case, there is little you can do to stop it, except to keep your drooler away from people it annoys. If the onset is sudden, check to see that nothing abnormal is lodged in your dog's mouth; if it is extreme, check with a veterinarian. If there is no physical reason, assume the overflow of saliva may be an emotional problem, a habit, or a reaction to excitement and fear. If it is the latter, eliminate the source. If the drooling is an emotional problem or a habit, it can be stopped by taking cotton balls and placing them under your dog's jowls every time he starts. They feel unpleasant in his mouth and may stop the drooling. A taste of Tabasco every time he drools may also help eliminate this reaction. If there is a physical basis to the drooling, these techniques usually won't work, but they are worth a try. When the body receives an unpleasant response to the drooling secretion, the flow may just stop.

Sexually Related Problems

Some male pups "show their lipstick" when petted or excited. These erections are simply an emotional response to handling—really an involuntary reflex that is best ignored. With the onset of sexual maturity at about six months, however, a dog may show precocious sexual habits. At this time some dogs start mounting objects to masturbate. It is most common in dogs ranging from six to eighteen months of age, and naturally enough is seen far more in males than females. Pillows are favored, as are children and the legs of owners. (Children often mistake such action for play and unwittingly encourage the dog's behavior.) Reprimand your dog harshly for any such behavior. It may appear amusing when a puppy behaves this way, but even a mini-sized pooch that decides to mount a visitor's hand is embarrassing. Whoever catches the dog in the act—or whomever he is directing the action toward—should slap him hard across the flanks or throw something at him every time he starts. This will deter most dogs.

Be especially sure to warn children not to tolerate, let alone encourage, such actions. If it is simply an adolescent urge, it will go away with a little correction, but will not normally go away by itself. In fact, since it is often one of the first signs of domination in dogs, it may grow into a major aggressive problem if not checked.

When they reach sexual maturity, some oversocialized dogs have a real longing for their owners, rather than for other dogs. Females like this are difficult to handle when in heat. Their male counterparts get turned on when being petted by someone. The person being longed for must reprimand the dog for any overt advances and make the animal realize you are not its sexual partner.

Other troublesome problems include nymphomania in females and an overdeveloped sexual drive in males. A male of this type will, if allowed, roam all over looking for an accommodating female; a female of this predisposition may mount and show male sexual activity. She seems to be in heat almost all the time, and is usually very nervous. Either case could arise because of hormonal imbalances; if so, it should be treated by a veterinarian. Punishment and restraint will help cement the cure.

Pseudopregnancy is a common emotional problem with females that occurs following ovulation. Though no real gestation occurs, the physical symptoms may vary from just a simple enlargement of the teats to all the physical symptoms of a real pregnancy. The bitch may even go through the motions of labor, then take some object as a surrogate puppy and care for and guard it faithfully. To avoid the psychological trauma involved—along with the physical discomfort—the only real answer here is to have your female spayed, especially if she has had several successive false pregnancies. It's a favor to her psyche. Otherwise mate her, and accept the responsibilities.

For some unknown reason, certain dogs will attack any menstruating woman. Fortunately rare, this inexplicable vice is apparently incurable. This is a time when the only true cure is to put the animal away; or if you are really attached, kennel and keep him muzzled.

Traveling

Traveling has become a common occurrence for dogs. Knowledgeable people take their pets with them everywhere, and generally both pet and owner have a safe and happy trip. When traveling, never allow a dog to run free, lest he get lost in unfamiliar surroundings. This sounds logical, but it is too easy to accidentally open a door, or have the dog bolt in panic at an unusual situation.

Before taking a long trip with a dog, a visit to a veterinarian is always advisable. Besides, a health certificate is often required in traveling.

Camping

Camping out has become a big national pastime and the family dog often goes along. Dogs on a leash are usually the rule, but some areas do not allow pets at all. When a family goes camping, a normally well-adjusted dog can become quite excitable. Strange sounds, coupled with a new daily routine, can change a dog from a happy, friendly member of the family to a high-strung noisemaker. Your pet should behave with decorum, even in the wilderness. In fact, national parks enforce strict regulations such as no barking. Families planning on taking the dog along on camping vacations should check in advance to find municipal or privately owned campgrounds that permit dogs, and make reservations where possible. The automobile clubs in various countries publish a guide listing which camps accept pets.

Hotels

A number of hotels and motels allow pets, but the only way to know the restrictions is by calling or writing in advance. When making your own reservations, ask about your pet. Some may admit small dogs and guide dogs only. Some have special rules such as dogs not being left alone in a room; limiting them to a short stay; walking them in a special area; requiring the owner to assume responsibility for any damage; or charging something extra.

Keep your pet from causing damage and disturbing other guests. Always keep him on a leash in public places; and don't take him into the dining room, lounge, or pool area where he can disturb others. Don't permit your dog to sleep on beds, chairs, or bedspreads, but always bring along canine bedding. Never leave a dog alone and uncrated in a room where the maid may open the door and accidentally permit him to escape. If he must be left alone in a room, place a "Do Not Disturb" sign on the door and inform the maid or front desk.

Travel Regulations

If you're traveling overseas, every country—even regions within a country—may have little quirks, so call the nearest government agency to check on the regulations. Additionally, be sure to check if there are any rules governing the return home of your pet. The SPCA and animal protection agencies usually have publications that give information about traveling needs. The consulate of the country to be visited or the health or agriculture department of the region to be visited are the most definite sources of information.

You could end up spending more time getting a dog's papers straightened out than you do your own. Before traveling, get a health certificate signed by your veterinarian indicating good health and registering recent rabies and other essential inoculations. Attach it securely to the crate if the dog is being shipped, or carry it with you. Be sure to keep all relevant papers concerning your dog as secure as those concerning yourself.

There are some places that you cannot take your pet, no matter how many certificates you can produce. Some (like Russia) will allow no dogs under any circumstances, while others require quarantine in a special kennel for periods ranging from three to nine months. There is no way of getting around these regulations, and ignorance is no excuse. The fear of rabies and other infectious diseases is so strong that the regulations are strictly enforced. If you try to circumvent them, your pet could be destroyed. When going abroad, make plans well ahead. There are some rare exceptions to regulations, such as performing animals or those there only for short layovers. Special conditions may also exist for guide dogs for the blind, but for this information, contact the association for the blind in your area.

Cars and Your Dog

Since cars are an integral part of life today, your dog should become acclimatized to using them. But problems often arise from your pet's early experiences with cars. Perhaps the first ride your dog took was to the veterinarian where he received an inoculation, so that he now associates the car with a giant needle. It could be that motion sickness overcomes your pet the moment he enters the car. Or the excitement of new sounds, sights, and sensations may result in downright rowdiness.

You shouldn't just take off on an extended car trip without first getting your pet used to riding in the car. You have to show your dog that a car means good things. To teach your pet car sense, start by taking him into the car and sitting quietly with him. Soothe him if necessary. Then take him out on short drives. First simply go out of the driveway or around the corner, and next just around the block.

Motion sickness or car sickness is most frequent in puppies, but all dogs can suffer from it. Often it only happens until they get used to the motion of the vehicle. If you are going on a long trip, counteract it by first taking your dog out on an empty stomach. Be sure the car is well ventilated. At mealtime, give your dog his normal food—don't change it drastically or feed any highly seasoned foods. Saucerfuls of water can be given en route when you stop for exercise breaks (glucose added to the water can postpone hunger pains). Watch your dog: When he becomes uneasy and restless or starts to drool, stop the car and walk him around. Then to further ensure against travel sickness, don't feed or water your pet for a few hours before going out.

Some dogs only have to stand and look at a car several feet away for the saliva to start running down each side of his mouth. Such car sickness is usually due to nerves. Sometimes psychological car sickness can be cured if your dog is permitted to sit quietly in a motionless car. Associating something pleasant with the car—such as feeding him tidbits in a motionless car—can be helpful. He should be given plenty of air while riding, and should be allowed to sit up where he can see what is going on.

In some cases of persistent car sickness, your veterinarian may be able to prescribe something, but it is best to teach your pet to ride without any aids. If you must use medication, give it only until he gets used to riding. If you continue giving it, your pet will need larger and larger doses to do the same job. In some cases, static electricity in the car is the culprit in upsetting your dog's system. If you suspect this, try fastening a short chain or a special static guard to the car so that three or four inches drag on the road, grounding out static charges.

Don't let your dog jump around in the car. Hopping madly about is an invitation to trouble. He should sit or lie quietly and not annoy anyone, especially not the driver. Providing a blanket on the seat may make it more comfortable and give traction to your pet's feet so he doesn't need to regain his balance every time you hit a bump or turn a corner—and will keep the seat clean.

Quiet, firm handling will teach a dog what he can and cannot do. Don't allow him to be unruly, and make him behave properly from the outset, even if you have to reprimand him with a slap. Since you can't always train your pet and drive at the same time, have someone else drive, or take along a passenger who will keep him in place until he learns.

A lap dog, no matter how cute and regardless of size, needs to be forbidden from the driver's lap, or he could get in the way and interfere with the driving. Keep pushing him off firmly every time he comes onto your lap. Don't let your dog hang his head out of the window. This encourages him to jump out; his eyes and nose may inflame; or he may be decapitated by a passing truck. If you must allow it because your dog adores it, let him do it in moderate doses and either keep the window rolled up halfway or have someone hold him in place.

Most dogs consider the inside of an automobile their private domain and will take stern measures to protect this area against toll-booth attendants and gasoline attendants. To forestall contact, some drivers keep their windows closed throughout the transaction. Communication may be a little tricky under these circumstances; therefore, warn your dog when approaching and slap him back. The dog's first attempt to bark or move forward should be greeted with a sharp rap across the nose, hard enough to make him draw back himself. If he repeats the act, rap again smartly. After one or two lessons, done properly, the dog can be kept under control.

Leaving dogs unattended in cars is inadvisable. If you must do so, park the car where you can watch it at all times. Make sure it is in a shady spot; it doesn't take long for a closed car to heat up like a furnace. Since dogs don't sweat as we do through pores in the skin over our entire body, but only through the tongue, pads of the feet, and certain other select spots, they are more subject to heat stroke. Uninsulated cars can be equally devastating on an animal, so don't leave your pet for long on a cold day. But don't put the heater on when leaving the car unattended or it may fill with deadly fumes. Leave the window open only an inch or so to allow air in, but not your pet out. And always be sure that the door is locked to prevent theft.

Do not ever try carrying a dog in an automobile trunk or your dog could freeze, roast, or suffocate. Never try to control your dog by keeping a leash and collar on him in the car, even if you are with him. The collar could get stuck and entangle your dog so as to injure or even strangle him. If you absolutely cannot control your dog, you may have to resort to confining him when he is in a car. Crating or caging your dog in a container or barring off the back of your station wagon is the best solution.

Carrier or Crate?

If you don't drive, your pet is likely to have to be confined. Whether you travel by air, rail, ship, or car, your dog can go with you. Teach him to accept the form of confinement to be used. This means getting your dog accustomed to being in a crate or carrier *before* traveling, so that he will not be traumatized when enclosed on the trip. Your pet must learn to feel totally secure in his crate so he will be comfortable and relaxed when going through new places and situations. The main ways of transporting dogs are on a leash or in a crate or carrier.

The carrier is for carrying smaller pets, and it is to be in sight at all times. It should be large enough to allow the animal to lie down, sit up, and turn around in comfort. It should not be so big, however, as to be impossible to carry. Make sure the carrier is a good sturdy case with an extra-strong handle, so that it won't fall apart when picked up. Some dogs like the new transparent plastic tops, while others prefer to be in a darkened atmosphere. Therefore, if you get one with an open top, be sure there is a way to cover it. But if you do cover it, make sure there is adequate ventilation so that your dog will be comfortable. If your dog is of the mini variety, you could even teach him to stay put in a small folding bag or tote bag and to remain quiet and unnoticed on trips. For the really large dog, a leash or a shipping crate will have to do.

The crate is of much sturdier construction than a carrier. It is for use when a larger animal is going to be handled as baggage for shipment, thus it requires special care in selection. It has to be safe even when being roughly handled and stored. In a baggage hold, things might be stored atop it or might fall or be stacked against the side of the crate. A translucent or transparent crate is not a good idea; neither is a wire cage, except for use in transporting a dog in your own car. If extremely sturdy, a cage can be covered with heavy-duty canvas or plywood.

The crate must have a leakproof bottom. Ventilation holes should be plentiful, and on *all* sides—if one side gets blocked, the dog could suffocate or develop heat stroke if all the sides do not have adequate vents. The size of the crate depends on the size of your pet: It should be large enough to let him stand, lie down, and sit, but not so large that he gets slammed around. A small dog might be thrown about more in an overly large cage, while he will fare much better in a cage that gives him just enough room to turn around. The sides of the crate will support him, and he won't be tossed around so severely.

Any animal who's unsure seeks a dark, safe corner. Be sure you give your pet that security. Special fiberglass shipping kennels are available at airlines and other transportation means. These come in customized sizes to suit your pet.

Before traveling, get your dog used to the crate or carrier, so that he won't be traumatized when enclosed within it on a trip. A week or so before shipment, encourage your pet to eat and sleep inside. First keep the door open, and then close it. This will give your pet the feeling that this is another part of his home, and he will travel in it with a feeling of security. Tranquilizers might be used, but very often (especially on long journeys) the effects of the drug wear off too soon. There's nothing worse than a groggy dog in a half-doped condition sloshing around in his own mess, unaware of where he has suddenly found himself.

To prepare your animal to travel in a crate, don't feed him for several hours before traveling; water should be withheld for an hour or two. Before the journey begins, take your pet for a run so that he can relieve himself and stretch his muscles.

If you're using a crate, clearly print your name and address and the dog's destination on the crate itself, as well as on an attached tag. Any instructions for attendants—including whether the dog bites—should also be clearly printed on the crate and on the attached tag, along with a copy of your pet's health certification.

A health certificate from your veterinarian, containing a statement that the dog has recently been immunized against rabies, is an essential document to accompany any traveling dog. Records of hepatitis and distemper inoculations are also recommended.

Attach a collar and leash securely to the outside of the crate so the dog can be readily removed and controlled whenever necessary. If the collar is to be on him, be sure it's one that can't get caught on anything. You need a dog-license tag and an I.D. on the collar. A more permanent means of identification—a number tattooed inside your dog's ear—should be considered if you travel frequently. A water dish may also be included so the attendant can give a little water on stops if it is to be a long trip. Put some newspapers down and add a familiar toy to give him a further sense of security.

A sudden change of diet can cause digestive upsets, so when traveling, take along a few packages of your dog's regular food. Well-known brands can usually be obtained en route, but take a small supply to be sure. For the first part of your trip, taking along water from home is a good precaution: In some dogs, a change of drinking water may cause temporary diarrhea. Many people take bottled water on short trips since they don't like to have to take chances; be as careful about your animal's drinking water as you would be about your own. Bring along your dog's bedding, a small kit filled with grooming and safety aids, and pans for food and water.

Railroads, Ships, and Airlines

Some railroads that still have the service allow dogs in private Pullman space. A few even allow dogs into coaches, providing they are in a carrier and make no disturbance. Most, however, stipulate that a dog must travel in the baggage car, and allow the owners to feed and attend them en route.

Some shipping lines will take a pet dog on a one-way trip only if accompanied by an owner. Others will take them as unaccompanied freight. Regardless, however, dogs are not allowed in staterooms or public rooms; you must visit them in the caged area.

Almost all airlines will accept dogs, but each has its own regulations; check directly with the airline of your choice. Some will let dogs accompany you in the cabin and be counted as excess baggage. Permission is needed in advance, however, so make arrangements early.

Some airlines have a courier service that can spare your dog considerable trauma. A courier ticket is given from the main desk so that you may accompany the dog's crate right to the gate and hand it to the courier. This enables you to oversee that he is carefully loaded; the dog can be picked up this way at the other end of the line, too. Inquire about the various airline regulations.

It used to be that airline travel for dogs in the baggage compartment was really horrible. Now there is some effort to make sure that any animals traveling in the baggage compartments are okay, but you still must check to see that the luggage compartment is pressurized and heated. Airlines try to help, but they can't control the baggage compartment once in flight, so the dog will be all alone while you are getting cocktails to quell your own fears about flying. The modifications made in today's compartments have cut down on drafts and some of the dangers of extreme cold at high altitudes. There is no air conditioning, however, and there can be problems during layovers when the compartment is no longer climate-controlled. Care and vigilance on your part is the best protection your pet can get. Flying is a very fast means of transportation, however, especially on a direct flight.

All animals have an internal biological clock, and it takes a while for them to reset it when traveling by plane. If your dog visits a different time zone, his behavior, sleep patterns, and body chemistry are out of tune with actual time. This stress can cause your pet to catch cold, get an upset stomach, and display other physical symptoms.

Boarding Your Dog

Some pets are rotten travelers and would far rather stay behind. The quarantine regulations of certain places may not admit your pet. And it is best not to take dogs to underdeveloped countries, since they have few services for small pets and the unsanitary conditions could harm them. If your dog is going to be in the way or interfere with your pleasure, make stay-at-home arrangements.

You can use the services of a kennel or a dog sitter. If you select carefully, either one can be a good choice. (Do not send an ill dog or female in heat to a kennel unless under very special conditions. An older dog is also far better off at home.) Ask friends with pets about good services they have received. Check the place out thoroughly to be sure it lives up to your expectations. Be sure a kennel is clean and well ventilated. The cages should not be crowded, and each dog should have his own separate quarters (unless from the same household). It should be bright and friendly. Adequate walking services or runs should be provided. Check before selecting, call well in advance for reservations, and once you find a good place, stick with it.

Do not leave your pet in a kennel too long, because an animal cooped up in a cage for a long time may become psychologically upset. When sending a dog to a kennel or sitter, remember to leave a slip of paper with your pet's name, what he usually eats, the amounts and time of feeding, his exercise periods, any particular foibles or quirks, plus any medical abnormalities.

To teach your pet to accept boarding, leave him for just a day or so on trial. Then leave him for a few days, then a week or so. The familiar surroundings will help your dog relax readily when left there. Leaving one blanket, or a toy for him so he won't be too lonely, can be helpful. But don't send a load of toys so your pet has no room for himself.

Ten

HEALTH, GROOMING, AND BREEDING

Veterinary Care

Every dog needs a veterinarian to follow his health care. To start off, stress in shipping can leave an animal susceptible to certain diseases. A puppy who looks playful can still be harboring a cold, severe gastrointestinal infection, or pneumonia. Thus a visit to a vet is one of the first things any animal should have. Humans rarely get worms from dogs; these parasites usually prefer to stay in the host rather than going to another species. The zoonosis diseases that are communicable from animal to man include certain types of mange and rabies. There are certain inoculations that every pet needs—he should be immunized against distemper, rabies, infectious hepatitis, and leptospirosis. The proper age and schedule for vaccinations should be determined by your veterinarian. Usually these need to be given at an early age, followed by regular boosters to keep up the protection.

Distemper, hepatitis, and leptospirosis immunization is usually given in a series of combination shots; and then rabies vaccination is given at six months of age. All dogs need this protection regardless of size, age, breed, and life-style.

Distemper, an inflammation of the brain, kills over half the animals infected. Infection comes through an airborne virus and it usually occurs in young dogs. Early signs are high fever, muscle twitching, watery discharge from the eyes and nose that turns to pus, dry and crusty nose, coughing, labored breathing, attempts to vomit, and diarrhea. Recovery from the disease gives permanent immunity, but as a result your pet may lack coordination and circle and drag his hindquarters, twitch certain parts of the body, or have fits. Newborn pups get immunity to distemper from colostrum—a thin watery fluid the mother secretes—which must be absorbed in the first day of life—but this protection only lasts from three to nine weeks, so they need the inoculation. It is important not to take your dog out until he has his shots.

Infectious canine hepatitis is marked by fever, enlarged

297

and congested eye and mouth membranes, no appetite, list-lessness, and abdominal pain. In early life a pup picks up the virus from feces and saliva of an infected dog, and later in the urine. A preventive vaccination is best.

Leptospirosis is shown by fever, abdominal pain, black and/or tarry diarrhea, and congested oral and eye membranes. It causes kidney and liver disfunction.

Rabies, a virus that attacks the central nervous system and can affect all warm-blooded animals, has horrible symptoms. It is passed on through a bite, scratch, or abrasion by an infection in saliva. Usually it is transmitted in the form of a bite. It shows itself in changes in temperament, first by extreme affection or seeking seclusion, and then in viciousness, hyperexcitability, and inability to eat. Fear of water, glassy stare, fear of light, and eating of unusual objects are also seen.

Dog bites are therefore a cause for concern as a source of infection. Rabies is always fatal if not cared for promptly. Fortunately, there is time between the bite and the beginning of the disease, so preventive measures can be taken. Any dog bite should be examined by a physician and the incident reported to your health department. Do not destroy the dog, because he must be examined before it can be decided whether the animal is rabid or not.

Deviations from normal habit patterns tell you if anything is wrong with your pet. In general, if your pet refuses to eat food for any extended period of time; if he has sudden continued diarrhea or vomiting; if he eats a lot, seems hungry all the time, but loses weight; consult your veterinarian. A dog's temperature is usually 101.5°; anything higher is sometimes the first sign of trouble. To take your pet's temperature, use a rectal thermometer. Puppies may have a higher temperature by a degree or so—102° to 103° is safe. Once over 103° it is time to consult your veterinarian immediately; the same is true for temperatures less than 101°.

Keep the vet's telephone number handy for emergencies, and take your dog in for regular checkups and inoculations. Always take your dog to the same doctor so he can get to know your dog just as your own doctor knows you. Since feces can indicate the health of your pet, have a stool sample examined yearly. Microscopic examination is needed to check for worms; then the proper medications can be prescribed.

Behavior in the Vet's Office

Every dog will at some point have to go to a veterinarian's office. In fact, your dog should really go at least once a year. Anywhere near a vet's office, unfortunately, most dogs behave abominably. One look at a veterinarian's waiting room shows the average reaction of animals to the place: cringing in the owners' arms, hiding and trying to blend into the walls, nervously panting and drooling, screaming from the inside of a carrier. The problem is that dogs pick up all the nervous vibes from you, those owners, and from other animals, so they get scared.

To counteract your pet's fears when going to the office, take along a couple of dog biscuit treats or other tidbits, and give your dog one before and one after. This way your dog may come to associate the place with treats rather than with the jab of a hypodermic needle. But no matter what, you must be firm and insist that regardless of the emotional reaction, your dog has to tolerate discomfort. No veterinarian will treat a dog that bites, and a pet that screams and squirms cannot be examined properly. If your pet misbehaves, reprimand him firmly. The basic obedience command of stand for inspection is a big step in teaching your pet to behave in a civilized way. Through this, he'll learn to stand still while being examined. If your nervousness and the nervous behavior of the other animal patients and their owners does upset your pet, do not overcomfort your pet to calm him, or that may encourage even more hysterical behavior. Just act as normally as possible; try to get your pet to do likewise.

Grooming

A dog's skin is an organ of his body, forming a protective layer over the bones, muscles, and internal organs.

The skin has few pain receptors and is sparsely supplied with blood vessels. (However, certain unprotected structures such as the ears have an increased blood supply.) Dogs don't get welts when bruised, since the skin is affixed very loosely to the flesh and muscles beneath it. This way, the epidermis can slide beneath a blow, affording greater protection from injury.

The skin also contains a number of glands: All dogs, whether male or female, have five pairs of mammary glands. Dogs don't have too many sweat glands, and those few they do have are situated around the pads of the feet, around the anus, and in the tongue. The anal glands, situated in sacs on either side of the anus, discharge a rancid, long-lasting liquid in situations of extreme terror or excitement, and are analogous to the scent glands of skunks. These can be a nuisance to the dog himself, however, because they can easily become blocked, causing the dog pain and necessitating treatment.

Near the anal glands is the now-useless, atrophied tail gland whose original secretions were used as a marking tool, and which on some breeds is still marked by a triangle or stripe one-third way down the tail.

Hair is basically determined by heredity, and can adjust to a new environment by increasing in density, but not in length. Certain emotional states like fear and anger activate tiny muscles in the skin that lift the hairs on a dog's back until they stand on end—a reflex that is the equivalent of human goose-flesh. A dog's skin is subject to many of the same diseases and injuries as human skin. In dogs, it does, however, have a protective coating of hair all over it—except for the hairless breeds, and even these need care. Both the skin and coat need to be cared for properly because of their constant exposure to the perils of everyday life.

Though they can occur in any dog, skin irritations such as eczema and parasites such as fleas and ticks are most common in dogs that are unkempt and subject to poor hygiene. Any unusual skin condition requires veterinary care, but prevention is usually possible with a small amount of attention from you. Grooming isn't a fancy or difficult business. It's just a matter of helping your pet keep clean. When you groom your pet dog, you're not pampering him; you are protecting his health and well-being.

Cosmetic grooming consists of basically unessential surgical processes that people have performed on their pets for a whim or to fit arbitrary standards that have been set up for certain breeds. Docking—the cutting of tails—is said to improve the appearance of certain breeds. Some dogs are born with a normally short appendage, others are not. Cropping consists of cutting off a portion of the ear flap so that the ear stands up. These adjustments are usually done so that a dog will adhere to the standards of his breed.

Professional grooming is essential for some dogs. Different styles of clipping for the various breeds are very fashionable. For some dogs going to the beauty parlor for grooming is a necessity. If this is the case with your dog, select your groomer carefully. Get recommendations from satisfied friends. You want to make sure good treatment and no drugs are used. Check the facilities and equipment for cleanliness. Carelessness can cause clipper burns which need to be treated with Vaseline or calamine lotion to soothe.

You can clip your pet yourself, but be careful. Many persons have hurt their dogs through incompetence. If you must do it yourself, get good clippers and do not hold them too close to the animal. Long-haired dogs, if trimmed, need special thinning scissors with a blade on one side and a comb on the other that thin out the hair. Wire-haired dogs like Airedales and their smaller cousins need to be plucked, not clipped; this requires a special technique that can be learned only by watching.

Bathing

A New York couple has been granted a patent for a dog-washing machine. However, bathing is not something that needs to be done too often. In fact, too-frequent bathing may be harmful because it removes the natural oils and encourages a variety of skin problems. Three or four baths a year are probably more than sufficient, depending on the kind of life your pet lives. Frequent brushing is more important. Without veterinary advice, don't bathe puppies, bitches more than four weeks pregnant, ill animals, or dogs with any skin complaint. However, an occasional bathing can aid in maintaining good health and cleanliness.

Comb and brush your dog well before bathing. The temperature of the water should be warm but not hot. Fill the basin or tub so it reaches halfway up the dog's legs. Pour the water over the dog gently or use a hand shower in a tub, or even soak him under a well-regulated faucet. Use a mild soap or shampoo you would use yourself, unless your veterinarian recommends a disinfectant such as a flea bath.

Soap from the dog's rear forward, and be careful about the eyes and ears. When done, rinse thoroughly to remove all the soap from the coat. If you do not, it will appear dull and sticky rather than shiny and glossy as it should. Dry thoroughly with a rough towel in a warm place without drafts, and keep the dog indoors for several hours.

A dry shampoo is fine for in between major baths or in an emergency. However, the best results are achieved on short-haired dogs; it is less successful on long-haired ones. Use any inert powder or bran. Rub it in, leave it for a short while, and then brush it out. A rubdown with a damp towel is also helpful between baths.

Once you take him outside after a bath, be sure to put him on a leash, because the first thing he will probably do is to try to roll in the first filth he finds. A washed dog is often socially ostracized from his canine pals until he smells like his old self again.

Paint on the coat requires special treatment. Try to wipe off as much as you can with a dry cloth. Gin applied first and then soap and water might help get some off. If your pet is really covered, get him to a veterinarian. If a dog's coat is covered with some obnoxious substance, bathing is needed. Covering the affected parts with tomato juice for about fifteen minutes will often neutralize the odor until you get around to the bath. Tomato juice is so good it will even neutralize the odor of a skunk.

Brushing

Brushing is the most usual form of grooming. It keeps the coat in good condition and stimulates the skin. Even short-haired dogs need regular brushing, and for long-haired breeds whose coats can mat and tangle, it is essential. All dogs shed, and one way to cut down on this is to brush your pet regularly.

Since all dogs require brushing at one point or another, it is best to get your dog used to it early. Some dogs have such bad dispositions they will not permit even their owners to comb and brush them. The way to prevent this attitude is to start the training early. Place your pet on a table or sit on the floor with him and force him to accept the grooming. Be firm and insist. If your pet is hesitant, one person should hold him while the other does the work. Or you can set up a special grooming table the way professionals do. Simply tie your dog's lead to something above his head so that he is forced to stay in a standing position. Your dog will struggle for only a short while if you insist. Once he realizes he is not getting his own way, he will quiet down and learn to accept the brush.

For short-haired breeds, you need a stiff brush with short bristles and a hound glove or chamois cloth. Additionally, you need a pair of special dull-pointed grooming scissors. A short-haired dog needs to be brushed once a week. Brush him first, then wipe him down with the hound glove or chamois cloth to add luster and give the coat a flat lie. Take the scissors and trim out excess hair and dirt from between the pads of the feet. Be sure to brush gently, or you may pull out too many live hairs with the dead ones. It is not advisable to brush against the grain or lie of the hair (except as a means to fluff up hair on certain long-haired breeds after they are thoroughly groomed). Use a cloth if your dog objects to a brush over the face.

Long-haired breeds need a stiff brush, with the bristle depth dependent upon the length of the hair, plus a steel comb with rounded teeth. Grooming for long-haired dogs needs to be done two or three times a week. First try to remove the mats by hand, and if it is impossible, cut them out. Then take the brush and brush thoroughly, being sure to penetrate to the undercoat. After this, comb out the coat to make it fluffy.

There should be a regular time and place for grooming if possible. Do it in good light and spread out newspaper to catch debris. Small- to medium-sized dogs do well when held on a table, and doing it at the right height will help avoid strain on you.

Brushing can also help cut down on dandruff caused by the scruff or scales formed by dead skin. Increasing the fat in the diet or adding fatty acids can also help eliminate these conditions. However, an excess of dandruff should be checked out with a veterinarian to be sure there is no underlying medical cause. If you let your dog's hair get too gnarled, nits and lice may live there, and your pet's skin could get covered with irritations you can't see or feel. While brushing your pet, be sure to check on his skin condition, keeping an eye out for skin diseases and parasites.

Removal of Parasites

Fleas, ticks, and other parasites such as lice are not uncommon on dogs. Keeping the pet properly groomed will help prevent them. Many people put flea collars on their dogs, but these have to be used with care because some can cause irritation due to their strength. They can be especially toxic when wet. Before using, leave out for a day or so to allow some of the potency to wear off.

Once fleas or other parasites are on your pet, you may have to work hard to remove them. Removal of ticks is important to you and your dog since they carry diseases which affect both humans and animals. The safest way to remove them is to use tweezers. Do not crush ticks with your fingers after you remove them because this may spread germs to you; burn them with a match to destroy them.

If infestation of fleas is severe, get in touch with a veterinarian. Otherwise try a nontoxic disinfectant to kill them when your dog is bathed. Powder is another solution, but in shaking it on you must keep it out of your pet's eyes and nose. Take a veterinarian's advice on the type to use. Just keep in mind that reinfestation is easy from the dog's bedding or even your house. So clean the sleeping area thoroughly, and if necessary, fumigate the house. Keep it up until everything is clean.

One of the most common complaints people have about their pets is that they smell. The location of the odor indicates the various grooming problems and necessities. If it is from the front end, it could be teeth tartar, his diet, or even kidney trouble causing the bad breath. It could also be a dirty or infected ear.

Ears

Ears are another grooming chore. Here, however, some dogs require more attention than others. The more hair in the canal, the more likely it is to become infected. Droopy ears develop problems because there is no air circulation and dirt becomes trapped. The ear flap and external ear canal area are extremely important because they dampen out noises and provide protection for the delicate middle and inner ears which are the centers of balance and hearing. The flap is vulnerable to cuts and bites, while the canal is readily accessible to germs and parasites such as fleas, ticks, and mites. A dog's balance is controlled in part by the semicircular canals of the ear. Though this system is not terribly refined, ear problems can have a devastating effect on a dog's sense of balance.

The normal ear canal is pinkish, smooth, and slightly moist or waxy. Never probe the ear itself, but clean the outer ear carefully. Put cotton around your finger, moisten with mineral oil or alcohol, and gently wipe out the areas that you can see easily and get at directly. Since hair can block the canal or trap bits of dirt to cause irritation and infection, pluck these hairs out once a month by pulling what you can grasp between the thumb and forefinger. Do not cut them. If you can't do it, let a good groomer or veterinarian do it for you. A few drops of olive oil in the ear canal will wash the dirt or debris up to the outer flaps where you can easily wipe it away. Don't dig, just let the oil do its work. You can't see the canal, so you might actually push something into it or hurt it in some way.

If this remedy doesn't clear the problem, seek professional advice. Symptoms of problems involve tilting or shaking of the head, pawing and scratching at the ears, discharge and matted hair round the ear, odor about the ear, reddened flap, tenderness to the touch, refusal to eat, and whimpering. Check for cuts, bruises, or lumps around the ear: Mites, lice, or even a single flea can cause a dog to scratch his ear until he draws blood. If not treated, they might cause major problems in the middle and inner ears. Prevention is really a matter of grooming. However, there are some ears that have to be operated on to rework the canals to prevent constant problems.

Eyes

Eyes also need attention to be sure they are okay. Excess tearing is the most common problem, especially with long-haired dogs. Conjunctivitis or red, inflamed eyes are a product of today's pollution, and some dogs seem to have it constantly. Less often dogs get problems with eye injuries; any kind of sores or discharge requires prompt attention. Dogs with protruding eyes have the highest rate of eye diseases.

Check for anything unusual about the eyes: excess tearing, irritation, or foreign objects in the eyes. Wash them out with a mild boric acid solution. Do this by moistening a sterile cotton pad and squeezing it gently into the corner of your pet's eye while holding his head up. Never use soap and water near your pet's eyes; it hurts and stings him just as it would you. If they do accidentally become irritated by soap, sprays, or any other noxious substance, squeeze warm water into them from a cotton ball to wash it out. Since hair over the eyes can affect vision and cause irritations, trim regularly unless needed for show.

Most excessive tearing is a hereditary characteristic of certain breeds. It can streak the hair from the corner of the eyes and darken it. The condition does not bother the animals, but you can help clean it by washing the area with boric acid solution and removing the sleepiness from the corner of the eye every morning. A veterinarian can improve your animal's tear-drainage system by removing the gland of the third eyelid. It is a delicate operation, but relatively simple with a fast recovery—and it works. The third eyelid helps keep the eye moist and serves as protection. An eyelid defect may be the cause of the tearing problem; it could also be a misplaced lash or hair rubbing against the eye, an allergy or something in the eye, an infection, or a blockage in the tear duct. Therefore, constant tearing warrants a veterinarian's look.

Nails

Dogs normally have five nails on each front paw, and four on the hind paws. The extras are dewclaws, which grow above the foot on the inside of the leg and are vestigial digits or nails of a once-useful toe. Certain dogs even have double dewclaws, and some breeds have them on the hind feet as well. They serve no purpose now, and often have to be surgically removed from active dogs lest they get snagged and cause an injury.

Nails grow in rapidly, and since dogs no longer wear them down by running around on rugged terrain, you have to keep the nails in shape. If you don't take care of the nails, they are apt to catch and break off, because they become brittle as they grow longer. This causes pain and often medical problems. Nails can even grow in a circle and thus into the foot pad. Too-long nails force a dog to walk flat-footed and splay-toed. And the pounding of long nails against the ground as he walks can be annoying at best and painful to your pet. Usually the nails need clipping or filing once a month.

Get yourself a pair of dog nail clippers and if necessary, a strong nail file. In clipping, be sure to avoid the quick, which is that red line running through the center of the nail. It is the part of the nail containing blood and nerves, corresponding to the dark pink part of your fingernail. A cut or injury to it causes profuse bleeding and pain. On dogs with clear or white nails it is easy to see, but on black-nailed animals, you can only guess. Have someone shine a good light behind the nails so you don't cut into the quick. The thing to do is to trim almost to the quick line, wait a few days, and then trim again. This will make the quick recede.

Some people even advocate cutting right into the quick to forcibly shorten it. If the quick is ever cut—deliberately or accidentally—the bleeding is profuse and hard to stop. The best first aid is to take a bar of soap and press it right into the nail.

For jagged nails or ones that are still not quite right even after clipping, use your file. When filing, however, draw it only in one direction from the top of the nail downward in a round stroke to the end of the nail or underneath. While clipping your pet's nails, examine the feet for cuts or infections, and remove tar or other substances with the appropriate cleanser and then wash it off thoroughly with warm water.

Teeth

People are often under the impression that a dog's teeth take care of themselves, and that dogs with bad teeth are unusual. This is wrong. Dogs are susceptible to gum disease and rotting teeth just like humans.

Since dogs must use all four legs for locomotion, they use their jaws to hold and carry objects. However, a dog's jaw has so adapted that it is relatively poor at manipulation. Dogs don't even chew their food that much; they just tear it into pieces small enough to swallow. Therefore, a dog's teeth are constructed for killing prey and tearing it apart. The front teeth are for piercing, the back for cutting flesh.

Once a pup loses his temporary teeth, they are replaced by a single set of forty-two permanent teeth that are normally completely grown in by the end of the seventh month; most are in by the fifth. Some toy breeds keep their puppy teeth after their permanent teeth erupt; if this happens, they should be removed by a veterinarian to prevent premature loss or a faulty bite. Dogs also develop cavities, and perhaps more importantly, form potentially harmful and unsightly tartar encrustations which—along with entrapped food particles—can cause bacterial infection. In turn this can lead to receding gums, loosening and possible loss of otherwise good teeth, and/or foul-smelling breath. The effects of the infection associated with tartar on teeth may stay localized in the gums, but more often it gets into the bloodstream. If this happens, the constant low-grade infection can become a cause of certain heart and kidney diseases. Dental disease can also cause abscesses and sinusitis in dogs, resulting in watery eyes and swelling of the face. Crowded teeth can cause teeth and gum problems, and these dogs should be checked regularly. Refusal of food, drooling, grinding teeth, pawing and rubbing at the mouth are all indications of gum infections or dental disease.

Check to see that your dog's teeth are not becoming covered with tartar deposits. Over a period of months or years, accumulations on and around the teeth can become hard, like cement. Being sure to avoid cutting the gums, scrape it off, using an orange stick used for manicuring. Or gently lift off the tartar with your fingernails. If there is an excess, a veterinarian should take care of it.

You can prevent the problem of heavy tartar formation if you clean your animal's teeth every two or three days. (Otherwise you need a vet to clean them once every six months.) To clean them yourself, use a special dog's toothbrush or a child's toothbrush and baking soda. A dog doesn't need bones to keep his teeth clean; in fact, he might even break teeth on them. Dogs do enjoy chewing, however, so give your pet rawhide bones.

Try to get your dog used to the activities he will have to accept when living with you. If you want to brush your dog's teeth or groom him, get him used to accepting it. For example, take a toothbrush and put it in the pup's mouth, or brush the dog's coat soothingly. Start from the first day to get your dog used to as much as possible of everything he is going to be involved in.

Anal Glands

An often-neglected hygiene problem is caring for the dog's anal glands. Perhaps the reason for this is because even the subject is distasteful to most people. It is, however, a necessary part of your dog's grooming. When brushing and doing other normal grooming, look under the dog's tail to see that there aren't any soiled mats of hair or a swelling around the anus.

The anal glands are the two small glands that are inside the rectum vent. These will sometimes become enlarged, and in order to prevent infection and abscesses from forming they have to be emptied. Indications of the need are the dog's rubbing or scooting along the floor, difficult defecation, or excessive licking. To empty these glands take the dog to a veterinarian or do it yourself. Hold your dog's tail in one hand, and take a couple of tissues or paper towels in the other. Using an upward and outward motion, apply gentle pressure with the thumb and middle finger to the glands located at four and eight o'clock. If you do it in the bathtub or sink, it is less disagreeable because the fluid excrement with its offensive odor can be washed quickly away. With older dogs this problem becomes more pronounced and thus needs increased care. It only takes a few minutes to do and can save you and your pet discomfort and aggravation.

Breeding: Pro and Con

Dogs can produce from one to twelve pups once or twice a year. It's true that having puppies can be a wonderful occasion for the entire family. It's equally true that it can be a nightmare if you can't personally keep and rear the offspring, or can't find acceptable homes for them. There is an over-abundance of dogs around now, and more strays are being produced daily. Too many people with good intentions assume they will have no trouble finding homes for their pups. They are usually wrong, and are seldom willing to take on the same responsibilities they would if planning to adopt the same number of dogs that you anticipate in a litter. Since there should only be as many pets as there are good owners and homes, think carefully before breeding your dog.

There are so many misconceptions about breeding. Some owners think that a male dog will be oversexed if he's never been bred, and believe breeding the pet will stop the problem. When the dog is bred he actually becomes more aware of females than before. Another reason given for breeding is that it is good business. However, if you think you can make money by raising pups from a single purebred bitch, don't plan to retire on the proceeds.

The best way to prevent problems is to have your female spayed, or be sure to keep her isolated during her heat cycle. If your female does accidentally mate, hormone injections within a couple of days are usually successful in terminating an unwanted pregnancy. If an animal is in good health, however, spaying is the preferred way of ending pregnancy.

Spaying and Castration

Neutering a pet means either spaying a female or castrating a male. Spaying is perhaps the most frequent operation performed on dogs. Thus *spay* is a term used to describe the operation of removing the ovaries from the female animal. Usually the uterus and two horns are removed at the same time. The operation is difficult, but not so hazardous as to make one hesitate. Spaying prevents the heat cycle, eliminates the nuisance of a male's attentions while she is in heat, and prevents pregnancy. It also prevents diseases of the uterus, ends false pregnancies, reduces chances of developing breast tumors, and stops the pet population explosion through birth control.

Some veterinarians recommend you have your dog spayed before the first heat, which occurs at six to seven months. Others recommend that the dog wait for one heat to make sure all develops properly. Studies show that spaying before the first heat (estrus) prevents the dog from developing any mixture of mammary tumors later in life. Anywhere from five to seven months, just prior to the first heat, is a good time, but not during the actual heat. It is an operation requiring general anesthesia, and the animal stays in the hospital twenty-four to forty-eight hours. Spaying should never be done while the female is in heat, or hemorrhaging can occur during surgery.

A vasectomy is a method of sterilizing where the vas deferens or sperm-carrying tube is tied and severed. This is desirable for those people who object to the visibility factor of the operation on their male pets. However, while a vasectomized male might stop breeding, it doesn't help his roaming or sex drives and activities. Castration stops the male sex hormone, testosterone, by removal of the testicles. If removed before they begin to produce testosterone, prior to five months of age, the chances of arresting the appearance of hormone-related aggressiveness are greater than waiting until full sexual maturity is reached. Once triggered, some aggressive habits become permanent, so the most effective castration is done at around three months. Castration of a dog can be difficult because the sac containing the testicles is lined profusely with blood vessels that seem to bleed forever. Thus the surgery requires skill and care.

For advice about neutering your pet, the person to consult is your veterinarian. Personality changes from spaying and castration are minimal except for becoming friendlier homebodies. Once back from the hospital, your pet's temperament and behavior will soon return to normal.

Which Mate for Your Dog?

If you insist on breeding your pet, whether for pleasure or profit, go about it properly and breed only superior dogs. Your pet should live up to certain expectations, as should your pet's prospective mate. To avoid inferior pups, select two dogs whose bloodlines favor each other. Seeking the advice of someone familiar with breeding will enable you to learn what points to look for and what faults to overcome in your particular breed.

Eliminate dogs that display such traits as viciousness or overtimidity. Check out all the possibilities of congenital defects. Have a veterinarian X-ray the hips of larger dogs to make sure everything is fine. Try to make sure there are no hereditary problems with hips, eyes, elbows, testicles, and overshot or undershot jaws. All the things you should look for when selecting a healthy puppy apply here. Even if there is the slightest suggestion that the undesirable trait in question is inherited, seriously consider not breeding.

Never breed a very small female dog. A show bitch is not always the same as a healthy, big brood bitch. With smallish dogs, in fact, the male should be smaller than the female to ensure the bitch's safety. Be certain your female is in good shape. Have your veterinarian be sure she has had all her inoculations. He should do a fecal examination and she should be wormed thoroughly. Do not breed a run-down or over-weight bitch; it will only cause complications.

If you want a good mate for your female, you will usually pay a stud fee, to be arranged between you and the owner of the dog. In lieu of a fee, you may agree to give up the pick of the litter, but you—the owner of the dam—own the pups. If no pups result from the mating the fee is usually returnable, or you may try again during the next heat. You probably won't pay anything for a friend's dog, but will have to take potluck on pedigree and quality. There is never a guarantee, but there are so many unwanted pups that it's best to pay a stud fee in the long run to be sure you are going to have at least a good shot at special, desirable ones.

The Mating

Female dogs go into heat twice a year, though in some colder climates dogs have only one cycle per year. The first heat or estrus cycle usually occurs anywhere from between six to twelve months of age, though some bitches do not come into heat until a year and a half.

The cycle lasts for about three weeks and is not hard to recognize. Beforehand, the vulva—the external sexual organ below the female's tail—becomes swollen, and there will be a white discharge. There then follow three distinct phases, each lasting about a week. In the first, a blood-tinged discharge appears, ranging from light pink to dark red. After this, another week passes before a female will accept a mate and show willingness by wagging her tail. For a few days, varying from five to twelve, the female will be willing to be mated; then the swelling slowly decreases and everything returns to normal.

A female should not be mated until her second or third heat, when her internal organs have completely developed; but she should be bred at least once before she is five years old. If too old or too young when first bred, your pet may have complications in whelping. Do not breed her more than two out of every three periods. However, she can continue to have pups as long as she comes into heat and remains in good health.

A male may breed when less than a year old. He should not be bred too frequently, but he should be able to continue to mate until a ripe old age. The mating should take place a certain number of days after the first show of color, usually just after the white vaginal discharge has stopped and the bleeding starts. And more than one service, though not essential, is smart—on the tenth and twelfth or the eleventh and thirteenth days of the cycle. Some even recommend three matings, on the ninth, eleventh, and thirteenth days. Mate her once on each day, and let her rest in between.

It is always best to have the male visit the female's environment. It is sometimes suggested that the female should be taken to the male, since he'll feel more secure on his home ground, but this is advisable only if the dog is kept outdoors. If mated in his own turf, a male will continue to smell the female after she has gone and will urinate over her scent to "claim" her. If you are going to take your male dog to a strange female's house, bring him a couple of times before the mating to accustom him to the place.

Most dogs will mate instinctively the first time in the right situation. With some dogs there is no foreplay whatsoever. Others go through a whole ritual—running with each other, sniffing and licking each other's anal and genital areas, and engaging in some friendly play-wrestling. When ready, the female will present and display herself to a male; when she is fully receptive, she will move her tail to one side. When the male mounts and clasps her around the sides, she stands motionless. With the male's ejaculation, the pair becomes "tied" by the expansion of the end of the male's penis and the constriction of the vulva around it. Never attempt to pull the animals apart; it can cause physical injury to either or both. This locking together of the two dogs may last for fifteen minutes or longer. Conception can occur without this happening, but it prevents semen leakage, thus increasing the chance of a fertile mating.

When they first become tied, clear sperm-free fluid which is slightly alkaline is released to ensure the optimum alkaline environment sperm require. Once the passage has been prepared, the fluid becomes filled with sperm, making it slightly milky. Millions of sperm are discharged at each service, but since only one can be accepted by each egg, the number of pups depends on how many ova a female releases.

The enlarged bulbar end of the penis will gradually reduce, and the animals will separate. The best help you can give is to leave them alone. If either or both are nervous, prevent panic and stop them from hurting each other by some gentle, soothing talk.

Some monogamous female dogs will accept only one specific male of their choice and may violently refuse others. This seems to be a trait inherited from the wild, since many canines show this tendency. In general, however, females are relatively indiscriminate in their willingness to accept mates. Failure to mate is usually due to nervous bitches who refuse all males for psychological reasons. Overattachment to humans can cause a bitch to refuse to mate. Dogs raised in isolation also often have problems with their sexual behavior. Males may refuse to breed if fearful or in a strange place. Some bitches, especially young ones, are shy and nervous when approached by a prospective sire. Immaturity can also cause problems, but may resolve itself after a short while.

Familiarity with the prospective partner often prevents pairs from mating, due to the social structure within the male and female hierarchies. Social dominance influences sexual behavior to the extent that a dominant female may not allow a subordinate male to breed her, while a dominant male may be unable to breed with a fearful female who rolls over submissively. And merely by his presence, a dominant male dog may inhibit socially inferior males from copulating. Isolation is often the way to try to eliminate some of the problems.

Physiological problems can also lead to failure in mating—even if copulation actually occurs. Some dogs are infertile, and there are impotent males. There are many reasons for this; some are hereditary and others result from physical illnesses. A hormone deficiency, malnutrition, excess weight, or the effect of an infection can all result in infertility or smaller litters. Some animals need to be bred in natural surroundings; other times they are better away from home.

If assistance is required, make sure both dogs know you, or you may get bitten out of fear or frighten the dogs even more. Usually it is best to leave the dogs to their own devices unless they're so emotionally upset as to become vicious. If the situation looks impossible, separate them and try another mate or skip it until the next heat.

Artificial insemination can be the answer to many problems; but when used in breeding, registry is accepted only under special conditions—that is, if you tell anyone. This procedure needs to be done by a veterinarian under sterile conditions. The male is made to ejaculate into an artificial rubber vagina with a test tube at the end. The semen can then be introduced immediately in its undiluted form into the female; otherwise, it is diluted and refrigerated or deep-frozen for later use.

After the Mating

The best time to diagnose pregnancy is three to three and a half weeks after breeding. At this stage, the veterinarian can feel pups as tiny lumps or bumps. Before or after this, it is more difficult. If the bitch carries the pups high in the back of her ribs, it may be hard to tell if she is pregnant or not.

The nipples usually show the first change. They will become red and slightly puffy, though they will not fill out until the seventh or eighth week. The abdomen itself may not swell until the fifth or sixth week.

Immediately after mating, when there is even a possibility of pregnancy, you should follow certain procedures to be sure all will turn out well. The normal gestation period runs from fifty-eight to sixty-five days, with sixty-two to sixty-three days being the average. During this time your pet's life-style should not change drastically. She needs to receive plenty of good exercise, but as she gets heavier with the pups, she won't want to do as much and so must take short, frequent walks.

Plan the expectant mother's nutrition with a little care and common sense. She needs to eat enough food to provide ample nourishment for unborn pups, and also to maintain her own health. Do not let her get foolishly fat, but a lean and languid look is not wanted either. For the first four or five weeks of her pregnancy, there is no need to change her normal meal consumption. During the sixth week her food consumption should be about sixty percent greater than normal. Add this additional amount gradually, starting at about the fifth week. If you increase it too early, the excessive weight can interfere with the normal delivery of pups. During very late pregnancy you must give four, five, or even six smaller meals daily because she won't have room for a single large meal. And during the last week, make the food on the soft side. The addition of supplementary vitamins can ensure that proper nutritional needs are met.

During pregnancy, schedule periodic checkups with the veterinarian to be sure everything is fine. Your bitch should definitely go in for a five- to six-week checkup. Find out where your veterinarian will be at the expected time of whelping. Perhaps if the dog is small, or if this is her first pregnancy, or a probable difficult pregnancy, you should ask your veterinarian to assist the delivery.

Toward the end of the gestation period, set up a place for your pet to have her pups, and prepare your house for the new arrivals' stay—for the next eight weeks or so. (If you don't prepare an area, your dog will begin to select her own.) Give your pet plenty of time to get used to her whelping quarters, and make sure they are in an area she'll accept.

Since a dog will naturally defend her offspring against strangers, be sure the birthplace is away from traffic in your home. Make sure it is in a secluded, warm, safe, dark, and quiet place. There should be enough room so your dog can stretch out comfortably in any direction. For a small dog, prepare a wooden or cardboard box with high sides and an old blanket for a cover. For a larger dog, set aside an enclosed area. Put thick newspaper in the bottom so it can be cleaned easily. The newborn pups have to be ensured of freedom from noise, excitement, and handling. At least for the first few days they should be protected from outward disturbances.

The Birth

To prepare your dog for birth, wash her udder to remove any parasite eggs from the skin and orifices of the nipples. Clip excess hair around the nipples. Be sure the birth area and all equipment is sanitized, but not overly chemicalized so as to smell or create fumes.

You can tell when it is time for birth, not only by counting the number of days that have elapsed since the mating, but also by your pet's actions. The female will wander restlessly around and pant nervously. Her temperature will drop to as low as 97°. When she's about to deliver, your dog may reject her meals or regurgitate her food. When this happens, you can be pretty certain the pups will arrive within twenty-four hours. There may be a mucous discharge.

When the actual delivery begins, be sure your pet isn't distracted by everyone watching her, or you may stop labor and bring on complications. During this time, your pet is better off taking care of things herself. Just hang around to make sure there are no complications requiring your or a veterinarian's help, but be very discreet about it. Disturb her as little as possible.

Labor pains and straining start about an hour or so before the actual whelping, which may last for only a half hour or up to six to eight hours. One puppy may even arrive twenty-four hours later. The rate of expulsion is generally irregular. The number of pups depends on many factors ranging from your dog's size and specific breed to individual characteristics such as health and the number of times she's been bred.

The water bag breaks and lubricates the birth canal just before the first pup comes through. Generally the puppies are born headfirst and abdomen down. Each is enclosed in its own individual placenta sac. This placenta is an organ that grows in the uterus of the mother and surrounds and protects the young. In delivery, one placenta or afterbirth is expelled for each pup. The mother then opens the sac and chews the umbilical cord where the placenta or afterbirth is attached to the pup. It is normal for her to eat the placenta, then clean and stimulate the newborn pups.

If a pup's rear comes first, it is not abnormal and is usually uncomplicated. And sometimes there is a dry birth when the pup is not covered with a placenta, which the mother passes separately.

If all seems to be going well, avoid any kind of handling or interference. A bitch delivering is best left alone. The slightest interference could disrupt the normal sequence of birth and her immediate reactions to the newborn pups. The presence of a strange person may delay delivery. The rule, therefore, is to keep away and observe discreetly, intercepting only when there is a real problem. For your first delivery, however, it is always good to have a veterinarian within easy reach, or at least an experienced person familiar to your bitch with you.

If the bitch is hyperactive and/or hysterical, if a pup is stuck halfway out of the birth canal, or if she ignores the newborn pups, you do have to step in to help. Bitches occasionally cry out when a pup enters the birth canal; some may require reassurance and gentle handling. Hysterical reactions may be due to a combination of fear and pain. If a pup is stuck, you can assist by taking and helping each pup out with a rough towel as the mother labors. Don't do it in a forceful way, but just give some added assistance.

If a pup is delivered with the enveloping sac intact, break and peel back the membrane that surrounds it. Then cut the umbilical cord: Snip it off with sterile scissors, leaving about one and one-half inches, and dab it with iodine. If bleeding continues, tie the end with a string and apply an antiseptic.

If the mother doesn't stimulate the pup by licking to initiate a cry and expel excess fluids from the upper respiratory tract and establish spontaneous breathing, you'll have to do it. Take a cotton-tipped swab and remove the fluid from the mouth. Rub the body gently with a towel to stimulate the breathing and flow of blood. Often a pup needs a vigorous pat and massage to start breathing.

Sometimes a pup will arrive with no sign of life. If you feel a pulse beat under the forearm, start the pup breathing by blowing steadily into his mouth—this way the lungs can be sufficiently expanded to supply necessary oxygen. Then suck and expel your breath. Inhale and repeat. Slap the pup vigorously, then swing it slowly back and forth ten times. Wait a second or two for a gasp. If there isn't one, swing again.

There are times in birthing when a veterinarian's assistance is needed. After a couple of hours of straining, no evidence of a pup's imminent arrival means you should call a vet. If the mother makes frequent attempts to urinate or labors with her head thrown back and mouth open, call a vet. Hypoglycemia, the rapid fall in the blood-sugar level, may cause superficially hysterical reactions and can be fatal. Appropriate veterinary advice should be sought immediately.

If there are several dry births and the placentas are retained, infection may follow that requires professional help. In fact, many veterinarians recommend a checkup right after whelping to make sure all the pups are out. If the discharge from the mother after birth becomes bright red, flows abundantly, or lasts more than two weeks, contact a veterinarian.

After eating a number of placentas, female dogs often have digestive upsets. In the wild, this afterbirth would serve as her only food for two or three days after she gives birth, because she wouldn't leave the family; it also acts as a laxative. But with our modern dogs that are so well fed and cared for, there is no need for this extra food. Therefore, if it is a large litter, remove the placentas if you are present. If the mother gets hold of them and eats them, as she usually does, give her some castor oil to clean her out.

With some pets, you have to make definite arrangements with your veterinarian before delivery takes place. If your dog has some kind of pelvic injury, a cesarean birth is needed. Toys and minis are so small they often need this kind of birthing procedure. Dogs with heavy shoulders and narrow hips often have pups with forequarters larger than their narrow pelvic passage will allow. Many veterinarians would rather operate early than have a difficult, dangerous forceps delivery. So if possible, all dogs should be taken to a veterinarian for advice. After the operation there may be some swelling around the stitches, but that's about it. These dogs may go home in a few hours, though usually the vet will keep them a few days. If your bitch requires more than one cesarean, spaying is the best answer.

Postnatal Care

The mother will care for her new family herself for the first three to four weeks. She will keep the brood clean; and as long as the puppies are warm and getting enough to eat, they will be quiet and sleep most of the time. If they aren't happy, however, they won't hesitate to let everyone know. Your main concern is the mother's needs and keeping the temperature at the right level. Pups can't control their body temperatures during the first week or two of life, so during the first week, keep the thermostat at eighty-five, then down to eighty degrees. As long as the mother seems to be managing, it's best not to handle the pups or interfere in any way. Many bitches resent their pups being touched, especially during the first few days. The whelping area or box should be a quiet place that remains undisturbed.

Teats of nursing mothers should be examined daily. Clip the hair around the nipples, and if the teats are raw and cracked, apply a bit of oil. If one gland is swollen much more than the others, it may be that the milk duct is blocked. Try to squeeze a bit of milk through, and milk it until partially empty. After a few days, if unmilked, the teat will dry off. If you can't get any milk through the opening, apply a warm, wet pad for a few minutes and gently massage it with some olive oil. If the duct doesn't open, take her to a veterinarian to see whether there is an infection. If there never was an opening, the vet may try to make one.

Within a few hours of birth, each newborn pup will choose a teat for itself. If the mother isn't producing her milk by then she may need an injection by a veterinarian. If she suddenly dries up before the litter is weaned, a vet is needed. If the pups are not getting enough milk, they'll let you know by whining, acting restless, and scattering about the box. Your veterinarian can help with food supplements. If the mother has a large litter and hasn't enough nipples to go around, be prepared to supplement the feeding of the entire litter. (Use the techniques covered under Orphans.)

The secret to successful lactation is keeping the mother strong and well nourished. A nursing dog has to eat a lot of food and drink a lot of milk or water. Supplements can be especially helpful at this time. If you don't take care of the dog's nutritional needs, the pups will drain her reserves, and you could end up by the time she finishes nursing with an emaciated dog. For the first few weeks give her all she can eat, making sure that the food is on the soft, moist side for a few days. If she becomes constipated, milk of magnesia is effective.

Through the pups' first two or three weeks, their mother stimulates their urination by licking, and also eats up all urine and feces that the pups pass. By two or three days after birth, the pups' umbilical cords drop off. The proper time for docking tails and removing dewclaws is three to five days. You should clip the nails of all the pups to prevent damage to the mother. If worming is necessary, do it at four or five weeks, or wait until after the weaning, because the medicine can upset young intestines.

Mastitis or mammitis is an inflammation of one or more of the milk glands, which arises after pregnancy. The swelling may localize itself into an abscess and drain pus. The breast is hot, painful, and swollen; and the mammary tissue is sometimes discolored. Other symptoms include depression, increased temperature, loss of appetite. Pups nursing at the infected gland will cry, become listless, and die.

Prevention is largely a matter of clean bedding, clipping

the hair around the breasts, and washing and drying them. (If teats are chapped, you may have to oil them.) Treatment is aimed at overcoming the infection. The breast is milked frequently and taped to prevent nursing. Until you get to a veterinarian, bathing with warm salt water and using hot and cold packs is the only home remedy.

A constant weak cry is a pup's signal of distress, and you should seek out the problem—perhaps a cleft palate (a split in the roof of the mouth) or another deformity. One of the signs of a cleft palate is milk coming out of the pup's nose; the pup needs to be destroyed since it will never be properly nourished. If any pups are sick, take them to a veterinarian and get his advice. If they must be put away, have your veterinarian do it painlessly with an injection.

If one of the litter dies, its particular teat should be partially milked. If the mother's milk must be ebbed prematurely because all her litter dies or if she is found to be unfit to nurse, feed her only small amounts of food and limited liquid at each meal. A dose of epsom salts or some other salt might help relieve her bloated feeling. Dry up the mother's milk by rubbing the breasts with camphorated oil. If there is lots of milk, gently squeeze it out by hand. Just be very gentle, because massaging stimulates milk glands and increases the flow. A solution that your veterinarian might prescribe will help halt your pet's milk supply.

Orphans

If the mother dies, or the quantity or quality of her milk is inadequate to feed the litter, you should get a foster mother who is lactating properly to take her place. But in attempting to have the pups adopted, be careful in introducing them, or the new mother may reject or kill the intruders. Rub the orphan all over with milk from the foster mother and/or droppings from her natural offspring. Keep the prospective foster mother away from her own litter for a couple of hours. When she lies down to give suckle, hold the orphans near the spare teats. Repeat a couple of hours later until the new pup gains acceptance.

If no such dog is available, you're faced with the problem of being a canine nursemaid. You have to keep the pups' bellies as full as possible without forcing them to eat. For hand rearing these orphans, you need an adequate substitute for the bitch's milk.

A number of commercial formulas are available. If you can't find any, perhaps your veterinarian can help. A good temporary formula is made from one cup of evaporated milk, one cup of water, one tablespoon of corn syrup, a pinch of salt, plus extra vitamins (usually of the prepared soluble variety like children's). Cow's milk is inadequate; if you must feed them on cow's milk, add cream to it. The consistency of cow's milk is not as rich as dog's, and pups require a great deal of cream since seventy percent of their energy is derived from fat at this age.

You will find the feeding recommendations—based on the weight of the pup—on the labels of commercial formulas. Usually you feed them as much as they want, and the schedule is often based on the quality of the formula: five to six times a day for the first five weeks of life; and afterwards, three times daily, plus the weaning food.

The stomach-tube method is preferred for feeding. Your veterinarian can supply one and show you how to use this. It is easy, painless to the pup, and has the safest quantity control. There's no danger of the pup inhaling or choking on milk, or swallowing air. If the pup is very small, you can use a medicine dropper. Later, a doll's nipple and bottle or one designed for premature infants can be used. Hold the pup in a horizontal position so the milk will not enter his lungs. Do not feed too fast, or the mixture will go down the trachea. The frequency of feeding is more important than the amounts; a pup will get diarrhea if overfed. Never feed more than a few drops at a time to start, and allow the pup to swallow it before giving more.

Until they can urinate on their own, after feeding you will have to bathe the genital area with cotton balls dipped in warm water to stimulate evacuation, then wipe again. You'll also need a suitable environment with proper temperature maintenance. Pups are susceptible to temperature changes, so keep them in a draft-free box in a warm room. A well-insulated hot water bottle may help, but be sure to refill it constantly. The first three weeks are the most trying.

Weaning

Weaning is the separation of the young from the mother, or in the case of orphans, from the substitute mother. Start weaning at two, three, or even four weeks of age, depending on the size of the pups, the number of the litter, and the milk supply available. Now you will be the provider of food. Wean gradually so as to slowly decrease the pups' dependence on the mother's milk. Her milk will slowly dry off, and the food you offer the pups in weaning should increase, as should the mother's intake.

Start off with a shallow dish of tepid milk. Teach each pup to lap by pushing his snout down in the food for a second. Don't hold it there, or the pup will choke. Usually he will lick the food off his muzzle and look for more. You can help the pup to start eating by having him lick your fingers first, then put your finger right into the food so they continue to lick finger and food, too.

As the pups start lapping milk, gradually start mixing in good-quality commercial food, dry or moist. (Select the puppy variety, if possible.) Make sure that it's well mashed to start with so that it is palatable. Give two of these meals a day at first; by the end of the weaning, boost it up to four. As the weaning proceeds, decrease the amount of milk you use to thin out the consistency of the food. Thus by the time weaning is over at eight weeks, you'll just be giving the solid food, plus water on the side. Feed all that the pups can eat in these meals. You can add supplements in the way of vitamins or wheat germ.

If you don't start weaning, the pups may mob the mother, who in turn will regurgitate food for them. Sometimes a mother will do this anyway, but she may not if you cut back on her food. During the weaning period, mothers need serious consideration. It is a period of approaching separation for her from her pups. If for some reason you need to wean quickly, separate the pups from their mother during the day for three to five days, but leave them with her at night. During the day, the hungry pups learn to eat on their own more rapidly. But by nursing at night, the pups will maintain the proper fluid balance and prevent congestion of the mother's breasts.

Normally the pups are ready for separation from their mother at seven weeks or so. After the pups have been weaned, the mother will naturally have exhausted her milk supply. On the day that you feel is right to be the actual weaning time, cut out all fluids from her diet for twenty-four hours. This will help stop her milk supply.

If possible, don't take all the pups away from the bitch at one time, or she will certainly be upset and may even become ill. Remove them one at a time with intervals of some days; and if possible, let her keep the last one until she shows signs of tiring of it.

If Your Dog Is Lost or Stolen

Make a list containing your dog's date of birth, sex, breed, coat length, hair texture, unusual aspects, color, eyes, ears, markings, tail length, weight, length, height, license number and renewal date, and inoculations. This will be an easy reference guide to the essential descriptive information about your dog. You can have your pet tattooed and register the dog's number with a registry service. It's a great help not to have to rely solely on memory, so keep a good photograph in addition to your list and keep them together.

Try to prevent loss by never allowing your dog out of sight in new surroundings. Training a dog to stay close and not to wander is your best insurance against his getting lost. But dog-stealing is rampant, either for value of the dogs themselves or to hold them for ransom. It is up to you to make sure your pet is not stolen, so do not leave him tied up outside stores, in cars, or anywhere unsecured. Still, a dog may become lost or stolen no matter how much care you take to prevent it. If so, contact the SPCA, police, humane societies, and newspapers; also post notices. If you offer a reward, be sure to give it only after the pet is returned, and not on the promise of same.

If a dog wanders out of sight in a strange area, your best bet is to stay where he originally left you in the hopes that he will return. Since dogs tend to return to the freshest scent, he may be able to track his way back.

In the wild, dogs don't just wander around aimlessly. They live on a very large range, which they constantly recircle, and thus they have a good sense of direction. Perhaps because of their incredible perceptiveness to even the minutest signals, certain lost or abandoned dogs have found their way home to owners who have moved hundreds, even thousands of miles away. Most dogs are familiar with the specific odor of the exhaust and contents of their owners' particular cars, and may even have detected traces of odor left as a moving van passed. Positive reinforcement may come when a dog sniffs places where the owners got out of the car to rest. (Perhaps the dog even saw the direction in which the owner moved when starting.) Additionally, dogs have an internal clock that can gauge when regularly scheduled events such as feeding are due. It's not clear whether this ability is innate, but it is probably learned through acute observation.

Indeed, dogs may use a sort of time sense to navigate: The sun never shines the same way at any given time on different places on earth, but varies according to the time of day and the season. Each square mile is different in relation to the sun, so each receives sunlight at a slightly different angle. It is thus possible that dogs are able to find where they live by "reading" the differences between what they see and the expectations of their internal clock.

Exponents of ESP also point to a dog's frequent foreknowledge of impending natural disasters. However, the warning system is probably their honed senses' ability to pick up low-level stimuli. The most frequently used argument for ESP ability in dogs is an animal's ability to foretell his owner's unexpected return. In such cases, however, the dog simply hears the owner's usual returning-home sounds: an elevator moving, a door opening, a car pulling up.

Dogs learn the odor of the persons, places, and objects they are regularly in contact with, so they might backtrack if home is not too far away. It is known that dogs backtrack home for shorter distances by leaving a scent trail from the pads of their feet; and in a new territory, a dog increases his urine and feces marking. By spiraling circles or zigzagging, lost dogs find their way home. So if possible, have someone else stay near your home in case he returns there.

The Older Dog

As your dog ages, he will need special attention and care. Like yourself, your pet is subject to the degenerative changes of old age. It happens faster in dogs than in humans since the life span is shorter. Larger dogs generally start aging at seven to eight years, smaller breeds from ten to eleven. Fourteen is a good old age, but there are wide variations.

The vet can point out what is best for your pet; just realize that things are changing and watch him. If he's overweight, reduce him gradually. Cut down exercise so that instead of a run, you give him a walk. Get a good diet from your vet and don't change it until he says to do so. Avoid boarding older dogs; cut down on stressful situations and excitement. In fact, try to keep his life pretty stable. Do not, however, upset him by completely changing his life-style too soon.

Old dogs tend to become constipated, so make sure to give short, regular exercise. This will help encourage elimination, but if there is chronic constipation, give a mild laxative or one recommended by your veterinarian.

Old dogs can definitely be taught new tricks, but may be slower to catch on. Just as with children, there are various dog types—clowns, bullies, doormats—and each requires different techniques. But the brain center of the nervous system of dogs is relatively small—two and one-half ounces for a forty-pound dog—so don't expect overnight miracles from your pet. Patience is a prerequisite, because you have to put time into teaching your dog. To reinforce training takes constant repetition of commands. Therefore, be prepared to repeat the same thing intermittently for weeks, if necessary.

The Unwanted
or Ailing Dog

A good-bye is not always based on necessity. If you decide to get rid of your pet for some reason such as a change in living conditions, boredom, or nuisance, try to place him in a good home. Abandoning pets is cruel, irresponsible, and illegal; yet it is done by otherwise self-respecting citizens. Once you take in a pet, you are responsible for his welfare, so make sure he is well cared for and happy. If you can't solve the problem yourself, ask for help.

When your dog has problems, do not immediately consider euthanasia. The increased knowledge in veterinary medicine can do much to help your dog. But when necessary, euthanasia is a painless, gentle death. A veterinarian injects an intravenous substance that puts the animal to sleep first, and then stops the heart.

This kind of good-bye, this parting with a pet who is either too old or too sick to enjoy life with you anymore, is painful to everyone. If your pet is hopelessly ill and suffering, the greatest kindness you can offer is a painless sleep. But unfortunately, there have been some rare cases where dogs are destroyed inhumanely, or not destroyed, but sent to laboratories. Therefore, even if you can't stand to hold the animal when it is being done, make sure you at least see the body.

Most people are distressed by the problem of disposing of

a dead pet. The many commercial pet cemeteries are a waste of money and space. If you live in the country or have a friend who does, burial is the answer. Otherwise a veterinarian can help make some arrangements for the disposal, and animal welfare societies will also accept and dispose of dead dogs.

Index

Index